America

MW00332075

American Hangman

A Biography of Amos Lunt, the Executioner of San Quentin

TOBIN T. BUHK

McFarland & Company, Inc., Publishers
Jefferson, North Carolina

LIBRARY OF CONGRESS CATALOGUING-IN-PUBLICATION DATA

Names: Buhk, Tobin T., author.
Title: American hangman : a biography of Amos Lunt,
the executioner of San Quentin / Tobin T. Buhk.
Description: Jefferson, North Carolina : McFarland & Company, Inc., 2022. |
Includes bibliographical references and index.
Identifiers: LCCN 2022036877 | ISBN 9781476685922 (paperback : acid free paper) ∞
ISBN 9781476646015 (ebook)
Subjects: LCSH: Lunt, Amos, 1846-1901. | Executions and executioners—
California—Biography. | Hanging—California—History. | California State
Prison at San Quentin—Biography. | BISAC: BIOGRAPHY & AUTOBIOGRAPHY /
Law Enforcement | SOCIAL SCIENCE / Death & Dying
Classification: LCC HV8658.L79 B84 2022 | DDC 365/.92 [B]—dc23/eng/20220811
LC record available at https://lccn.loc.gov/2022036877

BRITISH LIBRARY CATALOGUING DATA ARE AVAILABLE

ISBN (print) 978-1-4766-8592-2
ISBN (ebook) 978-1-4766-4601-5

Front cover: The sheriff fits the noose on one of the condemned men while
the other man makes his final speech. County hangings were often lengthy,
drawn-out affairs, whereas hangings at San Quentin—from the entrance
of the condemned man until the drop—consumed
just minutes. (author's collection)

Printed in the United States of America

McFarland & Company, Inc., Publishers
Box 611, Jefferson, North Carolina 28640
www.mcfarlandpub.com

Table of Contents

Biographical Timeline

August 16, 1846	Born in Newburyport, Massachusetts
May 1864	Enlisted in the 3rd Unattached Massachusetts Regiment
Late 1868	Traveled to California, settled in Santa Clara
August 22, 1874	Married Mollie Milstead
October 1, 1881	Divorced Mollie Milstead
October 18, 1881	Married Laura J. Martin
May 13, 1883	Lottie C. Lunt born
December 22, 1883	Purchases saloon in Santa Cruz
June 6, 1884	Sells "Clipper" saloon to M. O'Keefe
March 1885	The "House No. 10" affair
June 1, 1886 (until 1889)	Becomes a police constable in Santa Cruz
September 20, 1886	Amos Lunt, Sr., dies
April 2, 1887	Arnold E. Lunt born
May 8, 1888	Becomes chief of police of Santa Cruz
July 1889	Removed as Santa Cruz chief of police
July 1889 (until 1890)	Resumes duties as a constable
May 1, 1891	Hired as a guard at San Quentin
February 1, 1894 (until 1899)	Appointed hangman of San Quentin
January 27, 1899	Relieved of duties at San Quentin
March 22, 1899	Testifies at the Brandes murder trial
October 7, 1899	Resumes his duties at San Quentin
October 23, 1899	Suffers breakdown; sent to the Napa State Hospital
September 20, 1901	Amos Lunt dies in the Napa State Hospital

Preface:
Enter the Hangman

(Friday, April 20, 1894)

It was a warm, spring day in April when condemned wife-slayer Patrick Sullivan met the hangman on the scaffold at San Quentin. A *San Francisco Call* reporter described the sunny morning as "an ideal spring day ... great patches of bluebells made queer effects on the brown rolling hillsides. The birds twittered and chirped cheerfully, and the waters of the bay, hardly stirred by the reluctant breezes, glistened brightly in the hot sun and reflected the white and blue sky above."[1]

Patrick Sullivan's execution would proceed with military precision. As the third man to stand over the trap on San Quentin's gallows, Prisoner #15866 would benefit from a procedure perfected during two previous hangings and from a hangman who was a quick study with a noose.

At 10 a.m. on Hangman's Friday, the spectators arrived by train and made their way to the prison gate, where each man presented a black-bordered, personalized invitation signed by Warden William Hale. The warden, eager to avoid a spectacle, limited attendance to about 30. The audience would include newspapermen from San Francisco and San Rafael, physicians who wanted to attend for scientific reasons, and lawmen who wanted to watch justice enacted at the end of a rope. Most of them came from Northern California, but one man made the journey all the way from Nebraska. James Sage, the chief of police of Plattsmouth, wanted to witness a hanging, and Hale obliged by sending him a black-bordered ticket.

After collecting the invitations, guards shepherded the spectators to the old brick factory building at about 10:30 a.m. In small groups, they rode the freight elevator to the fourth floor, where they waited in a room populated by rocking chairs left over from a time when the building housed the prison's furniture factory.

The guards escorted the group into the gallows room, a spacious gallery containing the prison's scaffold. A noose, waiting for Sullivan, dangled motionless from a rope suspended over a massive wooden crossbeam.

The men—an eclectic mixture of physicians, county sheriffs, and news reporters—circled the scaffold. In hushed tones, they discussed what they were about to witness. The sheriffs spoke about retribution at the end of a rope using colloquialisms such as "swing"; the reporters discussed much of the same but in a different vernacular containing terms such as "expiation"; and the doctors, using a vocabulary foreign to the other two groups, chatted about the amount of time it would take for the last beat of the condemned man's heart.

At 10:45 a.m., William Hale entered the room. Standing on the bottom step of the scaffold, he addressed the crowd with a brief introduction to the procedures and the dramatis personae who would play a role in the ensuing scene. Following the condemned man's last wishes, Hale said, there would be no autopsy. Sullivan, an 11th-hour convert to the Catholic faith, had entrusted his remains to the Catholic priests—Fathers Lagan and Dempsey—who would stand with him on the scaffold. Dr. Isaac Le Roy Mansfield, the prison surgeon, would monitor Sullivan's pulse after the drop and make the pronouncement of death. Death Watch guards Fitch and Miller would tighten the leather straps.

And Amos Lunt, the hangman, would place the noose around Sullivan's neck and drop the black cap over his head.

When finished with the introductions, Hale explained why the group would have to leave the room for a few minutes. Once the room was cleared, three guards whose identities they could never know would take their place in a small box at the back of the scaffold. During the hanging, these three men would each cut a cord. Two of the cords were dummies, but one released the trap that would send Sullivan plummeting downward. None of the guards would know which cord was the "live" one, and no one but Hale would know who they were. To keep their identities secret, they would be hidden in what the *San Francisco Chronicle* reporter described as a "little box like closet on the scaffold."[2]

With the three cord cutters ensconced in their "little box like closet," the spectators reentered the gallows room at 10:50 a.m. They clustered around the front and sides of the scaffold, close enough to hear every word uttered from the platform above.

While the spectators angled for a better position from which to view the hanging, Warden Hale passed through the iron doors leading to the death cells to inform Sullivan that his time had come.

*   *   *

On the other side of the doors, the "Hangman of San Quentin" made the final preparations in a sequence of steps that would end with the prisoner shooting through the trap. At the hangman's direction, Death Watch guards Fitch and Miller began fitting Sullivan with the bindings that would inhibit movement of his arms and legs. Sullivan stood still as one of the guards looped a leather belt around his waist and pulled it tight, while the other guard fastened a leather strap to each arm below the elbow and then buckled them to the belt. Once Sullivan was standing on the trap, the guards would add a strap around his ankles and tighten the bindings.

With Lunt watching, Fitch and Miller affixed the straps. Under the wide brim of his hat, his icy blue eyes remained fixed on Sullivan with the deep, penetrating gaze of an artist studying his subject. At 5'11" tall, the hangman stood half a head taller than Sullivan, who stood just a hair under 5'8".[3] Hangmen like Lunt learned to pay particular attention to things like height, weight, and the thickness of a man's neck.

*   *   *

At 10:58 a.m., the spectators heard the chanting of priests behind the iron door separating the death cells from the gallows room: a signal that the death procession had started. A few seconds later, the metal groaned as the door swung open to admit the death march. Warden Hale and his right-hand man, Captain John C. Edgar, led the procession of two Catholic priests, Patrick Sullivan flanked by his Death Watch guards, and the hangman—a tall drink of water wearing a wide-brimmed hat. From the perspective of the pigeons roosting on the rafters, the death march formed the shape of a cross with the dead man walking in the center.

The *San Francisco Chronicle*'s representative described the condemned prisoner at the exact moment he entered the room. "Sullivan was ghastly pale, but walked with a firm step."[4] His colleague at the *Call* offered a more detailed sketch of Sullivan's demeanor. "After them [the priests] with face of ghastly pallor and unshaven beard came Sullivan, walking steadily and slowly with something of the rolling gait of the sailor."[5]

Both reporters noted the steadiness of Sullivan's step. This short walk to the scaffold indicated how the condemned man would fare in his last moments. Sullivan vowed to "die game," but a faltering step might hint at a possible hairline fracture in the condemned man's stoic façade. Men had been known to collapse physically and mentally on the scaffold, a scenario that would complicate matters for Lunt.

The *Call* reporter thought he noticed the crack in Sullivan's façade as he eyed the gallows.

"He [Sullivan] looked furtively around the chamber, scanned the faces of the people and then a look of fearful despairing agony crept into his eyes as they fell upon the gallows upon which he was to die."[6] To the reporter's surprise, and to Lunt's relief, Sullivan's knees held.

The *Call* reporter's words suggest a sense of respect for Sullivan. "Still he did not falter. He surveyed the apparatus with intense earnestness as if trying to discover whether it were strong enough to bear the ordeal. As he walked slowly up the scaffold steps he felt the handrails and the fastenings and on reaching the platform cast a critical look on the beam overhead from which hung the nearly stretched rope. Something of satisfaction gleamed through his stolid features as the firmness of the structure forced itself upon him."[7]

Sullivan, his gait hindered by the leather straps binding his legs, shuffled forward to make his final remarks, while the hangman stood next to the noose dangling motionless from the crossbeam.

A sketch in the *Chronicle*'s feature story depicted Sullivan at the rail while making his final remarks, his broad shoulders half-concealing the figure—merely an outline in the artist's rendering—standing behind him.

It is an appropriate symbol of the man who would feel more comfortable working behind the scenes in the shadows of San Quentin's gallows than on the scaffold in full view of the public.

He was the hangman of San Quentin, and his story has been largely concealed by the dust of over a century and obscured by the mythos that grew up around his legend.

Until now.

Introduction

The Hangman's Odyssey

While researching historic crimes in old newspaper copy, I stumbled across "The Haunting of Amos Lunt," a full-page feature detailing the career and eventual mental breakdown of San Quentin's infamous hangman. Lunt stood toe to toe with some of the wildest murderers of the Wild West—the hitman of a Chinese gang, a sociopathic serial killer, several jilted lovers—the ghosts of whom apparently came back to haunt him. Their unearthly screams drove him from his spot by the watchtower to an insane asylum and ultimately to the grave.

I, too, heard a voice—not the wailing of souls dropped through a trapdoor to oblivion but that of a man begging for his story to be told. And what a story: a former police officer who became the hangman of San Quentin after a series of ironic reversals worthy of an O. Henry short story: two botched hangings and a prison warden who did not have the stomach for executions but nonetheless had to preside over them. "The career of Lunt as a hangman was a remarkable one," a reporter later noted, "and a full history of his life at the prison would read like a ghastly romance."[1]

As the hangman of San Quentin, Amos Lunt stood at the center of a controversy over capital punishment and subsequently became an object for both mythologizing and demonizing, depending on a particular writer's viewpoint. I wanted to investigate the man behind the myth and to identify the demons that caused his downfall.

Yet delving into the man who tied the nooses proved easier said than done. People then, as now, found the crimes and the men who committed them far more interesting than the law officers. Reporters wrote lengthy descriptions about these headline villains, who have survived in near photo-realistic descriptions. Conversely, the men who stood guard at the prison, and especially those tasked with additional duties before, during, and after hangings, remain mere silhouettes standing in the background.

Thankfully, Amos Lunt was a media magnet. He liked to tell stories,

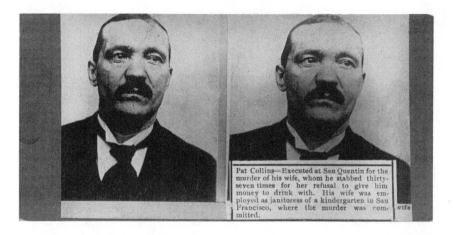

Pat Collins—Executed at San Quentin for the murder of his wife, whom he stabbed thirty-seven times for her refusal to give him money to drink with. His wife was employed as janitoress of a kindergarten in San Francisco, where the murder was committed.

While law officers not named Wyatt Earp or Pat Garrett received little if any attention, prisoners hanged inside the state penitentiary at San Quentin remained subjects of public fascination years after their executions. The curious could gaze upon the visage of condemned murderer Patrick Collins with this stereopticon (author's collection).

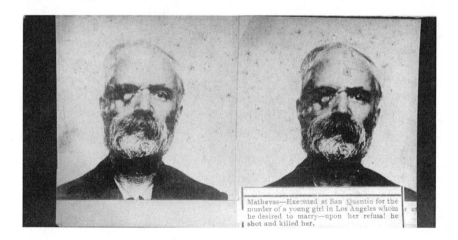

Mathevas—Executed at San Quentin for the murder of a young girl in Los Angeles whom he desired to marry—upon her refusal he shot and killed her.

Another gallows curio, this stereopticon contains the mug shot of Edward Methever, condemned for murdering 25-year-old Dorothy McKee in Long Beach in July 1899. Consumed with desire for the attractive brunette, who did not feel the same way about her 60-something admirer, Methever attacked McKee on the beach, shooting her four times at point-blank range: twice in the chest, once in the neck, and the coup de grace to the head. He tried to cheat the hangman by shooting himself in the temple and succeeded only in blowing out an eye. He met his hangman, Frank Arbogast, on the San Quentin gallows in May 1901 (author's collection).

which made him a goldmine for reporters, who would make the trek to San Quentin and attempt to excavate a good story or two from the loquacious guard. Eventually, as the hangman of San Quentin, he would materialize in newspaper coverage, although he would receive far less ink than the men he hanged.

Resurrecting a Long-Dead Lawman

Before he became "The Hangman of San Quentin," Amos Lunt left very faint footsteps in the historical record. As a saloon owner and later a police officer, his name occasionally appeared in one of the early Santa Cruz newspapers. Chronicling the pre-scaffold era of Lunt's life from these news blurbs is like assembling a picture puzzle without all the pieces. Rather than fill in the gaps with speculation or fictionalizing, I have presented the early eras through a series of anecdotes. Actions, after all, speak louder than words, and these anecdotes best represent the man behind the newsmaker.

Almost as soon as Lunt began tying nooses, he became a figure of fascination for newspaper reporters. As the final act in the sordid story of a headline crime, a hanging at San Quentin always generated interest in the Bay Area. Naturally, writers turned their attention to the person entrusted with the terrible task of executing the law's ultimate punishment. For a public used to hangings done by county sheriffs or faceless vigilantes, this new face of official retribution became one of endless fascination that climaxed with Alice Rix's full-page profile of the San Quentin hangman.

Yet newspaper stories of the era present a double-edged sword for the historian. Coverage of hangings, and of the hangman, reflected the ambiguity of the public toward capital punishment. Some viewed hangings as a barbaric throwback to a more primitive world, whereas others tended to view them as just punishment for some truly hideous crimes. Reporters reflected this dichotomy and broadcast their own biases in their descriptions of the man responsible for tying the noose.

Journalist Frederick F. Runyon, for example, described Lunt as "a cold-blooded fellow" who "apparently had no feeling."[2] Runyon's colleague Pete Dotz, on the other hand, viewed the hangman as a sort of mythic hero. He later said of Lunt, "Probably in all my newspaper experience, I have never met a person that so quite impressed me as Amos Lunt, the hangsman of San Quentin."[3] Biases aside, both Runyon and Dotz solicited sensational stories from their San Quentin source, and both writers later bragged about learning how to tie a noose from the official "hangsman."

This "yellow journalism" also presents a challenge for the historian. Newspaper editors sent reporters and sketch artists to San Quentin on Hangman's Fridays. As a result, they left a vivid chronicle, albeit one that tended to emphasize the macabre. Reporters relished describing the minute details of a condemned man's final moments, such as the spasms that followed the drop or the changing color of his hands (from ecru to cyanotic blue).

These details have left an invaluable record of what occurred during hangings, but the writers and their editors did not stop with a fact-filled chronicle. They added red pepper to already spicy stories in dozens of ways. In a nod to the pseudo-science of phrenology, they read the contours of a condemned man's head and studied his facial features, where they found evidence of his guilt (or innocence). They parsed the word choice in a condemned man's final statement, noting which words he stressed, and offered an interpretation. They found the symbolic in the coincidental, such as the dove that flew out of a window at the exact moment the trap opened, sending a man hurtling to his death.

Separating fact from fiction involves comparing news accounts published in a no holds barred competition to sell papers. Nowhere is this cutthroat competition more on display than during the hanging of Theodore Durrant, billed as the criminal of the (19th) century. Durrant's final moments made the front pages of all the major Bay Area papers, and reporters tripped over each other as they followed every footstep taken by Durrant's parents. Accounts in all three major area papers—the *Chronicle*, the *Call*, and the *Examiner*—repeated Durrant's final remarks, and all three accounts differed. These newspapers left a legacy in print, but determining which account is the most accurate becomes impossible in some instances. The only relevant fact is that the accounts vary.

Eventually, even some editors grew squeamish about the graphic details emerging from San Quentin. The editor of the *Call*, in a move to curtail his publication's attempts to commercialize gore, decided to stop printing art depicting the final moments of the condemned.

Rather than shy away from this attention, Amos Lunt tended to court it by periodically speaking to reporters. Pete Dotz later described him as the source of "a hundred thrilling yellow stories." As a result, Lunt's footprint in the historical record becomes a little deeper and a little more defined after 1894, when he began hanging men. Despite this flurry of media attention, the behind-the-scenes work—the work overseen by Lunt as the hangman—remains obscure. While people wanted to know what transpired in the final seconds of a condemned man's life, they cared little—or dared not ask—about the machinery behind an official execution.

The Duffy and Sullivan Records

Reporters who attended hangings wrote lengthy and detailed descriptions of the doomed felons, including their demeanor en route to the gallows, their demeanor once standing on the trap, and their final words, but they seldom discussed such mundane things as an inmate's height or weight—vital statistics when analyzing the physical dynamics of a hanging. Only on rare occasion did they mention, let alone discuss, the single most important factor in determining the success of a hanging: the length of drop.

While their after-action reports provide a vivid re-creation of hangings, these missing facts create a gap in understanding the dynamics that went into planning successful executions. This gap can be partially filled with two sources, which are vital in understanding what occurred during early hangings conducted at San Quentin. Both records originated with long-time prison employees (see Appendix 2 for a detailed analysis of these sources).

During a lengthy career that included a 12-year turn as warden of San Quentin, Clinton T. Duffy collected objects and compiled records related to the prison. Several items from his collection reside in the Marin History Museum, including an album of executed prisoners. The entry for each prisoner contains a mug shot along with basic information about his crime and, most importantly, his height, weight, and length of drop. A duplicate of this compilation is held in the California State Archives under the title *Execution Books, 1893–1967.*

Daniel Sullivan, whose 40-year service with the prison spanned five decades (1879–1919), walked a beat on "Murderer's Row" and later assisted with hangings under Lunt's successor, Frank Arbogast.[4]

During his time at the prison, Sullivan compiled an album—*Album IV*—that contains entries for inmates of "Murderer's Row." Like Duffy's execution record, each entry contains a mug shot and a brief description of the condemned man, including height, weight, and length of drop. Unlike Duffy's execution record, *Album IV* also includes entries for inmates (like Anton Vital) who escaped the death penalty for one reason or another.

Entries in *Album IV* also contain a piece of information not contained in Warden Duffy's compilation: a classification denoting the outcome of each execution. Most are characterized as "successful" or "highly successful," although two contain epithets such as "about right" and "head nearly severed," and in two instances, no outcome is recorded at all—a provocative silence discussed at length in Appendix 2.

These sources contain two pieces of information in particular that make it possible to understand the science behind early hangings at San Quentin: the inmate's weight and drop.

Unfortunately, they do not provide information about the men responsible for calculating the drop. This involves a little extrapolation from contemporary newspapers.

Lunt and the Drop

The "drop," the determination of which represents both the art and the science of hanging, is the key factor in creating a quick, painless death for the condemned. A hangman's acumen is dependent on his knack for calculating a proper drop.

Amos Lunt's drop calculations figure prominently throughout this work, particularly in Part II, which documents his work as the San Quentin "hangman." However, Lunt may not have been the only one involved in making these critical decisions.

Other guards at the prison may have helped Lunt with gallows preparations in his early days as the hangman, although who did what behind the scenes appears to have been a hot potato; no one apparently wanted to acknowledge taking part in this aspect of the hangings. Neither official prison records nor newspaper accounts of the earliest executions name those responsible. Even Lunt's role did not become clear until September 1895, when William Hale named him as the hangman who "makes and carries out all the arrangements, and to him is due the general success of executions."[5]

An article published in 1899 suggests that up until the Durrant hanging, Captain W.C. Jamieson calculated the drops, although this is most likely a misrepresentation of Jamieson's role in the San Quentin death machine. The reporter may have mistaken Jamieson's later responsibility of placing the black cap over the condemned man's head for a more significant role and subsequently misreported it.[6]

Although it is possible that "Turnkey" Jamieson helped Lunt with calculating the drops during the earliest hangings, it is unlikely that he played anything more than a supporting role in gallows preparations. While Lunt's pre-hanging work features prominently in newspaper coverage from long before the Durrant execution, Jamieson's supposed role in the prelude to a hanging is mentioned just once, and that instance occurred after Lunt's tenure as hangman had ended.

On the other hand, considering Hale's comments about Lunt's role in 1895—"makes and carries out all the arrangements"—combined with the warden's silence about Jamieson's part in any of the procedures, it appears evident that Lunt began calculating drops, possibly in consultation with the prison physicians and perhaps even Hale, as early as 1894.

In fact, several comments Lunt made about his responsibilities as hangman make little sense if anyone else calculated the drop. His remarks about "an ordinary neck and well-stretched rope" during an interview in 1895, for example, or a curious incident that occurred in court when he eyed the prosecutor and said he would estimate a 5'8" drop for the man.

Newspaper stories, such as the *Chronicle*'s account of the Allender execution (which preceded the Durrant hanging), leave no doubt as to who made the critical calculations. "Lunt will give his man a 'six-foot drop,' as he gruesomely expresses it," the *Chronicle* reporter noted, "rather a longer distance than in ordinary cases, but Allender is a slim fellow, and carries very little flesh."[7]

"Amos Lunt, the hangman," wrote another reporter, "visited Durrant's cell this afternoon for the purpose of taking his measure and determining the length of the drop. The machinery of the gallows was tested and everything found to work smoothly."[8] Following the messy outcome of the John Miller hanging in 1898, an *Evening Sentinel* reporter noted, "It is a wonder that his head was not pulled off, though hangman Amos Lunt gave him but a five foot drop."[9]

These reporters knew Lunt well and often ventured to the watchtower for a conversation with the hangman, who never failed to provide fodder for a yellow story. As voices familiar with the inner workings of San Quentin's death house and its operatives, they provided an accurate insight as to who did what behind the scenes.

Wire or Rope?

In the 1890s, the electric chair began to replace the scaffold in some states, supposedly because it offered an alternative with less of a chance for the type of error that might occur when the hangman makes a fatal error in judgment.

By the late 1890s, both Ohio and New York had installed electric chairs in their penitentiaries. William Kemmler, who hacked his sweetheart to death with an axe, became the first person to die in an electric chair when he took his place in New York's hot seat on August 6, 1890. Seven years later, Ohio inaugurated its own version of "Old Sparky" with 17-year-old William Haas and 38-year-old William Wiley, who both went to the chair on April 21, 1897. Haas had raped his boss's wife and, fearing she would talk, cut her throat. In a violent, drunken delirium, Wiley shot his wife. California's miscreants, however, would continue to face the hangman until 1937, when the gas chamber finally supplanted the rope.

Writing just a few months before Kemmler's execution, Dr. W.F. McNutt heralded the virtues of hanging in a short article titled "Noose

❧ SOUVENIR ❧

ELECTROCUTED:

No. 1—WILLIAM HAAS, of Cincinnati, electrocuted April 21, 1897, for the murder of Mrs. William Brady.

No. 2—WILLIAM WILEY, of Cincinnati, electrocuted April 21, 1897, for the murder of his wife.

No. 3—FRANK MILLER, was electrocuted September 3, 1897, for the murder of Mrs. Saluda Miller, of Franklin county.

No. 4—ALBERT FRANTZ, electrocuted November 19, 1897, for the murder of Bessie Little, at Dayton.

No. 5—FRANK EARLY, was electrocuted May 14, 1898, for the murder of his wife at Cincinnati.

No. 6—CHARLES NELSON, electrocuted November 4, 1898, for the murder of James Zimmerman, of Wood county.

No. 7—BRUNO KIRVES, electrocuted August 17, 1899, for the murder of his daughter Emma, at Dayton.

No. 8—RICHARD GARDNER, electrocuted November 9, 1900, for the murder of Ethel Long, of Ross county.

No. 9—ROSSLYN FERRELL, electrocuted March 1, 1901, for the murder of Eugene Lane, in Union county.

No. 10—EDWARD RUTHVEN, electrocuted June 21, 1901, for the murder of Officer Shipp, of Cleveland.

No. 11—JOHN BENNETT, electrocuted April 15, 1904, for the murder of his wife at Oberlin.

No. 12—CARL BERG, electrocuted June 3, 1904, for the murder of John Guibord, at Wauseon.

No. 13—MIKE SCHILLER, electrocuted June 17, 1904, for the murder of his wife at Youngstown.

No. 14—MOSE JOHNSON, electrocuted June 18, 1904, for the murder of Wm. Test at Portsmouth.

No. 15—ALBERT WADE, electrocuted July 14, 1904, for the murder of Kate Sullivan near Toledo.

No. 16—BEN WADE, electrocuted July 14, 1904, for the murder of Kate Sullivan near Toledo.

No. 17—CHAS. STIMMEL, electrocuted July 22, 1904, for the murder of Joseph Shide at Dayton.

No. 18—ALFRED KNAPP, electrocuted August 19, 1904, for the murder of his wife, Hannah Goddard Knapp, at Hamilton.

No. 19—ALBERT FISHER, electrocuted October 7, 1904, for the murder of Wm. Marshall, at Toledo.

No. 20—LEWIS HARMON, electrocuted Oct. 28, 1904, for the murder of Geo. Geyer, near Columbus.

No. 21—OTIS LOVELAND, electrocuted Nov 25, 1904, for the murder of Geo. Geyer, near Columbus.

No. 22—WM. NICHOLS, electrocuted Dec. 9, 1904, for the murder of Alf. Minard, near Kenton.

No. 23—HERMAN HAMILTON, electrocuted Mar. 24, 1905, for the murder of L. Culver at Portsmouth.

☞All orders for souvenirs should be addressed THOS. EDMONDS.

FROM THE O. P. ANNEX,
PRICE, 25 Cents.

The state of Ohio replaced hanging with the electric chair. For 25 cents, visitors to the prison could purchase a cabinet card containing mug shots of the first 23 men to take their place in the state's hot seat (author's collection).

or Battery?" "We know that when the spinal cord is snapped off, as it is in a properly conducted hanging, there can be no pain. Besides the shock to the brain after the drop must cause immediate unconsciousness. We also know that after such a sudden and complete congestion of the vessels that supply the brain with blood unconsciousness follows so close as to be practically instantaneous." Dr. McNutt surmised that improperly conducted hangings led to the change in New York but he continued to promote the age-old method over the new-fangled device and predicted that the electric chair would lead to even more botched executions.

"Of course there are times when mistakes are made and death is caused by strangulation instead of by the breaking of the neck. But such things as that are mishaps. If execution by electricity ever becomes general, I think there will be more cases of bungling than there are with the gallows." Dr. McNutt cited "erratic" batteries and faulty wiring as possible culprits. "Death may be the least bit quicker," he concluded, "but the chance of a mishap is greater. I suppose that this change in the mode of execution in New York was caused by a number of bungled hangings, for unless there is awkwardness and bungling about a hanging death is sudden, sure, and practically painless. In the great majority of hangings there is little or no physical suffering. The limbs may twitch or jerk, but that is no sign of agony. It is what is known as reflex action, mere muscular contraction. The man is practically dead when he reaches the end of the rope."[10]

One common theme runs throughout Dr. McNutt's article: hanging, when conducted properly, creates a quick, painless death. According to one writer, whose formulae led him to conclude that only three-quarters of a second elapsed from the opening of the trap to the end of the drop, an effective hanging provided a near-instantaneous death with just a fleeting moment for the condemned man to agonize over the inevitable.[11]

The strangulation cited by Dr. McNutt as the failure in any hanging took place with regularity before English hangman William Marwood pioneered the "long drop" in 1872. Before Marwood began tinkering with calculations for creating a perfect, neck-breaking fall from the scaffold, hangmen gave little thought to length of rope. The result was often disastrous for the condemned, who did not die the "instantaneous" death celebrated by Dr. McNutt but rather a slow, painful death.

The hangings of the Lincoln conspirators in 1865 provided a chilling example of what can occur when the fall fails to break a subject's neck. Two of the four people hanged that day in the yard of the Old Arsenal Penitentiary (Washington, D.C.) died quickly; two did not. Of those two, one of them—Lewis Powell AKA "Lewis Payne"—put on a sickening show later reported by a *New York Herald* journalist who wrote a gut-wrenching description. "Payne slowly draws himself up till he assumes for a second the shape of a man sitting in a rather low chair, his thighs forming a similar angle with the portion of his legs from the knees downwards. He straightens again, but the broad chest heaves and swells, and there is a sort of writhing of the body on the hips. It is twenty-six minutes and fifteen seconds after one. Six minutes and a half have they swung there, and again a spasmodic curving of the body and bending of the lower parts proves Payne still alive, but it is the last." This grisly animation turned the writer's stomach, who pleaded, "If death must, for the safety of society, be inflicted on the assassin, for the sake of civilization let some more summary means of inflicting it be devised."[12]

Following similar bungled hangings in their respective states, lawmakers in New York and Ohio evidently believed that the electric chair could provide the "more summary means of inflicting" the death penalty. Unlike their colleagues out east, California legislators did not opt for the wires, which put more pressure on the men tasked with preparing the ropes.

Amos Lunt and the Art and Science of Hanging

The witnesses who gathered around the scaffold to watch Patrick Sullivan die witnessed the final scene in a drama that began hours earlier, most of which occurred off-stage and thus off-limits to the press. These backstage preparations always ended with a pine box carried out of the building by a contingent of prison laborers, but a successful execution required a prescribed sequence of steps, mathematical precision, and keen knowledge of biodynamics.

This was the work of the hangman, Amos Lunt.

Just a few hours earlier, Lunt had weighed and measured Sullivan to determine the distance he must drop through the gallows trap to achieve the desired effect: the noose knot striking the neck with enough force to either fracture or dislodge the third, fourth, and/or fifth cervical vertebrae, crushing the spinal cord and rendering painless—if not immediate—death.

A mistake in calculating drop would most likely lead to one of two outcomes. With too little rope, the victim would die a slow, painful death by asphyxiation. With too much, the fall might jerk the head off his shoulders. Either outcome was a painful one for the condemned and the other for the spectators who came to witness the supposed majesty of justice.

The victim's weight was the vital factor in this macabre mathematics.

When preparing for a hanging, the critical calculation involves determining the distance a subject of a given weight must fall to achieve the proper neck-breaking velocity. It is a relatively simple equation: foot-pounds of force divided by weight. P.J. Sullivan weighed 215 pounds. If Lunt estimated a force of 1,075 foot-pounds, then Sullivan's drop would equate to five feet. These figures represent the science of hanging.

Lunt always waited until the last practical moment, usually a few hours before the hanging, to weigh his subject. While Sullivan's height would not likely change in the days leading up to his execution, his weight might fluctuate if he lost his appetite while in the death cells or, conversely, ate well. Death house meals were more ample than those served to the general population, so some condemned men gorged themselves before taking their last walk, while others tried to avoid it by going on a hunger strike and thus cheating the hangman.

An effective drop, however, seldom came down to a simple mathematical equation. Often, biomechanical considerations such as the musculature (or lack thereof) of a subject's neck factored into the decision. As he would later explain to a reporter, Lunt despised thick necks, the kind that sat on top of broad shoulders. He much preferred slender, thin necks, which were easier to snap.

*   *   *

A proper, effective execution by hanging involves a precise, methodical sequence of steps, any one of which could doom the entire procedure if done improperly.

In a piece appropriately titled "Placing Nooses on Necks"—a brief profile of Warden William E. Hale, Amos Lunt, and executions at San Quentin—a writer for the *San Francisco Examiner* chronicled just a few of the many considerations that go into a successful hanging.

> Hangmen are very particular about the style of neck submitted to them. A long slender neck is always preferable. Short, stout necks cause no end of trouble. The knot does not sit well on them and the victim often dies of strangulation instead of a broken neck. To break a neck is the sole aim of a hangman who knows his business. To effectually break a neck the noose should be placed over the head before drawing on the black cap. The rope should then be well drawn and the knot snugly fitted in the hollow behind the left ear. When the black cap is in position the noose should be drawn tight and the signal to spring the trap given immediately afterwards. If these precautions are taken, Warden Hale and his chief deputy say the execution will be perfect in detail and general effect.[13]

According to contemporary reports, when the California state legislature made executions the responsibility of prison wardens and not county sheriffs, the decision came in part to mollify the growing number of people who sought the abolition of capital punishment. Over the previous five decades, just about every community experienced either an official hanging performed by a sheriff in the courtyard of a county jail, or an unofficial lynching conducted under a tall tree or from a bridge truss by a vigilance committee.

Often, inexperienced hangmen—whether the local sheriff or the local bartender—botched the job by giving their victims too little rope, which left them writhing like a fish on the end of a line. These poor wretches suffered an agonizingly slow death. It might take up to 20 minutes for the dancing rope to become still.

In a few instances, an overly liberal amount of rope led to the bloody spectacle of a near decapitation or possibly even pulled the head off doomed man's shoulders entirely. Such a messy outcome left the closest spectators speckled with arterial spray and a bitter taste in their

In May 1877, an angry lynch mob dragged Francisco Arias and Jose Chamales from their jail cell to a bridge over the San Lorenzo River, where they hanged them for murdering a local carpenter. The bodies were left in situ until the next day, providing local photographer John Elijah Davis Baldwin with an opportunity to capture an image of the morbidly curious posing alongside the dangling corpses. Afterward, the bodies were cut down, the rope sectioned, and the pieces distributed. Baldwin sold copies of the photograph at his Star Gallery in Santa Cruz (author's collection).

mouths. Such displays quickly transformed God-fearing townsfolk, who attended hangings to witness God's justice, into death penalty opponents.

During an interview in 1895, Lunt answered the death penalty critics

The hangman's nightmare! When notorious outlaw Black Jack Ketchum was hanged in Clayton, New Mexico, in 1901, the hangman erred in giving a seven-foot drop to the 193-pound bandit. The rope, which had been coated with soap, tore Ketchum's head from his shoulders. In this photograph, taken immediately after the botched hanging, Black Jack's still-hooded head is sitting next to his decapitated body (author's collection).

when he defended hanging as a humane and painless punishment, if done correctly. His words provide a fascinating insight into the mind of a seasoned hangman and the intricate, behind-the-scenes work necessary to achieve the desired, clean neck-break.

"There was a man in prison here who once tried to commit suicide by hanging himself," Lunt explained to a wide-eyed reporter from the *San Francisco Examiner*.

> He was cut down in time, however, and resuscitated. He told me he felt no pain at all when he dropped. His troubles began when they brought him back to life. If he had understood his business they could never have revived him. I don't think the men feel the least pain after shooting through the trap. That is, providing the job is properly done.
>
> With an ordinary neck and well-stretched rope death would be painless. I am never nervous or sensitive in any way during a hanging. I look at it as a part of my duty. I always take pains to place the knot closely under the left ear and see that everything is in proper shape before I motion to the man in the box to cut the three strings which spring the trap. Capital punishment is an excellent law, and hanging, to my mind, the best way of putting men to death.[14]

PART I

From Boston to San Quentin (1846–1894)

1

Go West, Young Man

(1847–1886)

Sirens (1846–1861)

The man destined to become the hangman of San Quentin was born in Newburyport, Massachusetts, on August 16, 1846, the first son of 26-year-old sailor Amos Lunt and his 20-year-old wife Mary (nee Longfellow), who wed the previous November.[1]

The small coastal settlement of Newburyport, nestled alongside the banks of the Merrimac River, grew to prominence as a center of shipping and shipbuilding. While local salts engaged in commercial fishing, during its formative years much of Newburyport's economy depended directly or indirectly on the transatlantic slave trade. The town's distilleries converted imported molasses into rum, which local shipping interests transported across the Atlantic. Some ships constructed in Newburyport ferried slaves across the Atlantic, which meant that maritime interests in the small northern town participated in two legs of the triangular trade. The thriving industry employed hundreds of local men, including Amos Lunt, Sr.[2]

During this early phase of his life, Amos, Sr., moved very lightly through Newburyport society, leaving only very faint footsteps in the historical record. His only newsworthy moment came when he posted a $5 reward for a missing wallet containing the princely sum of $32.[3] In 1848, the couple welcomed a second child with the birth of John T. in July.

In 1849, Amos Lunt, Sr., heard the sirens calling him west and joined the growing migration to California, leaving his wife (at the time pregnant with their third child, Charles) and two young sons behind in Newburyport.[4] He settled in San Francisco, where he went to work lightering, or moving cargo from ship to ship. The difficulty in reaching the West Coast before the advent of the transcontinental railroad meant that the patriarch would remain geographically cut off from his family, and Amos Lunt, Jr., would spend much of his youth separated from his father.

There seems very little doubt that Lunt, Sr., did not travel west to escape a loveless marriage. All the evidence supports a bond of deep affection that linked Amos and Mary despite the distance separating them. It appears that absence only made their hearts grow fonder. In 1851, Lunt made the arduous and time-consuming trip back to Massachusetts, where he spent the next six months getting to know his three sons: five-year-old Amos, three-year-old John, and six-month-old Charles.[5] He also attempted to persuade Mary to return with him to California.[6]

Mary decided to have a go at frontier life and traveled to San Francisco, but she did not care for the climate and promptly returned home to Newburyport.[7] She may have considered the Barbary Coast—with its saloons, bordellos, and constant influx of hard-drinking miners—an inhospitable place to raise a family. Their split may have been more than geographical; Amos would not see Mary again until 1868—17 years later.

A few months after Mary returned to Massachusetts, Amos, Sr., left San Francisco and headed into the mountains. He spent the next few years mining in Tuolumne and Sonoma Counties.

The Civil War of Amos Lunt (1864)

Amos Lunt, Jr., spent his formative years in a community deeply divided about the issue of slavery. Although several prominent citizens had prospered from the fruits of slave labor, a strong abolitionist movement took root in Newburyport. This created a deep rift dividing Newburyport's citizens in the years leading up to the Civil War. Preachers delivered fire-and-brimstone sermons about the evils of human chattel while increasingly nervous maritime scions spoke out in favor of the status quo and the importance of preserving States' rights.

By the outbreak of hostilities, however, the atmosphere in Newburyport was decisively pro–Union, and the town's men queued up to enlist. "At the close of the Civil War we found," noted George Creasy, author of *The City of Newburyport in the Civil War,* "that it [the city] had not only promptly furnished all the men it was called up on the State to provide, but had actually exceeded by more than one hundred and fifty men … all demands made upon it"[8]

Too young to serve during the first three years of the conflict, Amos Lunt, Jr., missed most of the war. In May 1864—two months before his 18th birthday—he mustered in as a private with the 3rd Massachusetts Unattached Volunteer Infantry, tasked with manning the state's coastal defenses.[9] While his father swung a pickaxe in California, Amos Lunt, Jr., shouldered a rifle and stood guard over Fort Lee, a stellate-shaped stone citadel in Salem, and Fort Pickering, a 17th-century stone fortress on Winter Island in Salem Harbor.

Walking along the parapets of the ancient masonry must have created a sense of ambivalence for Lunt. The duty took place far from the action, yet Fort Lee's eight-inch colombiads served as a constant reminder of the combat raging in the South. The bulky cannons stood at attention, ready to repulse an attack that would never come.

However tedious, the service made a deep impression on Lunt. Although he mustered out of service without ever seeing combat, he would become an active member of the Grand Army of the Republic. Lunt served honorably until the end of the war, when he mustered out of service in Boston.[10]

Go West, Young Man (1868–1874)

In 1868, Mary Lunt attempted to reunite the family by traveling to California. With the Transcontinental Railroad still a year from completion, the arduous journey involved either a lengthy voyage around the always-dangerous Cape Horn or a ride over a combination of railroad tracks and wagon wheels.

Mary made the trip with her two surviving children: 22-year-old Amos and his 18-year-old brother Charles. John T. Lunt had died of unknown causes prior to their departure for California.[11]

Mary and the boys reunited with Amos, Sr., in Santa Clara County. After a year there, they relocated to Santa Cruz County, where both junior and senior worked in the lumbering business.[12] Amos Lunt, Jr., spent most of the next decade involved with logging in one capacity or another.

The Two Wives (1874–1883)

In the early 1870s, Amos Lunt, Jr., met, courted, and married Mollie Milstead from the tiny mining settlement of Washington in Nevada County. The marriage between the 27-year-old lumberman and the 24-year-old miner's daughter took place on August 22, 1874.

The marriage atrophied and died sometime in the late 1870s. Although still legally married to Mollie, Lunt lived alone by 1880 and considered himself single. He settled in Corralitos, a small town nestled on the banks of the Pajaro River, where he may have tried his hand at farming.[13] He remained married on paper until October 1, 1881, when a judge granted him a divorce from Mollie.[14]

Less than three weeks later—on October 18, 1881—35-year-old

Amos Lunt married 26-year-old Laura J. Martin. The timing is curious and suggests the possibility that Lunt and Martin went through a shotgun wedding, although their first child to survive into the historical record would not arrive until 1883. The couple remained in Corralitos, where Amos took a job as a clerk for the Watsonville Mill & Lumber Company.[15]

The year 1883 was a momentous one for Amos and Laura Lunt. On May 13, Laura gave birth to a baby girl, Lottie C.; Amos quit his job as a clerk at the Watsonville Mill & Lumber Company; and they moved to Santa Cruz, where Amos purchased a saloon.

The "Clipper" (1883–1884)

In December 1883, Amos Lunt purchased a saloon, located in the lower market area "opposite the plaza," from H.C. Veatch.[16] Perhaps in a nod to his "mariner" father or those thirsty gentlemen from San Francisco who sailed to Santa Cruz each July, he named it "The Clipper."

Over the next few months, Lunt advertised heavily in both *The Sentinel* and *The Surf*, inviting his potential customers to "DRINK THE BEST!" and proclaiming "everything pure"—a thinly veiled criticism of other saloon-keepers who cut their whiskey with water. For the Clipper advertisement in *The Surf*, Lunt created a faux wanted broadside with the heading "999 Men Wanted to Drink at the Clipper Saloon."[17]

The Clipper had plenty of competition. In the late 1870s, Santa Cruz boasted some 55 saloons with names like "The Senate," "The Railroad Exchange," "The Banc," and "The Old Corner," which sported an oval bar in the middle of the building. Thirsty lumbermen could begin their binges at "The First Chance" and end them at "The Last Chance."

Along with dozens of taverns lining the thoroughfares, every hotel in town had a saloon. The most opulent belonged to the Pacific House, which sported a majestic mahogany bar fringed with a brass rail. Patrons who downed shots of whiskey at the bar could glimpse their reflections in the massive, 20-foot-wide mirror, encased in a baroque frame of black walnut, hanging on the wall in front of them.

In addition to pouring drinks, the saloonkeeper of the era also functioned as a banker, moneylender, gambling impresario, and sometimes pimp.

Names of small saloons like "The Railroad Exchange" and "The Banc" hint at one of these secondary functions. When lumbermen and other laborers wandered into town after hours on payday, saloon owners were happy to cash their checks. Unlike banks, saloons remained open

24-hours a day year-round, except for Election Day, when the law required them to close. Even then, most barkeeps simply shuttered their front doors but kept their rear doors open so politicians could sneak a bracer while monitoring returns.

The era's saloonkeepers cashed checks, but unlike their colleagues in the legitimate banking business, they did not extend credit and often tacked up cleverly worded signs notifying patrons of this fact: "In God We Trust, All Others Cash," and "To Trust Is Best, To Bust Is Hell, No Trust, No Bust, No Hell."[18]

Every watering hole from the opulent Pacific House saloon to Lunt's Clipper hosted games of chance, usually in the form or cards or dice. Whiskey and gambling sometimes made for a violent chemical reaction, leading to innumerable fights and the occasional shooting, which kept the local constables busy.

Contrary to the stereotypical image of the "Wild West" saloon, most taverns in Santa Cruz did not employ prostitutes. If a saloonkeeper did traffic with the demimonde, he kept that aspect of his business behind closed doors. "If girls had been about the bars in those days they would not have been seen from the sidewalk," noted old-timer and historian Ernest Otto. "Most likely a saloon keeper in those days would not have allowed them in his place of business at all."

As a boy, Otto delivered newspapers to area businesses, a duty that took him into the hazy, dusky world of the Wild West saloon. In a series of articles titled "Old Santa Cruz," the former newsboy describes the town of his youth, including a fascinating and lively narrative about the local bar scene. One piece contains a humorous anecdote that captures the atmosphere inside the area's drinking holes. The saloonkeepers always asked Otto to place the stack of newspapers on the bars because the thin sheen of tobacco-laden spittle covering the floor would spoil the newsprint. The inebriated patrons, Otto explains, struggled with their aim at the spittoons.[19]

Competition among the saloonkeepers was fierce, and each did what he could to attract customers. One tavern owner presented ostentatious displays of curios, including an array of nooses used in local hangings and lynchings.[20]

Lunt's foray into the saloon business lasted about six months. In early June 1884, he sold out to Mike O'Keefe, whom, in an ironic twist worthy of dime novels, he later arrested on an assault and battery charge.[21] According to Ernest Otto, Lunt left the bar-keeping business to pursue a career in law enforcement, but the election would not take place until the following November. More than likely, he decided to sell because he could not compete with the dozens of other saloonkeepers in Santa Cruz.[22]

The Second-Most Handsome Man
in the County (1884)

The Neptune Bath House was a majestic hotel that featured "hot salt water baths at all hours."[23] Located on a pristine stretch of beach, the romantic milieu became a popular place for dances, including a ball held in June 1884. The event culminated in a contest for the "Fairest Lady" and the "Handsomest Gentleman." The winners each received a prize: an ornately decorated fan for the lady voted "Fairest" and a pair of finely stitched slippers for the gentleman voted "Handsomest."

Audience members nominated their friends, and attendees paid a nickel for the privilege of voting. Eighteen-year-old Gertie Otto, sister of paperboy Ernest Otto, ran away with the competition, winning with a vast majority of 124 votes. In presenting the award, Mrs. Burke demurred. "It is ridiculous for a woman to make a speech," she said, "but I must say that you are fairer than the fan I present to you. If it was over a cup of tea I could say more."[24]

The contest for the "Handsomest Man," on the other hand, became an unexpectedly competitive affair. One attendee nominated Mayor Z.N. Goldsby. Another—Justice Spalsbury—praised the mayor for his service as a volunteer fireman and his good business sense, but pointed out that while a good city administrator, Goldsby fell short of the "handsomest" male in town. That accolade, Spalsbury said, belonged to young George Hastings, who many considered an Adonis.

What at first appeared to be a foregone conclusion—Hastings walking away from the competition wearing a new pair of embroidered slippers, ended when Amos Lunt's friends nominated him. A fierce but playful debate ensued. Hastings' friends hailed his virtues, and Lunt's friends countered with his. After the final tally, Hastings won the slippers by a nose, edging Lunt's 380 votes with his 395.[25]

*   *   *

As owner of The Clipper, Amos Lunt, Jr., became the de facto sheriff responsible for maintaining law and order in a volatile environment populated by a motley crew of loggers, miners, gamblers, and ne'er-do-wells. In a town with a nascent police department consisting of a lone constable who could not possibly patrol all the thriving nightspots, Lunt would have broken up dozens of fights between his bleary-eyed patrons. In this role as an unofficial peacekeeper, Lunt was a step away from a star, a nightstick, and a tunic.

In the fall of 1884, Lunt decided to take that step by running for "Constable of Sea Side Township" as the Republican nominee. He campaigned heavily for the spot and placed regular advertisements in the local papers but lost a close race.

The 36-year-old ex-lumberman, ex-saloonkeeper found himself without a means to support his wife and one-year-old daughter. He would eventually pin the star to his jacket, but not until 1886.

"Amos Lunt must have sent them" (1885)

By mid–1885, Amos Lunt, Jr., had acquired a reputation for hedonism. Although nothing in the historical record suggests that he ever indulged in opium, he drank alcohol and snuffed tobacco frequently. While news reporters of the era tended to turn a blind eye to substance use, Lunt's use of tobacco became a matter of public record when the *Santa Cruz Sentinel* ran an amusing blurb in the May 22, 1885, edition.

"'Who could have sent me these beautiful flowers?' asked a prominent young man in the audience at the Opera House last evening, as he sniffed the fragrance of a bouquet. When he began to sneeze he mentally exclaimed that Amos Lunt must have sent them, as they were filled with snuff."[26]

The light-hearted tone of the blurb suggests that the writer intended nothing more than a playful jab at the former saloon owner, but it illustrates how the community had come to view the man who aspired to become town constable.

The "House No. 10" affair (1885)

In 1885, Amos Lunt, Jr., played a bit role in the "House No. 10" scandal. That March, Nellie Clark, Lottie Phillips, Frankie Adams, and Frankie Kern were arrested for living in "a house of ill fame." The case originated with an anonymous "complaining witness" who lost $20 while visiting "House No. 10." Convinced that one of the women stole the money, this complainant took his case to the local police. Frankie Adams and Frankie Kern skipped town, leaving Lottie Phillips and Nellie Clark holding the bag. Labeled "nymphs du pave" by the local press, the women each posted $25 in bail and began preparing for their moment in justice court.[27]

After Justice of the Peace John Pope Davenport determined that St. Patrick's Day did not qualify as a legal holiday and therefore a verdict rendered on that day would not trigger an appeal, testimony began in the cases of Lottie Phillips and Nellie Clark.

The trial opened to a standing room only crowd on Tuesday, March 17, 1885. A *Sentinel* journalist studied the women of the hour. "Both females were gaudily arrayed and closely veiled," he wrote. "Either would not capture a prize in a contest for beauty."[28] He described Phillips as "short and stout" and Clark as "tall and angular."[29]

The trial, with testimony from men who had heard about the goings-on inside "House No. 10" but swore they had no inside knowledge, scandalized Santa Cruz. Midway through the prosecution's case against Nellie Clark, an elderly man named William Pephfer took the stand. Inebriated, he slurred his way through this testimony, during which he said he visited the house, downed a few shots, and "cohabited with the defendant."[30]

Amos Lunt, Jr., entered the drama when he came forward and claimed that Pephfer had lied on the stand by stating that he had "cohabited" with Nellie Clark in "House No. 10."[31] Lunt's knowledge as to whether or not Pephfer had bedded Clark most likely put him inside "House No. 10" that night, linking him with known prostitutes and a notorious brothel. Whatever the case, his complaint greatly helped Nellie Clark's case and led to a perjury charge against Pephfer.

A single holdout against conviction led to a hung jury in the Nellie Clark trial. After the jury in Clark's second trial also failed to reach a unanimous decision, Justice Davenport dismissed the case altogether. Shortly afterward, Nellie Clark relocated to San Francisco. That April, she was arrested for vagrancy, and the following September, she and a woman named Flora Saunders stood accused of stealing $30 to $40 from a customer. Over the next few years, she faced numerous charges linked to prostitution.[32]

Walking the Beat (1886)

The year 1886 would be another watershed in the biography of Amos Lunt, Jr. In early June, he formally began his career in law enforcement when he obtained the long-coveted role as a town constable.[33]

Three months later, he lost the "Jr." when his father died at the age of 66. The elder Lunt worked at a local lumber mill up until a week before he died.[34] In mid–September, he had a stroke that left him partially paralyzed. He convalesced in Amos and Laura Lunt's Pacific Avenue home for about a week before passing away. His beloved Mary followed him two years later, in 1888, at the age of 62.

2

The Wild West of
Amos Lunt, Lawman

(1886–1890)

Amos Lunt's career in law enforcement began in 1886, when he joined a three-man police department that consisted of two night watchmen and Chief W.W. "Will" Clark.[1] As one of the two night watchmen, Lunt faced the daunting task of policing what could be at times a real Wild West town.

Over the next five years, Lunt became the key figure in several fascinating cases that illustrate both his personality and that of Santa Cruz in the late 1880s.

The Case of the Purloined Overcoat (May 1887)

The *Santa Cruz Daily Surf* called it "a shrewd piece of detective work by Officer Amos Lunt."[2]

In late April, a guest at the Ocean House Hotel reported the theft of a valuable overcoat and robe. Vincent Nolan, night clerk at the Ocean House, spotted a figure lurking around the hotel and saw enough of the man to give a sketchy description to Lunt. After searching every saloon and hotel in Santa Cruz, Constable Lunt concluded that the man had skipped town.

A week later, while strolling down Pacific Avenue with County Undersheriff Tom Dakan, Lunt learned about a prisoner who had just escaped from custody in the nearby town of Soquel. The description of the escapee matched that of the hotel stalker, so Lunt and Dakan made a beeline to Soquel. They found Constable Daubinbiss in Arana Gulch, where he had collared his escapee, Alex McDonald.

After eying the suspect, Lunt became convinced that Alex McDonald was the Ocean Hotel thief. The three officers dragged McDonald to Santa

Cruz, where they put him in front of Nolan. A quick nod of the head confirmed Lunt's suspicions.

While Dakan took McDonald to a cell, Lunt attempted to track down the stolen items. He learned about a resident of Arana Gulch who had recently purchased an expensive coat for pennies on the dollar. Lunt returned to Santa Cruz, put McDonald into a buggy, and drove him to Arana Gulch. For a second time, Lunt obtained a positive identification when the man fingered McDonald as the seller.

Amos Lunt caught his culprit and recovered the stolen goods.

Operation Red Light (November 1887)

Authorities allowed the use of opium in Chinese enclaves but prosecuted its use outside of those areas. In late 1887, Constable Amos Lunt became aware of a burgeoning opium problem outside of Chinatown, particularly among youngsters. Since they did not smoke the pipe in any of the Chinatown establishments, they became especially difficult to track. Lunt suspected that one of them operated a den or "joint" in his parents' house, possibly in a barn or loft.

In February 1887, Lunt managed to collar three teenagers, including Harry Jones, who admitted to using opium over the previous four years to help with "lung troubles."

Interviewed by a *Daily Surf* reporter, Jones explained the difficulty he had experienced in obtaining the drug due to Lunt's vigilance. "Jones ... said that he had some trouble to procure the drug, as officer Lunt kept a close watch on him, and to procure the opium he had to go over the fences, along sewers and under houses to certain dens in Chinatown, where a Chinaman gave him the drug, of which he purchased seventy cents' worth at a time."

"The vigilance of Officer Lunt," the reporter concluded, "is to be commended in unearthing this case, and bringing it to light as a warning to white opium smokers, if there be any, that the eye of the officer is upon them, and their 'joints' will soon or later be unearthed."[3]

Throughout the summer of 1887, Lunt and company busted several opium dens or joints. Those caught smoking the seductive weed usually spent 25 days in the county jail. Most received the message loud and clear. Most except for one stubborn purveyor of opium. Lunt suspected that the son of a prominent citizen ran an opium den somewhere in town, but his suspicions remained unconfirmed until November, when he and Chief Clark witnessed a buy.

They trailed the seller to the second story of barn, but as they stepped closer, a watchdog gave the den's occupants an advanced warning. Two men hobbled down the flight of steps, followed by a third, who cradled a shotgun. Quick on his feet, Lunt grabbed the man before he could raise the firearm, and Clark went into the barn, where he found the opium den. The two stars took the purveyor and his stash of opium to the county jail.

By the end of 1887, the three-man department had managed to sanitize Santa Cruz of opium use outside of its Chinatown.

Clark and his two constables also waged a small-scale war against "undesirables," sending a strong message to red light district denizens when they arrested ten "brutes," fined them $50 each, gave them an overnight in the tax-funded hotel, and then demanded they leave town.

In a brief history of the men who wore the star in Santa Cruz, former Chief J.E. Armstrong, who served two terms (1889–1890 and 1906–1910), described Clark as responsible for "the best cleanup of undesirables that was ever made by any chief in the police history of Santa Cruz. This was the arrest of 10 human brutes who were living off the earnings of the red light district. They were fined $50 each, and given 24 hours in which to leave town."[4]

Although W.W. "Will" Clark wore the star, the *Santa Cruz Daily Surf* attributed much of this clean-up to one of the two town constables. "Officer Lunt has on many occasions achieved a reputation on account of his ability to trace down offenders of the law and has been especially successful in ridding the town of low characters," gushed a *Daily Surf* writer in an allusion to the Ocean House theft case. "The town has been well-cleaned of tramps, pimps and other similar characters owing to Officer Lunt's energy and detective work."[5]

The Case of the Twenty Dollar Gold Coins (May 1889)

Amos Lunt put on the Police Chief's badge in 1888, beginning a tenure cut short less than a year later by a political scandal.

Chief Lunt's idea of justice did not always align with those of the establishment, which led to occasional clashes with authority. One illustrative incident occurred in May 1889 when he arrested Steve Avilla. Avilla and an accomplice named Juan Mesa rolled a drunk named Manuel Bedell and made away with over $70 in gold coins. Lunt caught Avilla, who claimed that Bedell had given him money to pay for drinks. Lunt, who did not believe one word of Avilla's story, reconstructed his movements after the robbery and discovered that the thief had changed several $20 gold coins into smaller denominations by purchasing items at local stores.[6]

Armed with this evidence of conversion, Lunt, in the words of the *Santa Cruz Daily Surf*, "extracted a full confession" from his suspect. According to Avilla, he and Mesa agreed to a 50-50 split of the take but, proving the adage that there is no honor among thieves, Mesa in turn robbed Avilla. To the Chief, it seemed like an open-and-shut case of grand larceny.

Rather than throwing the book at the malefactors, the Police Court judge handed down what to Lunt felt more like a slap-on-the-wrist punishment. Avilla pled guilty to petty theft and received 60 days behind bars. Mesa pled not guilty. After a brief trial, he received the option of 90 days in jail or a $90 fine. When he elected to pay the fine, Lunt lost his temper. "He [Mesa] offered to pay the fine immediately if allowed to go home, but Chief of Police Lunt was so aggravated at the manner in which justice (?) was dealt out that he refused to accommodate the prisoner and he [Mesa] was taken to jail."[7]

The historical record does not contain the judge's reaction to Chief Lunt's petulance, but the peace officer may have narrowly escaped spending a night in the county lockup.

During the summer of 1889, Chief Lunt became the subject of a putsch. On July 1, the city council voted for a resolution to remove Lunt as police chief. News items about Lunt's ousting do not state the reasons, but J.E. Armstrong, who replaced Lunt, offered a hint. "Amos Lunt then wore the star for part of one year, being duly discharged for naughty conduct. J.E. Armstrong (that's me) was appointed to serve the remainder of Lunt's term, which I did, and resigned in 1890."[8]

Armstrong did not define "naughty," but another news item, published in the *Santa Cruz Sentinel* a decade later, provides a clue. "At one time he [Lunt] was the Chief of Police in his city. He was a good officer, barring occasions when he drank more than was good for him, which were not often. Through this weakness he lost his billet."[9] He may have drunk himself out of the good graces of the townsfolk, who blanched at the idea of an inebriated police chief.

Lunt vowed to fight the legality of his dismissal, and for a brief time the town had two police chiefs. "The truth is," quipped a *Daily Surf* writer, "that though Santa Cruz cannot boast of two Dromios, she has two Chiefs of Police—Lunt and Armstrong—and both wear the star. The situation is a complicated one and may give rise to some racy scenes before it closes."[10]

The "two Dromios" comment—a reference to characters in Shakespeare's *A Comedy of Errors*—represented a scathing rebuke of the city officials. Shakespeare's "Dromios" were twin slaves. Constantly mistaken for each other by their masters, they were, in the words of the *Daily Surf* reporter, "both beaten all the time." The writer's allusion suggested that Lunt and Armstrong were the Dromios in the Comedy of Errors that was led by the City Council masters.

If the dispute led to any racy scenes, they escaped publication. Lunt's thunder apparently came without rain. In the end, he lost his star, which really amounted to a demotion. By the following week, Officer Lunt was back patrolling the mean streets of Santa Cruz. One of his first collars involved a familiar face.

In a twist involving several layers of irony, the former police chief dismissed for drinking arrested the man who had purchased his Clipper saloon five years earlier.

On Friday, July 12, William O'Connell stopped by Mike O'Keefe's saloon for a few drinks. When he conveniently forgot to pay, O'Keefe pistol-whipped him. O'Connell wobbled out of the saloon and grabbed the first officer he found, which happened to be Amos Lunt, who subsequently arrested the barkeep for battery.[11]

The Strange Case of the Wild Man (July 20, 1889)

Officer Lunt's courageous behavior went on display during the summer of 1889, when he tracked down and arrested the "Wild Man."

Stories about a bestial man inhabiting the thick woods around the city ran through Santa Cruz like wildfire during the summer of 1889. The man, described as a hairy troglodyte, harassed people who wandered into his woods. In late July, he accosted a young couple. The terrified teens later recounted their run-in with the legendary beast in a brief interview with a local reporter.

"I wonder if the wild man is anywhere about here?" the girl asked her beau as they passed through a wooded area beyond the fringes of town. Like some demented genie conjured by the question, the wild man materialized from the woods. "Yes, I'm the wild man," he growled, "and I'm after you." The Wild Man howled in laughter as the youngsters ran away.

The next day, Chief Armstrong and a small contingent combed the woods for the mysterious figure. On a hill above Wildcat Creek, they found his lair: a hollow underneath the stump of a cedar tree and covered with a carpet. The space—about four feet high and three feet wide—contained clear evidence of long-term habitation. A smattering of pots and pans indicated that the Wild Man apparently cooked his meals over a rough fire pit.

Armstrong managed to find the Wild Man's lair but not the Wild Man himself.

Something about the Wild Man and his behavior seemed familiar to Amos Lunt. He suspected that the beast was a habitual drunk named William Ramsey, whose heavy drinking binges transformed him into a raving maniac. Lunt may have even witnessed such a transformation when he operated The Clipper. Ramsey also had a tendency to disappear for weeks at a time.

Lunt, accompanied by a young man named Ben Skirm, went into the woods to test his theory. At the Wild Man's lair, Skirm spotted a pair of legs jutting out from under the carpet. "There he is."

"Hello, Ramsey, are you dead?" Lunt asked, half-joking.

"No, I ain't dead," came a gruff voice from under the carpet. "What do you want of me? You ain't going to arrest me again, are you?"

The shape that emerged from the hollow looked more like a wild critter than a human. His face was barely discernible under a film of dirt and sticky residue of tar weed mixed with sweat. Scratches from crawling through sharp underbrush crisscrossed his neck and arms. His tattered clothes hung from his body.

Ramsey explained that he felt comfortable living in the woods and only harangued people during periods of drunken delirium or the "jim jams," as he called them.

Lunt escorted the Wild Man back to town, where he would go in front of a judge for drunk and disorderly conduct. Apart from scaring a few passersby, he did nothing to warrant more serious charges. Before he could stand in front of a judge, Ramsey cleaned up his act. He washed, shaved, and put on a new suit of clothes. Then he posed for a photograph … wearing shackles and holding a club.

As usual, the *Surf* had nothing but love for Lunt. "The wild-man-of-the-woods sensation is no more, having been exploded by ex-Chief of Police Amos Lunt, now acting as constable," proclaimed the *Surf* correspondent. The reporter credited Chief Armstrong for "finding the lair," but "it remained for ex-Chief Lunt to discover the man and dispel the mystery."[12]

White Picket Fence (March 1890)

In March 1890, the 43-year-old lawman moved his family to a house on Pacific Avenue near Cathcart Street. A spacious front yard, surrounded by a white picket fence, gave seven-year-old Lottie and three-year-old Arnold a nice place to play. The colorful blooms of the garden and the flower-lined path delighted Laura Lunt. The move warranted a brief mention in the local society news. "Constable Amos Lunt and family have moved into one of the houses belonging to John R. Chace, on Pacific avenue, near Cathcart street."[13]

The Chalk Hill Road Gang (January–February 1891)

Lust's last significant action as a Santa Cruz lawman occurred in January and February of 1891, when he oversaw a chain gang of county prisoners constructing a road on Chalk Road Hill.

A reporter sarcastically commented about Lunt's detail. "Fourteen interesting specimens of the genus tramp were marshaled in glorious array under the leadership of Amos Lunt out to Chalk Road Hill where with the aid of a pick-ax and shovel they will reduce the proportions of that romantic upheaval."[14]

For the sharp-witted constable with a nose for clues and a tenacity for following them where they led, this chain-gang duty had to feel tedious. In three months, the former police chief would have a new position policing some of the most dangerous men in California.

3

Sheriff William E. Hale and the Sutton Debacle

(1888–1889)

While Amos Lunt policed the mean streets of Santa Cruz, Sheriff William E. Hale did his best to keep law and order in Alameda County.

Born in Massachusetts in 1842, Hale traveled west as a young man, his journey taking him to Gold Hill, Nevada, where he worked as a Wells Fargo agent. After his brief stint among miners, he continued west and settled in California. Running as a Republican, Hale won the first of three elections for sheriff of Alameda County in 1884, winning reelection in 1886 and again in 1888.

Hale liked the work of sheriff and made an excellent lawman, although he despised one particular facet of the position: as a county sheriff, he was responsible for the hanging of condemned convicts.

A year after California joined the Union, state legislators enacted the Criminal Practices Act, a law that empowered county sheriffs to carry out hangings. In 1872, capital punishment became part of the state's penal code, and for the next 20 years, official hangings remained the responsibility of local law enforcement. While vigilance committees and lynch mobs meted out frontier justice by administering ad hoc hangings, county sheriffs conducted the only officially sanctioned, legal executions.

During his tenure, Sheriff Hale presided over just two hangings, the second of which was such a disaster that it set into motion a chain of events leading to a change in how the state of California handled executions. It would also transform a former small-town constable into the hangman of San Quentin.

*   *   *

On Friday, January 6, 1888, 58-old Nathan B. Sutton took his place on the scaffold for the murder of Alexander Martin—the fourth official

35

hanging in Alameda County and the first since 1884.[1] The cause of Sutton's "necktie party" took place nearly two years earlier, on the morning of September 15, 1886, when Martin went to round up some cattle that had wandered onto Sutton's land. The bad blood between Sutton and the Martin family stretched back almost fifteen years and stemmed from several incidents when, Sutton alleged, the Martins allowed their stock to graze on his land. The feud came to a head when Sutton noticed his neighbor once again traipsing on his property. He charged the unsuspecting rancher and shot him in the chest with a Winchester rifle.

Indignant and unrepentant even as the hour of his execution approached, Sutton claimed to be the only man in California executed for defending his land.

The hanging took place in the southeast corner of the Alameda County Jail yard on a scaffold assembled 24 hours earlier.[2] From his cell across the yard, Sutton could hear the workmen hammering together the 71 pieces of Oregon pine and 50 bolts that made up the gallows. "A flight of twelve steps leads to the platform," noted the Oakland Daily Evening Tribune, "giving the ominous number 'thirteen' that must be counted before the death trap is reached."[3]

Official hangings always attracted a great deal of attention from the press. Journalists from around the area converged on the jail yard to marvel at the scaffold and its unique feature: a blind designed to protect the conscience of the men tasked with triggering the drop.

An Evening Tribune writer described the gallows configuration and the mechanism that would trigger the drop. "Three cords are stretched to a hole in a long box standing on end. One of these cords is attached to the weights. The other cords are dummies. They are cut at the same time the cord attached to the weights is severed, but none of the three men who cut them can tell which knife has released the weights that sprung the trap. The fall of the weights forces the iron rods back and the doors fall striking against the ends of the stays that have rubber bearings producing the 'dull sickening thud' that used to appear so frequently in the accounts of hangings."[4]

For the rope, Hale selected a 40-foot-long manila manufactured by the Tubbs Company. To soften the rope, he soaked it in oil. As for Hale's choice for noose, a journalist later explained, "It is a five eighth inch rope of twenty one threads, this size being preferable to the three-quarter inch sometimes used, as a noose turned in it will not 'render' or yield, the knot staying where it is placed. The three-quarter inch noose, it is claimed, is apt to slip around the man's neck and strangulation under these circumstances invariably ensues. The small role, if properly adjusted, will break a man's neck if the length of the drop is properly proportioned to the weight of the man. The larger rope if it does not strangle cuts the neck deeply and instances have been known where the head was severed entirely from the body."[5] After measuring and weighing Sutton, Hale calculated the drop as eight feet.

The ensuing drama would play to a crowd of 250 witnesses invited by Hale to attend the hanging, none of whom belonged to Martin's family; Hale rejected their application to attend Sutton's execution.[6] On the outside of the high board fence surrounding the jail yard, boys shimmied up trees or pressed up against the fence to peer through gaps between the boards or knotholes in the wood.

As the clock at the courthouse chimed twelve, all eyes focused on the door at the rear of the jail swung open and Sutton began his walk down a roped-off path to the scaffold. A representative from the *Oakland Daily Evening Tribune* (and one of Hale's invitees) described Sutton's dramatic entrance: "Then silence, and the crowd swayed backward as Sheriff Hale appeared at the door holding the left arm of Sutton, on whose face was a smile.... He exhibited no emotion whatever as he caught the first glimpse of the machinery of death—the stout beam overhead, the snake like rope coiling around it, the crowd assembled to see him die."[7]

His arms strapped to his sides, Sutton wobbled across the yard, up the flight of steps and onto the platform. He gave a brief speech, in which he thanked Sheriff Hale for his kind treatment and characterized himself as "the first man in the State of California that was legally executed for defending his property."[8]

Sheriff's deputies then pinioned Sutton's legs. Game to the last, the condemned man quipped, "Let me have the necktie, Mr. Woolsey." He reached for the rope, but Deputy Sheriff Woolsey gently pushed it away and slipped the noose over his neck.

"I took that collar off," Sutton said—referring to his collarless shirt— as Woolsey pulled a black hood over his head, "so's to give you a fair show."

"The hideous front of the cap at first wrinkled, filled with the short breath of the unfortunate man," noted the *Tribune* writer, "and the cloth stood out smooth like a little balloon."

Hale nodded, and three volunteers each severed a cord, one of which pulled back the V-shaped rods under the trapdoor. The floor fell out from under Sutton's feet with a dull thud. The eight-foot drop broke the condemned man's neck, but Hale had made two critical errors in his preparation that became obvious in the half-second it took for Sutton to reach the end of his rope: he miscalculated the length of the drop, and he failed to stretch the rope adequately.[9] The hemp had retained some play, and Sutton's body bounced at the bottom of the drop.

The *Tribune* writer gave a graphic description of the result. Leaving nothing to the imagination, he wrote:

As the body brought up, a noise was heard such as but few in that crowd have ever listened to—a sound that none of them ever wish to hear again. It was like the gurgle of wind and blood from the laboring chest of a dying man.

"God!" cried a man in the crowd, "it is blood!" Yes, it was blood—blood spurting from the left side of his neck—blood bubbling from the right side— blood welling from in front—rushing in a thick crimson torrent over the bosom of the dead man's shirt—blood staining the cruel rope as it cut deeper and deeper through the tissues, through the vessels and arteries, through the throat until it lay against the vertebra at the back of the neck. Blood that dripped, dripped from his feet, forming a sanguinary pool on the ground which sucked it voraciously, leaving only a dark, clotted stain in the moist sand. The crowd stood spellbound with horror. They could see that the rope had cut nearly through the neck, and they expected every moment that the head would leave the body and add this other touch of horror.[10]

The attending physicians examined Sutton's body. The noose had achieved its purpose, crushing Sutton's vertebrae and severing his spinal cord below the medulla oblongata, but the rope had cut clean through the soft tissues of his neck, leaving his corpse hanging from a thread, literally. In the words of one eyewitness, the "body being sustained only by a thin piece of skin at the back of the neck where the knot rested."

Despite the massive loss of blood from the severed carotid artery and jugular vein, a faint flutter remained in Sutton's chest, so his body dangled from a thread for a tense 16 minutes as the audience watched, horrified at the possibility that the thread might give way at any time.

A curious reporter watched as Dr. E.H. Woolsey raised the black hood and slid his hand into the gaping wound. "He removed several clots of blood and then proceeded to feel about in the gash until his fingers dripped with blood. As he did so, a whispering whistling sound proceeded from the wound."[11]

Scribbling notes as he watched Dr. Woolsey examine Sutton's body, the Evening Tribune reporter recorded the physician's reaction. Pulling his blood-streaked hands out of "Sutton's blood-gaping aorta," he remarked. "This is the way the just ought to die, I think it was an outrage to hang this man. Hanging is barbarous, anyhow." The disgust was evident in his word choice and tone, which the journalist described as "indignant."[12]

Dr. Woolsey's acerbic comments may have represented the collective feeling about Sutton's execution. Several spectators, sickened by the sight, darted out of the yard. Embarrassed and eager that none of the crowd would see Sutton's head fall, Hale ordered the rest of the audience out of the yard as well. "If you don't cut him down pretty soon his whole head will be off," Dr. Woolsey warned. "The rope is cutting his head off."[13]

The rope was severed before the sinews and tendons snapped under the weight of the dead body. Sutton's corpse was gently set into a coffin and quickly taken out of the jail yard, but the story did not end there.

News of the bloody fiasco appeared on front pages across the state. *The San Francisco Chronicle*'s coverage noted, "The execution was a horrible sight, for, on account of the unusual length of the drop—eight feet— the throat the unfortunate man was cut by the rope and the blood gushed forth in streams."[14]

The disastrous hanging even disturbed the dead man's final bequest. In a letter to Sheriff Hale, Sutton wrote, "I desire that my remains be delivered to the Medical Department of the University of California, and request that my bones be set up in the University, so that if any of my friends should ever come to this coast and so desire, they can take a look at what once was."[15] The University of California's Medical Department, however, rejected Sutton's corpse because of the damage to the neck tissues.

The near-decapitation fell short of the dignified death the audience expected. Hale was humiliated. He immediately began work on a bill that would the take the noose out of his hands by making executions the responsibility of state prison officials.

4

The Last Straw

Sheriff McDougall and the Eubanks Hanging (January 1891)

At about the time that Amos Lunt marshaled "fourteen interesting specimens of the genus tramp" on Chalk Road Hill, Santa Clara County Sheriff Giles McDougall began making preparations to hang convicted murderer James Eubanks. He stretched the hemp, measured the condemned, calculated the drop, and oversaw the construction of the gallows.

As a hangman, McDougall had considerably more experience than his colleague in neighboring Alameda County. By 1891, the 58-year-old sheriff had officiated over several hangings, but almost three years from the day of the Sutton debacle, history would repeat itself in Santa Clara when a fatal miscalculation led to another botched hanging.

* * *

James Eubanks murdered his 16-year-old daughter Ada in December 1889 because she refused to relinquish the money she had earned as a waitress at a local hotel called the Heath House. After downing a few shots at a saloon next door, Eubanks calmly walked into the kitchen of the Heath House carrying a shotgun and shot Ada in the chest at point blank range. He then tried to shoot himself, but while loading the weapon in a drunken haze, he put both cartridges into one barrel. When he pulled the trigger, he ended up with only a minor powder burn on his cheek.

Eubanks returned to the saloon, downed more whiskey, and went upstairs, where he tried to cut his throat with a straight razor. For a second time in the span of an hour, he failed in his attempt at suicide and only managed to cut a deep gash running the entire length of his neck. Sentenced to hang, he would expiate his crime in the prison yard of the county jail in San Jose in front of 200 spectators, including several journalists, who stood shoulder to shoulder to watch swift justice enacted at the end

The typical scaffold used in county hangings was a simple structure that could be assembled and disassembled quickly, such as this gallows used in Mercer County, New Jersey, shown in a photograph circa 1907. After a hanging, the scaffold was taken apart and the pieces stored, preferably in a dry, cool place. Humidity could cause wooden floorboards to swell and impede the quick release of the trap (author's collection).

of a rope. The hanging took place just about a year after the Sutton debacle shocked witnesses in the yard of Hale's Alameda County Jail.

A *San Francisco Examiner* described the condemned man on the Friday before his execution, scheduled for Monday, January 19, 1891. "He is fat, weight 200 pounds and is gradually overcoming his nervous dread of the ordeal plainly visible last week and he claims will bear up to the end with becoming Christian values."[1]

The correspondent described the physical dynamics of the impending execution. The gallows, stored in pieces in the cellar of the county courthouse, would be reassembled behind the 25-foot-tall fence of the jail yard. Sheriff Giles McDougall had made all the necessary preparations. "Sheriff

This rare sequence of photographs chronicles the public hanging of two unidentified men. Before California law shifted the responsibility of executions to state prison officials, county sheriffs conducted hangings. But without the services of a professional hangman, they often bungled them. In the first image, two condemned men, their arms strapped to their sides, walk to the scaffold erected on the outskirts of town (author's collection).

Spectators, including a man on a horse and a young boy, listen as one of the condemned men addresses the crowd. Only a select number of witnesses, and no minors, would be permitted to attend hangings inside San Quentin (author's collection).

McDougall has a new five-eighth inch rope which he is now testing with 300 pound weights," the correspondent noted.

After measuring and weighing Eubanks, who tipped the scales at 210 pounds, McDougall calculated the drop at five feet—an accurate measurement that resulted in a quick, painless death lauded by the *Examiner* correspondent. "Death was instantaneous," he wrote. "Not a convulsion followed the drop."

McDougall, however, did not account for the deep wound on Eubanks' neck when he calculated the drop at five feet. The result was disastrous. The *Examiner* correspondent sarcastically described the execution as "perfect in every detail" before detailing the macabre scene.

The sheriff fits the noose on one of the men while the other man makes his final speech. County hangings were often lengthy, drawn-out affairs, whereas hangings at San Quentin—from the entrance of the condemned man until the drop—consumed just minutes (author's collection).

Attending physicians feel the wrists of each man for a pulse. Note the leather straps used to restrict movement. After such hangings, the bodies would be left suspended, allowing curious onlookers the opportunity to take mementos, such as a piece of the rope or a lock of hair (author's collection).

"Eubanks was very fleshy, weighed 210 pounds, and the fall of five feet two inches re-opened the old self-inflicted wound in his neck, and nearly severed the head from the body."[2]

No doubt to the delight of his more morbid readers, the anonymous journalist gave a graphic description of what happened when the trap was sprung. "The head was nearly severed from the body. The vertebrae separated nearly three inches and the old wound, inflicted by himself at the time the crime was committed, was torn open, sending a spray of blood that soon covered the front of his black clothes. His body, weighing 210

Opposite bottom: Public hangings were popular. The crowd watches in tense anticipation as the sheriff makes last-minute preparations of tightening the nooses and fitting the caps over the heads of the two men (author's collection).

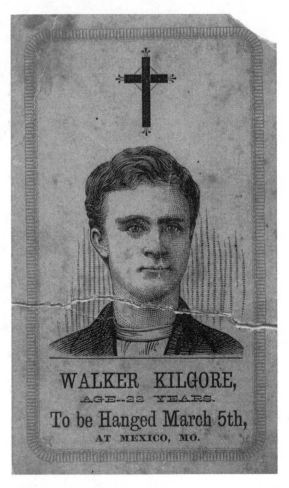

WALKER KILGORE,
AGE-22 YEARS.
To be Hanged March 5th,
AT MEXICO, MO.

Above and opposite: County hangings often drew large crowds. The limited space of a jail yard often forced the local sheriff to issue tickets or passes. When the hanging was conducted in an open space such as a field, attendance could run into the hundreds. This is a card advertising the forthcoming hanging of 22-year-old Walker Kilgore in Mexico, Missouri, in 1880. "Not less than five thousand persons surrounded the scaffold," noted the *Mexico Weekly Ledger*, "some in trees and some on the railroad bridge. We even noticed a great many women present." The scaffold, erected the night before the execution, only stood five feet high, which did not allow for a proper drop. The result was a botched hanging. "Seventeen minutes after the drop fell he was dead," wrote a *Weekly Ledger*'s on-scene reporter, "and had been hanging thirty minutes exactly when he was cut down by the sheriff…. His neck never broke at all. He died by strangulation. His tongue was clinched between his teeth, cutting it slightly. Discoloration of face very slight, and eyes not closed" (author's collection).

THE CRIME
The Doomed Boy Committed.

THE MURDER.

On the 27th day of January, 1879, Lorenzo Dow Willingham was shot and killed by Walker Kilgore. Willingham was on a load of corn-fodder at the time he was shot, but was afterwards found on the stile-blocks at the house of Mr. Krunkle, about 7 miles northeast of Mexico, in a dying condition. His last words were that Kilgore had shot him—that they were not in a fight, but that he was shot from the bush. Kilgore asserts his innocence, and claims that he shot in self defense. Willingham had a pistol, but did not use it.

CAUSE OF THE MURDER.

Willingham was hauling off some fodder said to belong to Kilgore. In fact, there had been "bad blood" existing between the parties for sometime, which finally ended in Kilgore killing Willingham. After the deed was committed Kilgore came to Mexico and gave himself up to Sheriff Glascock.

KILGORE'S BIOGRAPHY.

Walker Kilgore was born in the year 1857, on the Henley farm, on Skull Lick, about 10 miles northwest of Mexico, near where Reuben Pulis now lives. His father's name was Harlan Kilgore, and his mother was named Frances Kilgore, who was a daughter of old Sam Kilgore. Walker's mother (who was a cousin to Harlan Kilgore), was only 18 years old when Walker was born. She afterwards married Marion Kilgore—Harlan's brother—by whom she had another son, Alex. Kilgore, and who is half brother to Walker. Walker Kilgore is, therefore, the illegitimate son of Harlan Kilgore.

Dow Willingham's father was named Delone Willingham. During the war he was sent to prison at Alton, Ills., took sick there, was brought home and died in Mexico. Sarah Willingham (Dow's mother) now lives on the old "Lone" Willingham farm, about 7 miles north of Mexico.

Dow was about 35 years old at the time he was killed.

It has been stated that Kilgore and Willingham were cousins, but they are in no way related.

pounds, was suspended by the muscles at the bank of his neck, the rope having cut deep into the flesh."[3]

Eubanks' motionless body had dangled from the rope—swaying slightly as the momentum from the drop died—for two minutes when the attending physician approached with stethoscope in hand. He could not find a pulse but heard a slight flutter in Eubanks' chest, so sheriff's deputies waited until 15 minutes had passed to cut the rope.

While they gently lowered Eubanks' corpse into a coffin sitting next to the scaffold, a small crowd, including a local reporter, began to gather around the pine box. A hushed silence fell on them as a deputy tugged the black hood up and over the dead man's ears.

Then a collective gasp. "The throat was cut open eight inches across," the reporter noted.[4] From the jail yard, the undertaker transported Eubanks' body to his establishment, where he displayed it in the front parlor. Over the next few days, 2,000 curious onlookers paraded past the macabre display.

According to some sources, the Eubanks fiasco nearly unhinged McDougall. He subsequently lobbied for a bill that would make executions the responsibility of state prison officials and even reportedly sent letters to all county sheriffs urging their support.

Still reeling from the embarrassment of the Sutton hanging, Hale joined McDougall in a crusade to change how the state of California handled officially sanctioned executions.

The two sheriffs became prime movers in formulating a bill that shifted the responsibility for executions from the counties to the state. If the bill became law, the hangman's noose would pass from county sheriffs such as Hale to the wardens of the state prisons at San Quentin and Folsom.

5

Warden Hale and the Politics of Execution

(April 1891)

William E. Hale was about to become the victim of a cruel reversal of fortune. In a way, he had tied his own noose.

In November 1890, Hale ran for a fourth term as Alameda County sheriff but lost the election. A few months later, he traded his star for a desk when he became warden of the state prison at San Quentin.[1] The change of milieu must have come as a relief for the 42-year-old lawman; he had at last rid himself of the loathsome role of officiating over hangings.

Less than a month after taking the position, the new warden became the victim of a cruel irony when the bill he helped conceive—the bill that shifted the burden of official executions from county sheriffs to State prison wardens—became law. The statute proclaimed, "A judgement of death must be executed within the walls of one of the State prisons designated by the Court by which judgment is rendered."[2] California's new law took the noose out of the hands of county sheriffs entirely and made official hangings the sole purview of prison wardens.[3]

The law also did away with the public spectacles of past executions, which were community events attended by scores of morbidly curious onlookers, including children. The new statute limited the audience to a select few. Invitations, signed by local sheriffs, would become relics of a bygone era. Instead, the guest list for San Quentin's necktie parties would contain (excluding prison personnel involved in the procedure): the warden, a doctor, the state attorney general, one to two "ministers of the Gospel," no more than five persons invited by the condemned, 12 "reputable citizens," and "such peace officers as the Warden desires."[4] None of the spectators could be underage.

Designed in part as a response to death penalty opponents, the new statute contained a precise timeline to avoid lengthy lapses of time between a sentence and an execution. A hanging judge had ten days to deliver a death warrant to the county sheriff. Upon receiving a signed death warrant from the court, the sheriff had ten days to deliver the condemned prisoner to the warden of a state penitentiary for expiation of the sentence, which had to take place between 60 and 90 days from the date the condemned was received.

The sheriff who once officiated over the occasional hanging in Alameda now faced the daunting prospect of conducting executions for counties throughout the state.

Reporters reveled in the irony. In an homage to Gilbert and Sullivan's Mikado, one clever writer dubbed Hale the "Lord High Executioner of the State" and described his predicament.

> A bill signed by Governor Markham makes the Warden at San Quentin "High Executioner of the land"; not that he must swing a sharp-edged sword, like the chap in "Mikado," but he will be obliged to "swing" from the gallows all in the State who are condemned to death. Warden Hale does not relish his dark-bordered honor, but the joker in the case lies in the fact that he is the father of the bill. While Sheriff of Alameda he wished to avoid the unpleasant duty of hanging men. A brilliant idea struck him. Why not have a public executioner, as they have in other States. He worked long and hard to accomplish this, and at last got the matter in shape to present to the legislature. The bill was a sort of boomerang, for no sooner was Mr. Hale installed in office as Warden than the half-forgotten bill was signed, and now it devolves on Mr. Hale to do all the hanging for the State.[5]

The writer characterized the new San Quentin warden as the sole executioner for California, but the warden of the state prison at Folsom—Captain Charles Aull—would bear a similar responsibility. Because of the ten-day time limit for the delivery of the condemned, it appeared that geography would determine the place of execution; sheriffs from the "Bay" counties and south would send their condemned to San Quentin, while those from northern counties would send their condemned to Folsom.[6] However, executions did not begin at Folsom prison until 1895, and over the next five years, almost twice as many hangings would occur at San Quentin.[7]

6

The San Quentin Gallows
and Gallows Procedures

(April 1891–August 1892)

Over the first few weeks of April 1891, William Hale began preparations to fulfill his new duties as "Lord High Executioner."

First, he needed to find a suitable place to serve as a death house. Rejecting a proposal to erect the gallows in the prison yard, where the population could see and hear the proceedings, Hale selected a vacant factory building on the perimeter of the prison complex.

Hale later explained his decision. "You see, we have 1200 prisoners here, and, of course, they do not like this sort of thing. I selected the place for the execution with a view to having it conducted so quietly that it will not interfere with the work of the prison. At the hour of the hanging the prisoners will be at work as usual and as if nothing unusual was going on. It was suggested that they should be locked up in their cells and that the execution should take place in the prison yard so that they might all see it, but I did not favor that plan."[1]

The four-story brick structure once housed the prison's furniture factory, where convicts fulfilled the hard labor portion of their sentence by making chairs. When the manufacture of jute supplanted furniture in San Quentin's prison industry, most of the building became vacant. In April 1891, the building contained only a small machine shop and some rooms for storage.

The original plan called for building a platform over the elevator shaft leading from the first floor into the basement, which would provide a maximum drop of 14 feet. The platform, which would contain a trap door, would cover a portion of the eight-foot-square void but leave enough space to avoid obstructing the view of spectators, who would watch the proceedings from the cellar.

A curious *San Francisco Examiner* journalist described the proposed set-up: "The rope will be suspended from a heavy beam securely fastened to the rafters of the second floor, and the trap, of course, will be sprung from the main floor, so that the spectators below will not know who cut the rope."[2]

Next, Hale needed to find a location for the death cells, which would house a condemned man in the days immediately preceding his execution. As the date of a condemned convict's execution neared, he would be moved from death row into one of these cells, where a specially selected duo of guards—the Death Watch—would watch him around the clock.

Experience and common sense suggested a spot close to the gallows. Dead men walking tended to stumble during lengthy wobbles from their cells to the place of their execution. Such treks also complicated preparations; instead of pinioning the inmate's arms in the cell, the hangman would have to do this on the scaffold, which could only slow down the process, drawing out the condemned man's final minutes and exacerbating the potential mental anguish.

Hale eyed a small building adjacent to the vacant factory building for San Quentin's earliest death cells. Once inside San Quentin's new death cells, the condemned would be off-limits to morbid curiosity-seekers who flocked to every execution, collecting memento mori by cutting locks of hair from the deceased or slicing off pieces of the rope. "Condemned prisoners will be carefully guarded from the moment that the heavy gates of the main entrance close upon them until the moment of execution," a *San Francisco Examiner* journalist noted. "They will be, indeed, dead to the world when they pass under the Warden's jurisdiction and no morbid curiosity will be allowed to be gratified by putting murderers on exhibition to people who have no right to visit them."

Lastly, Hale needed to find a hangman to oversee executions, which following a long tradition would take place at 6 a.m. on Friday mornings. It would not be an easy task. Even seasoned lawmen blanched at doing the macabre work, which consisted in weighing and measuring the condemned for the drop, stretching the ropes, tying the noose, and overseeing the preparations on the fatal day. Hale also had to sift through a pile of applications from a motley group of crackpots and self-proclaimed avenging angels, few of whom had any experience in tying a noose.

The prison directors received a comic missive from John O. Sidner of Kern County, offering his services as official state hangman. Dated April 26, 1891, the letter was addressed to Honerable bord of Prisen directers.

> I here frum the papers that all men who dose a murder air to be hung in stait prisen and as most oficers think it onery bisines to hang people I herewith aply to you fur the job. I will hang every man you el me too fur $8

dolers apice. I once hulped too linch A man in minisoty. it was me that tide the not. So I no how to do it. My dady has soured on me and don't hulp me any mor becas I wodent mary the wimin he wanted me to mary an I maryed A pirt lockin girl that is hansum an we now have a lot of children to support. She will doe to surch the wimin prisoners as they can't hide eny thing frum her. We do in the best Siciety hear an you will help an onest family by given me the job. Anser this quick and have no red tape about it. i don't drink liker nur have no bad habbits, an I go to chirch every Sonday rite quick.[3]

The letter, which gave the "honorable bord of Prisen directors" quite a laugh, was signed "John O. Sidner." When the real John O. Sidner discovered that some crank had affixed his name to the letter, he became enraged and demanded an investigation.

Hale made an offbeat suggestion in response to the farcical letter: use inmates from the San Quentin population, many of whom would work for far less than "8 dolers" a head. For a few extra credits, the more hardened among them would not think twice about dispatching their fellow convicts. Predictably, the prison board rejected the convict-as-hangman idea.

*   *   *

The first death sentence issued under the new law came on April 8, 1891, when a judge condemned Dr. F.O. Vincent for murdering his wife in Fresno on December 18, 1890. Inebriated, Vincent shot his wife, who had initiated divorce proceedings because of her husband's "cruelty." He narrowly avoided a lynch mob but not an official death warrant, signed on April 8, 1891. The deadline for delivery to San Quentin—April 18—came and went while the case wended through the appeals process.

Because Vincent's crime predated the new statute, he went to the gallows not at San Quentin but at the Fresno County courthouse on Friday, October 27, 1893.

A reporter described the preparation for Vincent's execution. His description illustrates the complex calculation of the length of rope required for a quick hanging as well as the fear associated with the consequences of too much rope.

A bag of sand was attached to the noose and the trap sprung, the noose acting smoothly at each trial. The trap is sprung by means of a trigger arrangement beneath the floor. To the trigger is fastened a rope which is extended alongside the gallows, through the jail wall to a closet behind a door leading to the scaffold. The man who is to pull the rope will be stationed in this closet. At a sign from Sheriff Scott, the executioner, whose name will not be divulged, will pull the rope and send Vincent to eternity. The rope will be given seven feet slack, as Vincent is a light man, not weighing more than 120 pounds. There was talk first of having four feet of slack, and even this Vincent believed to be too much. He said he was afraid his head might be jerked off and preferred to take chances of strangulation. However, the authorities prefer their own judgement in this matter, and seven feet of slack it will be.[4]

The seven feet proved adequate for the lightweight man. The fall broke Vincent's neck.

Dr. Vincent did not earn the dubious distinction as the first man to drop down the elevator shaft at San Quentin, but by mid–May the queue of condemned began to grow. Five men languished in the San Francisco county jail under sentences of death, all for crimes committed before passage of the new statute. Pending their appeals, it appeared they would take "the long walk" to San Quentin's new gallows.[5] Two months later, the number grew to ten.[6]

Nonetheless, the death cells of San Quentin remained vacant. Due to a combination of factors—pre–1891 death sentences carried out at county jails, legal challenges to the new statute, death sentences overturned on appeals, and at least one death by natural causes in a county jail—almost two years would pass before the first condemned man mounted San Quentin's scaffold in March 1893.[7] Meanwhile, official hangings at county jails—like that of F.O. Vincent—atrophied as sheriffs disposed of condemned convicts whose sentences predated the new law.

* * *

When William Hale took over as warden of San Quentin, he faced two endemic problems at the penitentiary: opium and escapes. In his first report to the Prison Board, Warden Hale identified opium trafficking as the largest crack in San Quentin's walls, a problem enabled by the lax policy of "allowing visitors at any and all times." "One of the evils that may creep in through this channel is that of the opium traffic," Hale wrote, "which is quite extensively carried on inside."[8]

His crusade to end the midnight express and close down the illicit trade in opium resulted in a purge of personnel. "There will be a new deal all around," Hale promised.[9] He replaced all of the top officers and several of the guards. For captain of the yard and deputy warden, he tapped J.C. Edgar, and for a captain of the guard, he chose J.F. Birlem.

Hale created a new position, the "usher," who would function as a liaison between the inmates and the outside world. San Quentin's first usher, H.C. Hinman, would escort all visitors inside the prison and read all correspondence to and from the prisoners. As a chaperone standing between inmates and their visitors, the position of usher was intended to keep opium outside and prisoners inside the walls.

The new warden's axe fell particularly hard on the existing contingent of guards. After removing 12 of 60 men on duty, Hale reluctantly stopped swinging his axe to preserve whatever remained of the flagging morale among the staff.[10]

To patrol the wall and maintain law and order inside one of the most dangerous complexes in the United States, Hale appointed dozens of new guards, including a former police chief from Santa Cruz. Forty-four-year-old Amos Lunt formally entered the prison system on May 9, 1891.[11]

7

Off the Wall

(May 1891–June 1891)

When Amos Lunt first walked through the gates of San Quentin as an employee of the state prison, he entered a highly volatile, dangerous environment. Of the 1,272 prisoners behind the walls in June 1891, 355 (28 percent) had committed violent crimes, and 258 (20 percent) had committed murder. Of the 213 prisoners serving terms of 20 years or longer, 129 were serving life sentences. Teenaged convicts, the youngest of whom was 14, mixed with hardened criminals. The prison population's eldest statesman was 98 years old.[1]

While the majority of the inmate population was serving a first term, San Quentin was home to several career criminals, including 58 men doing at least a fourth stint in prison and one malefactor doing an eighth.[2]

One was the most troublesome inmates was Henry "Dutchy" Baker, who did a dozen stints in the prison's dungeon from 1884 to 1890. His first turn in the hole came May 1884, when he was caught attempting to escape "by cutting," which landed him in solitary for 20 days. His resistance to authority led to a second period of three days in the dungeon for "refusing to answer a proper question," and his predilection for edged weapons led to a third term of 20 days for possession of a shank.

Over the next few years, Baker's truculence led to numerous terms in solitary, including two for assaulting fellow inmates with knives. The year 1886 was a particularly troublesome one for Baker; he served six separate stints in solitary for various offenses.

In June 1891, Hale's sweepers caught Baker for "dealing in Opium." The prison board came down hard on the troublemaker; "On motion it was ordered that said Prisoner Henry Baker should forfeit all credits earned or to be earned in the future."[3]

Despite this mixture of dangerous characters, very few violent incidents occurred behind the walls of San Quentin during the first half of 1891. In the annual report, dated June 30, 1891, the new prison physician,

Dr. I.L.R. Mansfield, reported only one death from wounds. This number does not include the number of non-fatal wounds received during prison scrapes; Dr. Mansfield logged hundreds of "Calls for Treatment" during his first six months on the job but did not specify cause.[4] While Mansfield's ambiguity may hide the true picture of violence inside the prison, another factor may have contributed to a relative lack of violence: the prisoners were simply too tired for mayhem.

Inmates spent a portion of their day working off the hard labor portion of their sentences in one or more of the prison's industries. Most convicts worked one of three shifts at the jute mill, San Quentin's primary enterprise. Others worked, according to their skill or experience, in one or more of the prison's support or maintenance areas. They tended horses in the "Stable Department," looked after livestock at either the hog or chicken ranch, cultivated vegetables or flowers in one of the gardens, or worked in one of the skilled trades in the carpenter shop, the tin shop, and a myriad of others. The state penitentiary at San Quentin was a self-sustaining city walled off from the world.

Making sure that everything functioned according to plan and everyone remained inside, a legion of guards patrolled the walls, monitored the shops, and oversaw the farms. Approximately 75 guards maintained law and order among a population about the size of a large suburban high school, but instead of intractable teens, their charges included murderers, rapists, thieves, and con artists, some of the worst men in the Wild West. To police this motley group, each guard earned $50 per month.[5]

They rotated duties, but on occasion Warden Hale shuffled the deck to avoid the ennui that he believed bred complacency. The Warden found just such an occasion in 1892 when a routine inspection uncovered large quantities of contraband stashed in the laundry.

In his crusade to cleanse the prison of opium, the new warden had his most trusted officers conduct random searches on a continual basis. In addition to tossing cells, they swept the prison shops and other areas. When a sweep of the laundry uncovered enough tobacco and opium "to fill a large clothes basket" and a suit of civilian clothes apparently intended for an escape, Hale ordered Captain Edgar to reassign several guards as well as the officer in charge.

The discovery caused a stir that reached the ears of San Francisco reporters, so Hale gave a brief interview during which he explained that he often reassigned prison personnel to avoid carelessness. Such changes, Hale said, also preserved the health and well-being of the guards, and he used the example of a guard moved to a new detail because the man had developed eyestrain from staring across the bay for too long.[6]

During his earliest days at the prison, Amos Lunt policed the cafeteria, one of the more dangerous assignments for guards. With large groups of inmates clustered together, mealtimes presented the ideal opportunity for inmates to settle grudges and even scores.

When not on duty, Lunt enjoyed hiking the rugged terrain in the area—a hobby he began in Santa Cruz. The wide-open space provided an ideal escape from the prison walls and the ugliness contained within the closed community of the state prison. He became skilled enough at scaling the rock faces to earn the epithet "cliff climber."[7]

8

One Hot Summer

(July 1891–August 1892)

Amos Lunt had been on the job for two months when his family relocated from Santa Cruz in July 1891. Laura, eight-year-old Lottie, and four-year-old Arnold settled into San Quentin while a stone's throw away, Amos policed some of the worst offenders in the state.

That September, an incident that underscored the treacherous and volatile world behind the walls made headlines in nearby San Francisco. For the first time, Bay-area readers saw the name "Amos Lunt" when the former police chief single-handedly averted a full-scale prison riot.

*   *   *

Among his other duties, Lunt was in charge of seating prisoners in the dining hall during the dinner break at 4:45 p.m. Each afternoon, about a thousand prisoners shuffled into the spacious room from the jute mill and other work details. Like an usher at a wedding, Lunt's job was to seat prisoners at the tables lining both sides of a central walkway. The evening of Saturday, September 19, appeared to be like any other in the dining hall.

None of the six guards on duty that day noticed as Henry "Dutchy" Baker—a thief from San Francisco serving 15 years for a burglary conviction—crept behind James Bailey, who sat at one of the tables. Baker grabbed Bailey's head with his left hand, yanked it backward, and thrust a knife into the unsuspecting man's neck just below his right ear. His arm moving rhythmically like a piston, Baker jabbed his victim eight more times before Lunt realized what was happening.

"Sit down, boys!" he shouted and raced over to where Baker brandished the shank. Seeing Lunt approach, Baker slashed at him, the tip of his knife missing the guard by inches. Realizing the futility of resistance, he handed the knife to Lunt, threw up his hands, and surrendered. Twisting Baker's arm behind his back, Lunt escorted him out of the dining hall, while four convicts carried Bailey to the infirmary. He lingered for a few days before dying of his wounds.

The cause of the trouble remains obscured by time, but some real or perceived slight led to the deadly altercation. Once good friends and later cellmates, both Baker and Bailey entered the prison system following burglary and theft convictions in San Francisco. Both men transferred from Folsom in 1888, and both men became nuisances in San Quentin. They preferred to settle their scores with edged weapons, the chronicle of their prison scraps told by the scars crisscrossing their arms.

Lunt described the mess hall incident during the inquest, held in Captain Edgar's office on the prison grounds. "There was no trouble as far as I saw until the prisoners went into the dining-room at about 4:45 o'clock," Lunt testified.

> It is my duty to seat the men. Something over half of them had been seated, when I saw a man standing when the rest were sitting. I saw this man apparently hitting another in the neck or face. I ran to him and then I saw the blood spurting, and saw the knife in Baker's hand.
>
> I demanded the knife and he made a thrust at me. I lifted my stick and said: "Give me that knife." Then he handed it to me. I took Baker out through the dining-room and gave him into Gallagher's charge. Some convicts carried out the injured man and I went on seating the men. As I grabbed him, Baker said to the man he had stabbed, "You ----- -----, I've fixed you; you'll never threaten me again."[1]

Although the fracas may have left prison officials red-faced, it made a hero out of Amos Lunt. If he had not immediately taken charge of the situation, the inmates could have easily overpowered the half-dozen guards in the dining hall and the incident could have quickly devolved into a full-fledged riot.

*   *   *

In July 1892, Warden Hale once again began to prepare for San Quentin's inaugural execution, scheduled for August 5 at 5 a.m. when convicted slayer Anton Vital would stand on the scaffold.[2]

The 38-year-old Vital shot a Chinese man during a robbery in Bakersfield. J.A. Campbell, his accomplice, turned state's evidence, beat the murder rap, but pled guilty to burglary and was sentenced to 13 years behind bars. Convicted of first-degree murder, Vital was sentenced to the noose.

During the year and a half since the new law took effect, Hale changed the milieu that would become the prison's death house.

Rather than mount the gallows over the first-floor elevator shaft as originally planned for the execution of Dr. Vincent, Hale selected a spacious room at the north corner of the disused fourth floor for the scaffold.

The San Quentin gallows in a photograph from the Daniel Sullivan collection. Three guards stood in the box at the back of the structure and each cut a cord, one of which released the trap (Anne T. Kent California Room, Marin County Free Library).

This open space, capped by the trusses of the building's roof, offered enough clearance for the gallows and a small audience to gather around the frame and witness executions. As one reporter quipped, the room housed only a small population of resident "bats and night birds."[3]

The top corner of the building offered the most isolated spot available in the entire prison complex. The only way in or out of the room was through an exterior staircase running up the outside of the building from the ground level. A prisoner under a sentence of death stayed on "Murderer's Row" in another part of the prison, and as his Hangman's Friday neared, was brought to the top floor of the brick furniture factory and lodged in one of the "death cells." Once a condemned man entered the death house, he would not leave again until a gang of fellow convicts carried him out feet-first in a prison-issued coffin.

San Quentin's death house was composed of two areas—the death cells and the execution chamber—separated by a wooden partition. Two death cells, each about 20 feet square and lined with Oregon pine,

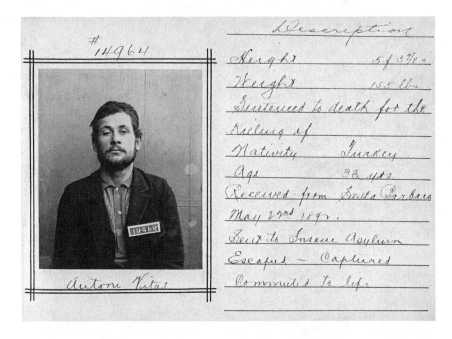

Anton Vital's entry in Album IV of the Daniel Sullivan collection. Questions about Vital's mental stability led to a commutation of his death sentence (Anne T. Kent California Room, Marin County Free Library).

straddled a central corridor with a vaulted ceiling. The proximity of the cells to the execution chamber cut down the "long walk," shortening the time of the proceedings. The positioning of the cells made it impossible for the condemned prisoners to see the gallows, although they could hear sounds coming from the other side of the wall, disquieting sounds such as the dull thud of a sprung trap and the oohing and aahing of witnesses.

While visiting a condemned man the night before his execution, a reporter described the structure of these rooms, which represented the final stop in the prisoner's journey from county jail to scaffold. "There are two 'condemned' cells, side by side," wrote a journalist for the *San Francisco Examiner*. "Three sides of each cell are formed of slats about four inches apart. By this arrangement the 'death watch' may see every movement of the condemned. The fourth side of the cell ... is the partition which divides it from the other wooden cabin. A few feet from the cell is a cot upon which the men on guard lie while they watch the prisoners."[4]

A wooden partition separated the death cells from a 100-foot-long void in which prison Captain Jamieson constructed a scaffold: an eight-foot-square wooden platform supported by four uprights and situated under a massive crossbeam. The "stairway to Heaven" consisted of 13 steps leading to the platform, the drop, and the dangling noose.

The first hanging at San Quentin drew considerable interest. A journalist from the *Examiner*, who toured the death complex on the eve of the Anton Vital hanging, described the set-up for his readers. "The scaffold was planned by Captain Jamieson and has been constructed of sound Oregon pine, to be framed with wooden pins, so that it may be taken apart if desired. It is a frame of four posts, connected by a platform at a height of eight feet. The platform is eight feet square and in the center is the fatal drop, a yard square."

The simple structure resembled hundreds of others like it throughout California, but San Quentin's gallows incorporated a feature used by Hale in Alameda: a blind that kept anyone from knowing whose hand had sprung the trap. A journalist described the set up.

"Three of the guards will stand with sharp knives near the point where the pully-box is fastened. From the upper end of the box three strings will appear. After all else is done, Warden Hale will command the guards to cut the cords and when that is done the weight within the box will fall, the trap bolts be drawn and Vital will go into oblivion, while no one will be able to say precisely which guard cut the string which precipitated the drop."[5] The configuration provided a mental balm for guards tasked with cord duty.

With the inaugural drop looming, Hale still had not decided on an executioner. He would have some time to contemplate the appointment, as Anton Vital's scheduled date with the hangman—August 5, 1892—came and went while his case snaked through the appeals process and serious questions about his mental state lingered.[6]

San Quentin's death house would remain dormant for another eight months.

First Drop and an Old Hangman Sets the Stage

(Friday, March 3, 1893)

After months of preparation and eager anticipation, San Quentin's first hanging would take place in 1893. Following a long-standing tradition, executions at the prison would take place on Friday mornings. The first would come on March 3, 1893.

Dr. F.O. Vincent, who would hang in Fresno on October 27, 1893, weighed 120 pounds and would be given a seven-foot drop. Jose Gabriel, destined to be the first man hanged at San Quentin, was five feet three-and-an-eighth inches tall, weighed 140 pounds, and was given a six-foot drop.[1]

Would it be enough rope?

* * *

As the first man to take the long walk to San Quentin's new death chamber, 60-year-old Jose Gabriel became a curiosity among newspaper reporters looking for a yellow story. A *San Francisco Chronicle* reporter attempted to interview "Indian Joe" a few days before his execution.

The reporter traipsed up the exterior walkway to the fourth floor, where Warden Hale had converted the former sash and blind factory into the prison's new death house and entered the hallway between the two death cells.

Gabriel lay asleep on a mattress in the corner of his cell, swaddled under two heavy gray blankets. "Captain Edgar pushed up the cap and pulled down the blanket, revealing a most brutal and repulsive face," the reporter wrote. "It was swarthy and wrinkled and covered with an irregular growth of short, black beard, but the features which dominated all others were the eyes, small, close set, snappingly bright and vicious.

"The savage scowled and grunted. When asked how he felt, he whined

Jose Gabriel, the first man hanged at San Quentin (Anne T. Kent California Room, Marin County Free Library).

in broken English that his stomach was bad, at the same time indicating the location of his discomfort by the motion of the hand."[2] Gabriel pulled the gray blanket over his head and grunted when the reporter attempted to ask him a question.

*   *   *

Gabriel was described as sullen and morose by the Death Watch—two guards watching the condemned man around the clock—and his nerves had become frayed by the sound of a 140-pound sack of rocks dropping from the gallows in the adjacent room.[3]

Jose Gabriel, alternately described in the press as "a Mexican-Indian," "a half-breed Indian," and "a savage," murdered elderly farmer John Geiser and his wife on their spread near Otay, about 15 miles south of San Diego. Gabriel sometimes did odd jobs for Geiser, who owed him payment for a well he had just dug.

After nightfall on October 16, 1892, Gabriel crept into Geiser's home with two makeshift clubs fashioned from two-by-fours and clubbed the couple to death. Sounds of the ferocious attack alerted a neighbor, who found Gabriel rifling through the Geisers' possessions. Caught with blood on his hands and subsequently convicted, Gabriel made this sole statement: "Ask them to hang me in the day and not at night."[4]

*   *   *

To conduct the Gabriel execution, Warden Hale enlisted the help of Colonel John W. McKenzie, a veteran peace officer and experienced hangman. McKenzie, a hero of the Mexican War, arrived in San Francisco with the wave of gold rush miners in 1849. Over the next few years, he played an active role in vigilance committees, where he may have first learned how to tie a noose.[5] According to some sources, he oversaw a prison bark anchored off Angel Island, a rotting hulk that served as an overflow for the small San Francisco calaboose.[6]

In 1854, McKenzie began a long career in law enforcement when he became a city marshal. Over the succeeding years, he played a variety of roles in the law and order of San Francisco, including chief of police, "Chief Jailor," and adjutant of the guard at San Quentin. As Chief Jailor, a position he held from 1858 to 1864, McKenzie acted as the city's hangman. "Colonel McKenzie," wrote an *Examiner* reporter, "was chief jailer at the County Jail and in that office he developed the skill in hanging men which has since then made him an indispensable adjunct to metropolitan executions."[7]

Because hangings at the county level took place infrequently, most sheriffs such as William E. Hale had very little experience with hangings, but during a career that spanned four decades, McKenzie had hanged eight men, making him one of the most experienced executioners in California.[8] McKenzie understood the dynamics of hanging.

"I have never had a hitch in any way [in a] hanging at which I have had charge," McKenzie bragged during an interview with a curious *San Francisco Examiner* correspondent on the eve of the Gabriel execution. He recounted his brief career as a hangman, providing a rare glimpse into the mindset of an executioner.

> The happiest man I ever hanged was Albert Lee, a son of United States Senator Thomas H. Benton…. He walked up to the drop singing, and had his neck broken in a most cheerful state of feeling.
>
> A man of the opposite sort was John Devine, the "Chicken." He cried and begged and had to be held up until the rope was made snug about his neck.
>
> I hung "Tipperary Bill," as they called William Morris, and also officiated at the hangings of James Whitford, James Clarkson, H. Russell, Wheeler the strangler, and Edward Bonney. They were all in San Francisco, except Bonney, who was hanged in Alameda county. I have had the best of success with all of my work, because I look after all of the little details that make an execution go off without a hitch, myself. I give them a long drop and make sure to have plenty of room under them, so that if the rope stretches they will not touch the floor. There is a great deal in stretching the rope. If it is not done it will be so

elastic that instead of being as rigid as a bar of iron it will give and not break the neck, but slowly strangle the man. Give me a good rope, well stretched, let me make my own knot and then let the drop be as I want it and there will be no trouble, no horror, but the most merciful death the law could order.[9]

To avoid a debacle such as the near-decapitation of Nathan Sutton during the last execution overseen by William Hale, McKenzie opted for the thicker, three-quarter-inch rope. For days leading up to the execution, he stretched the rope by suspending three buckets of nails from one end. By the morning of Gabriel's execution, the rope had become noticeably thinner and had stiffened.

McKenzie measured and weighed Gabriel (5'3⅛" and 140 pounds). The condemned man's thickly muscled neck concerned the veteran hangman, who calculated an eight-foot drop. McKenzie knew that every inch mattered when calculating a proper drop, but the San Quentin scaffold presented an unsettling limitation: the distance between the platform and the floor below restricted the maximum length of drop.[10] Achieving the longer drop necessary for lighter victims was possible only by either raising the scaffold or sawing a hole in the floor. Removing the floorboards directly under the gallows would increase the distance to 20 feet, allowing for a drop of any logical length, and accommodate even the heaviest of convicts.[11]

Hale decided to keep the current configuration, which vexed McKenzie, who settled on a six-foot drop. One reporter described the hangman's dilemma: he doubted that six feet would prove "sufficient for so light a man with so powerful a neck. As it was all the gallows would afford, he had to accept the inevitable."[12]

While McKenzie worked the ropes, Warden Hale prepared a guest list and sent out invitations to approximately 30 people, including several members of the press. An invitation allowed the bearer to pass through the front gate and into the prison yard, where the witnesses would gather until an escort took them to the gallows room just minutes prior to the hanging.

Passes to attend the Gabriel hanging, the first official execution in the history of San Quentin, became a curiosity. Under the headline "But a few hours left," the *Oakland Evening Tribune* reproduced the invitation Hale sent to the editor.

STATE PRISON, SAN QUENTIN,
March 3, 1893

Captain J.F. Birlem:

Pass editor OAKLAND EVENING TRIBUNE, or representative, through front gate to witness the execution of JOSE GABRIEL

W.E. Hale

* * *

At about 7:30 a.m. on the morning of Friday, March 3, 1893, the death watch guards—John Miller and T.K. Waters—roused Gabriel from his slumber. Throughout the night, his sleep had come in short intervals interrupted, he said, by the ghosts of Mr. and Mrs. Geiser. After downing a hearty breakfast of steak, ham, eggs, potatoes, and coffee, he changed into a new suit of clothes. Then he pulled on his boots.

The condemned man valued his boots. Gabriel made very few demands on his jailers during his time in the death cell, but he made one final request, which Warden Hale granted: he wanted to die with his boots on.

As Gabriel dressed, the sound of thunder echoed from the scaffold as Colonel McKenzie made his final preparations. He tested the trap and the rope by repeatedly hanging a bucket of iron weighing 160 pounds.

This ominous foreboding unhinged Jose Gabriel. He darted to a corner of his cell, faced the wall, and began muttering in Spanish. After a few minutes, he pointed to the wall and said, in broken English, "I like go out see where gone."[13]

At about 9:30 a.m., a reporter from the *Oakland Tribune* slipped into the death cell and attempted to scoop his competitors by prying a few last words from the taciturn convict. "What kind of night did you pass?" he asked.

"Very bad," Gabriel said. "The old man and woman came to see me."

"As he spoke," the curious reporter noted, "he pointed to the ceiling and the side of the room and indicated by his gesture that the place was alive with spirits."[14]

The writer, however, could not wrench another word from Gabriel, who responded to the reporter's questions with a sequence of grunts.

As Gabriel finished dressing, Hale's invitees gathered around the base of the scaffold and waited for the condemned man to enter the death chamber. Folsom Prison Warden Charles Aull, who would also oversee hangings at his prison, joined several sheriffs, prisoner officials, and state attorney general William H.H. Hart. Anticipation ran high, especially among the reporters.

Luke North, the *San Francisco Call* representative, described the view from San Quentin's deadly aerie. With his purple prose, the writer created a setting worthy of a gothic novel.

> From the north windows of those two dismal rooms one could see Mount Tamalpais, with the storm-clouds brooding over its peaks and the dense, purple blackness enshrouding it from summit to foothills. Tamalpais frowned and looked angry and mysterious.
>
> The south windows looked out upon a broad expanse of colorless water that was fast being lashed into white-capped waves by the storm-wind as it blew against the tide. There was a dense, heavy roar on the beach below.[15]

Meanwhile, in the adjacent room, death watch guards John Miller and T.K. Waters pinioned Gabriel's arms while Hale read the death warrant. Two priests stood by for moral support, to receive Gabriel's last confession and administer the last rites, but Gabriel refused to speak to them. He also refused the alcoholic bracer Hale offered as a nerve tonic.

As the clock struck ten, Gabriel, his arms strapped to his sides, entered the room and waddled the short distance from the death cells to the gallows, where Colonel McKenzie waited. The lack of emotion surprised the *Call*'s Luke North, who characterized the condemned man as the calmest one in the room. To the reporter's chagrin, the final moments of the dauntless man would not contain the type of breakdown that made good copy and tended to please readers who came to expect such a catharsis. "To the calloused sensation monger the affair was a disappointment throughout," he wrote. "The element of visible human suffering was missing. Some of those who witnessed it suffered more, externally at least, than did the principal."[16]

The *Oakland Tribune* writer was more critical than his colleague at the *Call*. Gabriel's head, he believed, told the tale of the man's depravity. "He was a moral monstrosity," he wrote. "He had an immense head, and a cold, cruel face, from which gleamed not the faintest trace of intelligence."[17]

Gabriel took his place on the trap, and Colonel McKenzie fitted the noose around his neck while Hale watched. Just five minutes had elapsed from the moment Gabriel entered the room.

With the final preparations complete, Hale snapped his fingers. McKenzie raised his hand, and the three designated guards each cut one of the three cords.

One of the severed cords released a weight that yanked the floor out from Gabriel's feet.

Gabriel dropped through the trap. His body jumped slightly as the rope pulled taught, stopping his downward momentum. A few slight convulsions and then he was motionless except for an almost imperceptible swaying.

The *Oakland Tribune* representative described the immediate aftermath of the drop. "The body fell with a jolt. For a few seconds there was not a movement, then the feet were drawn up and the body commenced to swing. The chest heaved, but not a sound escaped from the lips of the executed man."[18]

Dr. Mansfield, the prison surgeon, detected a slight flutter when he checked for a pulse. After three minutes and 45 seconds from the drop, Mansfield could no longer feel a heartbeat. Jose Gabriel was dead, but they left his body suspended for 12 minutes before cutting the noose and lowering it into a coffin. This was a necessary precaution. If they cut down

Gabriel while he still had a heartbeat, he could conceivably revive. Every hangman heard at least one horror story of a dead man who suddenly came to in the coffin only to be hanged a second time.

"Jose is now a good Indian," McKenzie remarked as he eyed Gabriel's lifeless body suspended from the rope.[19]

Following a cursory examination by Dr. Isaac Le Roy Mansfield (Coroner Edward Eden did not order a postmortem since cause of death was a foregone conclusion), a crew of convict laborers buried Jose Gabriel, still wearing his boots, in the prison cemetery.

Reporters from the four major area papers—the *San Francisco Call*, *San Francisco Chronicle*, *San Francisco Examiner*, and *Oakland Tribune*—all characterized the hanging as a success. All three noted that the fall broke Gabriel's neck, a conclusion supported by the Sullivan record (see Appendix 2), and by a medical examination of Gabriel's body just after it was cut down from the gallows.

The *Examiner* representative leaned over and studied Gabriel's face when Mansfield removed the cap. "When the mask was removed," he wrote in his blow-by-blow coverage of the execution, "it was observed that the eyes were closed, but that otherwise the face preserved the same appearance it had borne when Jose left the cell—it was no stolider, no more unmeaning than before the cap was drawn over it. There was nothing to indicate that death had caused a pang of suffering."[20]

That Gabriel did not suffer appeared to be of prime importance to the journalists, which underlines their disdain for the slow death by strangulation meted out by hemp committees and hemp parties. The writers, and their reading public, clearly expected a higher standard for hangings inside the state prison, which meant that Hale and his hangman faced enormous pressure.

Curiously, the same publication that heralded the Gabriel hanging as a success later condemned it as a failure. Writing about the Gabriel hanging in an 1895 piece profiling Warden Hale and Amos Lunt, a journalist for the *San Francisco Examiner* noted, "Jose Gabriel … was unfortunate in more ways than one…. In fact, the exit of the Indian caused a small tidal wave of objections and exceptions to sweep through the prison. The trouble was the result of negligence on the part of the hangman. The drop was wrong. Warden Hale removed the executioner without parley. It nearly broke the man's heart."[21]

In fact, Hale did not remove McKenzie but rather asked him to conduct San Quentin's second hanging, scheduled for February 1894. The condemnation was probably a piece of revisionist history designed to justify Hale's appointment of McKenzie's replacement—a relatively unknown guard named Amos Lunt.

PART II

The Hangman of San Quentin (1894–1901)

10

Learning the Ropes

Lunt Becomes Hangman
(Friday, February 2, 1894)

Twenty-six-year-old convicted assassin Lu Sing took his place on the trap. Warden Hale, the Rev. August Drahms, and Captain John C. Edgar stood in the corner of the platform and watched as Amos Lunt knelt down and made a few last-minute adjustments to the leather straps binding Sing's legs.

Sing looked down over the 15 witnesses gathered around the base of the scaffold. "Goodbye, all men goodbye, goodbye all."[1] His last words echoed through the cavernous room.

Warden Hale placed his hand on Sing's shoulder while Lunt gently slipped the noose under his chin. The Reverend Drahms stepped forward and gripped Sing's hand while Lunt slid the black hood over his head, then positioned the knot behind his left ear and pulled it taut.

All three men stepped back, and Hale raised his hand.

*   *   *

When it became clear that Lu Sing would be the second man to swing from San Quentin's gallows, Warden Hale once again turned to the hands that tied Jose Gabriel's noose. He named Colonel McKenzie as the hangman in July 1894, but on the eve of Sing's execution, Hale adjusted his plans.

The cause of Hale's last-minute change remains obscured by time and the lack of documentary evidence, but in an 1895 interview, Hale said that he first told Amos Lunt that he would act as Sing's hangman the night before the scheduled execution. If true, then Colonel McKenzie most likely made all of the necessary preparations. Hale would not have turned to a man with no prior experience in executions, the night before the hanging, to make the complicated calculations for a proper, neck-snapping drop.

It remains unclear as to why Hale tapped Amos Lunt as San Quentin's

Lu Sing, the first of 20 men hanged by Amos Lunt (Anne T. Kent California Room, Marin County Free Library).

hangman. Patronage may have come into play; both Lunt and Hale represented the Republican Party in their respective roles as county law officers, and party bosses may have helped secure Lunt a spot as a guard at the prison after his ouster from Santa Cruz.

Yet patronage seems like a long shot because the position of chief noose-tier did not come with any prestige or notable perquisites. It did not serve as a stepping-stone to greater political office. Lunt may have drawn the short straw. Or Lunt's dispassionate demeanor may have convinced Hale that he would have the ability to dissociate himself from the gruesome work done on the gallows.

It remains equally unclear who taught Lunt the fine art of hanging a man, although he probably learned his craft from McKenzie. Regardless, it would not take long for the apprentice to become the master. Over the next five years, Amos Lunt would hang over twice as many men as McKenzie did in 25 years.

* * *

In a short piece about the "art of hanging" titled "Placing Nooses on Necks," a *San Francisco Examiner* writer described how Amos Lunt became the premier hangman in California. In a nod to Hale, the reporter explained how the warden retained the title "official hangman of California," but "refrained from participation in the actual work of the hanging."

"I never do the mechanical portion of the hanging myself," Hale explained, "but I make it my business to be present at all of our executions. As official hangman I think it is my duty to do so."

He left the dirty work to the guard who single-handedly prevented a prison riot in the dining hall, whom the writer described as "eminently qualified for the unpleasant work." Lunt, Hale noted, "makes and carries out all the arrangements, and to him is due the general success of executions."

Or the failures. As the one in charge of "the mechanical portion of the hanging," Lunt became accountable for botched executions.

"To a man who takes any pride in the proper performance of his duties a bungle is always regrettable," Hale continued. "To the man who hangs men an unfinished execution is appalling. Some hangmen are content if they produce death by strangulation but, sentiment aside, death should be caused by a broken neck or the hanging is not properly done."

According to the article, Hale called Lunt aside on the evening of Thursday, February 1, 1894, and informed him that he had become the "Chief Deputy Hangman" of San Quentin and would perform his first hanging the following morning.

"I am ready to do my duty," Lunt replied.

"You understand," Hale warned, "there is no sentiment in matters of this kind. It is simply a case of have to. We are the creatures of the law and must carry out the order of the court."

"I will do my best," Lunt promised. The two men parted company; Hale went to dinner while Lunt made a beeline to the former sash and blind factory and began testing the rope that McKenzie most likely stretched ahead of time.[2] He also measured and weighed Sing to calculate the drop. At 5'5¼" and 120 pounds, Lu Sing would receive the same six-foot drop as Jose Gabriel, who weighed 20 pounds more.[3]

Amos Lunt's debut as a hangman occurred on Friday, February 2, 1894. The former police constable faced enormous pressure. Unlike lynchings done by vigilance committees in unpopulated forests or hangings conducted by county sheriffs behind prison yard fences, executions at San Quentin played to an audience of reporters from the largest-circulating newspapers in California. News of a botched hanging would reach thousands of readers within hours and provide ammunition for the growing population of death penalty abolitionists.

At 10 a.m. on Friday, February 2, 1894, a cadre of reporters boarded the freight elevator and rode to the former sash and blind factory. They came to see the hanging of an infamous assassin and the debut of San Quentin's new hangman.

* * *

Lu Sing's journey to San Quentin's gallows began the previous March, when feuds among members of San Francisco's Chinese community erupted into several violent crimes, which the papers dubbed the "highbinder war." Merchant Yick Kee, who owned four stores in the city, was marked for death by the Sam Yup Company (also known as the Suey Sing Tong)—one of San Francisco's six "Chinese associations"—and became the target of an assassination attempt on March 6, 1893.

A gang of five assassins lay in wait outside of Kee's Clay Street shop, and when they spotted Ah Kee—a man of similar build and appearance to their target—leave the shop, they tailed him to Stockton Street and ambushed him. All five "highbinders" began shooting at the frightened man. Several slugs struck Ah Kee in the back as he attempted to run away from the flying lead.

A squad of constables spotted Lu Sing running down nearby Jackson Street with a revolver in hand. During a short chase, Sing attempted to dispose of his smoking gun by tossing it into a crevice under a staircase, but he could not outrun the faster constable, who collared the suspect and recovered the pistol. They dragged Sing back to Stockton Street, where Ah Kee lay dying. He lived just long enough to identify Lu Sing as one of his assassins.

The overwhelming evidence led to a quick conviction followed by a death sentence, to the consternation of his defense attorney, John J. Coffey. "I do not believe Sing was guilty," Coffey said on the eve of his client's execution. "Two jurors who condemned him admitted they would not believe a Chinaman on oath. We had no money to properly carry on the defense— no money for the preparation of affidavits and the ordinary costs of the court. We have paid our own expenses in several instances, such as visits to San Quentin and the preparation of Sing's own affidavit." Coffey's complaints fell on deaf ears.

"I consider the hanging a judicial murder," Coffey concluded.[4]

Like Jose Gabriel, Lu Sing whiled away his remaining days by lying on a straw mattress in the corner of his cell, chain-smoking. He said very little to the deathwatch, but unlike Gabriel, he did not appear morose or sullen. He spoke freely to reporters but dodged questions about the murder of Ah Kee.

Sing did not appear to fear his punishment in the slightest. "You get sick, you die, all same," he remarked to the watch. "I get hanged all same."[5]

A series of delays pushed the execution date to Friday, February 2, 1894.[6]

*   *   *

Warden Hale, Captain Edgar, the Reverend Drahms, and Amos Lunt entered the death cell holding Lu Sing promptly at 10:30 a.m. on the morning of Friday, February 2, 1894. As Lunt fitted the leather straps on Sing's arms, the condemned man uttered, "Put them on good."

Five minutes later, Hale led Sing to the scaffold, followed by Lunt and three guards. One of the journalists in attendance described the condemned man as the procession first entered the room, serenaded with the singing of the pigeons who had taken up residence in the rafters. "He came out of his cell with an actual grin on his face, and never once, while arrangements were being made, seemed to show the least sign of nervousness or fear."[7]

Once on the scaffold, Lunt positioned Sing over the trap while three guards, designated to cut the umbilical cords tethering the condemned man to the world of the living, waited behind what one journalist described as a "sentry-like box" made from a wooden frame covered by a jute screen.[8] The cloth covering concealed their identities.

Hale placed his hand on Sing's shoulder, and the Reverend Drahms gently reached out and took Sing's hand as Lunt tightened the leather straps, fitted the noose, and slid the hood over Sing's head. Lunt worked deftly, making his final preparations in under a minute. Only two minutes had elapsed from the time Hale escorted Sing from the death cell.

As Lunt lowered the black cap, Sing said, "Is that all?" followed by "All right."[9]

*   *   *

The drama that took place in San Quentin's death house was enacted by a cast of characters, each of whom played a specific role in the procedure. For much of Amos Lunt's career as the hangman of San Quentin, the same actors would appear on center stage—the scaffold—to reprise their roles in repeat performances booked by the courts. Only the actor in the leading role—the condemned man—would change; for him, the show would be a one-night stand.

The man holding Lu Sing's hand just prior to the drop was the Rev. August Drahms, San Quentin's 44-year-old chaplain. Drahms, who emigrated to the United States from Prussia at age six, fought valiantly in the Civil War but turned down West Point in favor of the ministry. Before prison work, he owned and operated a newspaper, the *Sonoma Index-Tribune*.

Drahms' Catholic counterpart, Father Hugh Lagan, would attend all of the hangings during the Lunt era. The 41-year-old pastor of the church in San Rafael was a native of County Derry, Ireland, and spoke with an

Irish lilt. Sometimes Father Lagan stood on the scaffold, next to the condemned; other times, he would cede that duty to Drahms and stand on the periphery. Regardless of an inmate's spiritual preference, however, Lagan stood by with the Good Book in hand, poised to help when needed.

Sixty-year-old captain of the yard and deputy warden John C. Edgar was the elderly statesman of the group. He came to California from Belfast, Ireland, in 1852. In 1872, he won election as sheriff of Yuba County and went on to serve four successive terms. He entered prison service in 1879, when Governor George C. Perkins appointed him deputy warden.

Dr. Isaac Le Roy Mansfield, a 46-year-old physician from Butte County, California, replaced Dr. Durand as the prison surgeon when Hale took over in 1891. Mansfield began his medical training at age 16, but the Civil War interrupted his studies. He enlisted with Company B of the First New Jersey Infantry. After the war, Mansfield attended the Philadelphia School of Medicine, graduating with the class of 1869. He immediately left for California, settling in Wyandotte, where his father Jacob owned several orange groves. In addition to his medical practice, Dr. Mansfield dabbled in agricultural pursuits as a gentleman farmer, owning several olive orchards and orange groves.[10]

* * *

Executions would become the favorite show in town among journalists. All the major newspapers in the Bay area sent at least one journalist to each hanging, and their stories always occupied multiple columns, often with detailed art depicting the final moments before the trap dropped. Journalists from the *Oakland Tribune, San Francisco Call, San Francisco Chronicle*, and *San Francisco Examiner,* joined a dozen other spectators and watched as Amos Lunt nodded to Hale, who gave the signal by raising his hand.

The three guards behind the jute screen each severed their individual string, one releasing the trap and sending Lu Sing falling to the floor. The six-foot drop snapped Sing's neck, resulting in a slight but noticeable physiological reaction.

"There was quite a display of vitality," wrote one of the witnesses. "The chest heaved and the muscles of the limbs contracted with the reflex action, but the spinal cord had been severed."

An eerie silence fell upon the room. "An official opened the iron doors communicating to the larger room," wrote the *Examiner* correspondent, "and then an odd thing happened. A window in this room was open a few inches and a dove lighted upon the sill and flew in, and set up cooing that broke so strangely upon the silence of the death chamber that the officer was constrained to wave his hat toward the bird. It flew away, but returned at once with louder cries, and the deputy put it out and closed the window."[11]

Dr. Mansfield, assisted by two colleagues invited to attend the execution, stepped forward and measured Sing's pulse at 40 beats per minute. The pulse accelerated to 140 beats per minute before becoming irregular and then ceasing altogether at the seven-minute mark. After 15 minutes had elapsed, a team of three guards severed the rope and lowered Sing's body into a coffin.

An elderly prisoner, enlisted to help, became a curiosity for one of the attendant reporters. "He handled the corpse as tenderly as though it had been that of one of his own children and removed the rope from the neck with great care, as though fearful of hurting the dead man."[12]

As Amos Lunt watched with a cigarette dangling between his lips, Dr. Mansfield knelt down and swiveled the head, the movement of which indicated that Lunt's calculation of a six-foot drop had dislocated Sing's vertebrae. One at a time, each of Mansfield's assistants repeated the process, kneeling beside the body and gently rotating the dead man's head.

Lunt sauntered out of the room, a trail of cigarette smoke behind him. Several eyewitnesses noted the hangman's icy demeanor before, during, and after the hanging. He pinioned, noosed, and hooded the condemned with no more outward signs of distress than that of a man strolling through the park during a lazy Sunday morning. Amos Lunt's stoicism would become legendary in the years to come.

*   *   *

Lunt's first hanging went without a hitch. A few years later, an *Examiner* correspondent noted, "The work was well done. No one could take an exception to the manner in which the law was carried out. The drop was just right, and Sing shot into eternity without pain or struggle. Mr. Lunt received the congratulations of his friends and the Warden with modesty. He is of a retiring nature and did not like to force his claims as an expert hangman."[13]

11

Tight Rope

(Friday, April 20, 1894)

Forty-one-year-old Irishman Patrick J. (P.J.) Sullivan, scheduled to die on Friday, April 20, 1894, would become Lunt's second subject and the third man hanged at San Quentin.

A longtime sea salt, Pat Sullivan swore like a sailor (until a few days before his execution; he swore off cursing to placate his religious counsel) but did not drink like one. He enlisted with the United States Navy at age 19 and spent most of his youth cruising around the world on the *Brooklyn*. Like his fellow tars, Sullivan spent his time ashore in dives, but instead of drinking away his pay, he squirreled it away, managing to bank $8,900. He planned to use the money to open a "sailor's outfitting" store, but then he met Deanie "Belle" Taylor, a barmaid from Oakland who had recently left her husband. News accounts referred to Taylor as a "dive waitress," hinting that she had lapsed into the oldest profession.

Sullivan became enamored with Taylor, and using small gifts of cash and fancy clothes, nudged her into divorcing her husband. Before the ink on the divorce papers dried, the couple exchanged vows. Taking his wife's advice, Sullivan used his nest egg to open the Stag saloon on the Barbary Coast. Over the next year, the Stag did brisk business, and the newlyweds lived an Edenic life together.

Two widely divergent versions exist of the next chapter in the Sullivan tragedy.

In a version that made the rounds shortly after Sullivan's arrest for his wife's murder in 1892, he loses the Stag due to financial misfortune. Belle must work to support her deadbeat husband, who frequently beats her. After living in utter misery, Belle declares her intention to leave. Unable to take "no" for an answer, he stabs her to death.[1]

Another rendition, which circulated at the time of Sullivan's execution, has Belle Sullivan relapsing into her old habits of drinking and flirting with the Stag's customers. For a while, Sullivan attempts to drown his

Convicted wife-slayer Patrick J. "P.J." Sullivan (Anne T. Kent California Room, Marin County Free Library).

angst with whiskey, but then decides to separate his wife from sin by isolating her on a spread he had purchased in the country, away from the high life of the Barbary Coast.

Sullivan's gambit fails. Taylor continues to flirt with the bottle, and following one terrific argument, returns to San Francisco with $400 of Sullivan's money and a promise to reform. Sullivan trails her and discovers that she has taken up with another man. Following a brief reconciliation, she leaves Sullivan for good after selling several of his personal belongings.[2]

The strands converged at about 5 a.m. on November 18, 1892, when Sullivan crept up behind his wife as she sauntered down Pacific Street. In a savage frenzy, he buried a butcher's knife up to its hilt in her back. Shocked, she attempted to run, leaving a trail of blood in her wake. When Sullivan caught up to her, he plunged the knife into Belle's back twice, and as she fell to the street, stabbed her twice more at the base of her spine, tearing away three inches of scalp in the process. As Belle Sullivan lay dying, Sullivan repeatedly kicked her. She managed to utter a faint cry of "help," which brought a quartet of constables who restrained the manic assailant. Belle bled out en route to the hospital.

Sullivan arrived at San Quentin on March 6, 1894, for what would be a very short stay of six weeks. A heavyset man with the barrel shoulders of a pugilist and a series of scars over his heavy-brow ridge that suggested he was a man who occasionally attempted to impose his will on others, Sullivan did not appear the least bit sorry that he brutally murdered Belle. On the contrary, he made several remarks about how Belle deserved a knife in the back.

"I do not regret the death of that woman," he told the Death Watch the night before his execution. "I only regret that I killed her, not that she is dead." He echoed the sentiment to a cadre of reporters who interviewed him just before lights out—9 p.m. on Thursday, April 19. "I deserve what I am getting, not for killing that woman, but for being fool enough to get into such a scrape."[3]

In his final interview, Sullivan complained about his treatment at San Quentin. Warned about Sullivan's violent tendencies, Hale ordered him locked up in a solitary cell without furniture until he was moved into a more spacious death cell in the days prior to the execution. This chafed Sullivan, who bitterly resented the treatment. He characterized himself as a gentle soul. "Why," he said, "they could have left me with a baby in that yard and I would have done no harm."

The condemned man put on a jovial façade with the reporters. "I'm sorry, boys, that I can't send out and get a couple of bottles of wine. For that matter I'm sorry I didn't get done up over in the County Jail in Frisco. I wanted to hang there if I had to hang. Why, they don't know how to treat a fellow here."[4]

Sullivan's expanding waistline undermined his complaints. Plied with food during his time in a death cell, he ate heartily and jested, "I'll bet a dollar against a ferry ticket that I've gained ten pounds since I came over here from that cell."

Beginning on Tuesday, Dr. Mansfield sent two ounces of whiskey to Sullivan each day. The stout Irishman enjoyed his daily shots but refused to take a nip on his last day alive. He also refused the opiate bracer offered to him just before he went to the scaffold. "I want to go to the drop clear as a bell," he said, "so that no fellow can say I was braced up for the trip."[5]

*　*　*

Sullivan presented a new challenge for Amos Lunt. At a height of 5'7½" and a weight of 215 pounds, the stocky, broad-shouldered Sullivan outweighed Jose Gabriel by 75 pounds and Lu Sing by 95 pounds and presented the heaviest man to date hanged at San Quentin.[6] If Sullivan had weighed less than Sing's 120 pounds, then Lunt would have faced the same dilemma as Colonel McKenzie had faced when he prepared for the hanging of Gabriel: not enough room for an adequate drop of greater than seven feet.

A heavier victim needed a shorter—not longer—drop. With too little rope, however, Sullivan would thrash on the rope like a fish on the end of a line, a botched execution in front of the city's press corps. After weighing and measuring Sullivan, Lunt calculated a drop of five feet, one of the two shortest drops he would give during his tenure as San Quentin's hangman.[7]

*   *   *

For the convicted wife-slayer, Hangman's Friday came on April 20, 1894. The usual suspects gathered under the scaffold and waited for the "dead man walking" to make his appearance.

Sullivan spent much of the morning with his chosen spiritual counselors, Father Dempsey of San Rafael and Father Lagan of San Francisco. He appeared less contrite than proud, and his emotions did not break, even when Warden Hale entered his cell to read the death warrant a few minutes before 11 a.m.

For some reason, P.J. Sullivan developed a disliking for Amos Lunt. After Lunt fitted him with straps, Sullivan asked if one of the Death Watch guards—Fitch or Miller—could put the noose around his neck. When Hale denied the request, Sullivan asked if he could put the noose around his own neck. Again, Hale deferred to his hangman, who understood the intricacies of a proper hanging, which included placement of the knot.

Sullivan, it appeared, feared a botched hanging. "Say, Fitch," he requested in his final minutes before taking the long walk, "please go out and see that everything is all right, won't you? I don't want no mistakes, no rope breaking, like there was in New York last time." Fitch and Hale both left the death cell more to placate Sullivan than to inspect Lunt's preparations. Fitch returned a few minutes later to tell Sullivan that everything appeared in order.

At 10:55 a.m., Hale returned to the death cell. Sullivan's time had arrived.

As Fitch and Miller pinioned Sullivan's arms and legs, he warned, "You know my temper. You fellows put on the straps and put them on easy. If you don't get me irritated I'll be all right."[8] The two guards then fastened the straps on Sullivan's wrists and around his waist. With this final step completed, Sullivan was ready to meet Lunt on the scaffold.

With Hale in the lead, the death procession stepped toward the gallows. Sullivan, who maintained a show of bravado throughout his time in the death cell, began to crack when he eyed the scaffold. "He looked furtively around the chamber, scanned the faces of the people and then a look of fearful despairing agony crept into his eyes as they fell upon the gallows upon which he was to die," wrote the *Call* correspondent.

Sullivan paused at the top of the platform and stared at the crossbeam overhead with the noose hanging loosely, like a dead arm, over the trap. He turned, stood at the railing, and gazed down at the small crowd who came to watch him die. He tried valiantly to maintain his composure, but then a sparrow began chirping. The slight sound almost unhinged Sullivan.

"A look of such despair as once seen is never forgotten rested for a moment in the fixed eyes, then with an effort of superhuman strength he collected his faculties for the last talk he should ever make," noted the *Call* reporter. Sullivan's lower lip trembled, but he rolled back his shoulders, stood erect, and held his head high in an obvious effort to conceal his fear. It was such a pathetic spectacle that several of the onlookers grew pale.

A few of the spectators had last-minute doubts about watching the execution and started toward the door, but Sullivan stopped them. With a dramatic, sweeping gesture of his arm, he said, "Come in here, you fellows, and shut the door. I want you all in here." Then he scanned the audience for familiar faces. He spotted Dr. Mansfield. "I don't see any one here I know but the doctor. Come up here, doctor. I want to shake hands with you before I go."

As Mansfield ascended the steps, Sullivan noticed Dr. R.H. Brown, the city physician of San Francisco whom he came to know while lodged in jail. "Is that you, Dr. Brown?" he asked.

One of the heads below began to bob. "Ah, doctor, come up here and say good-by before I go off." As the physician climbed the stairs, Sullivan continued, "You've been a good friend to me and helped me all you could."[9]

Sullivan met the physicians at the top of the steps, shook each man's hand, and returned to the rail. He paused for a few seconds and began his final statement while Amos Lunt waited by the noose. Jose Gabriel and Lu Sing said very little before they dropped, but Sullivan did not plan to go out without a statement. The reporters pressed their pen nibs to their notebooks and waited for Sullivan to begin.

A great many people may think they would do better than me in the same fix, but as the Irishman says, they don't know until they are in the last ditch. Many have put me down as a cur and a brute, and they think they will never get down in the world, but they may after all. The newspapers have made me out much worse than I am, but all I ask from the reporters here is to give me a square deal. This is the shot in the bucket, you know. I freely forgive every one on this God's green earth, and forgive all as they should forgive me. God bless you all, as I hope he will bless me. And young men, I would say to you, beware of women and wine. As the Frenchman said, "Wine, women and song will ruin anybody." Whatever any one says they must say I am not dying like a cur. Good-by everybody.[10]

The Death Watch then began to fasten the leather straps. "Don't draw those straps so tight," Sullivan barked. He gripped a handkerchief in his right hand while the guards worked. When they finished, one of the priests pressed a crucifix to Sullivan's lips. He kissed it.

A curious scene occurred as Amos Lunt lowered the noose over Sullivan's head. He reiterated his desire to place the noose himself. Lunt leaned forward and whispered that Sullivan could not possibly place the noose himself with his arms strapped to his sides. As Lunt slid the black cap over Sullivan's head, he muttered, "You can't say I died like a cur."[11]

Amos Lunt lowered the noose, positioned the knot below Sullivan's left ear, and pulled it taut, eliciting an immediate gripe. "What in—are you pulling that knot so tight for?" he barked, his voice garbled by the drawn mask. He shot through the trap just as he finished his question.[12]

The hypocrisy of Sullivan's last words, in which he broke his promise to the padres and reverted to his salty language, was not lost on a *Chronicle* reporter, who wrote, "With an oath on his lips, uttered within half a second after he had kissed the crucifix, Patrick Joseph Sullivan, the wife-murderer, dropped through the trap."[13]

The five-foot drop did the trick. Sullivan's body hung motionless, the handkerchief still clenched in his right hand. "Not a quiver disturbed the flesh," wrote the witness from the *San Francisco Call*. "The hands did not even close in the usual convulsive grip of death. The handkerchief held lightly to the last in his right hand was still there after death."[14]

Dr. Mansfield stepped down from the scaffold to take Sullivan's pulse, which measured at a rate of 147 beats per minute within seconds of the drop. Eight minutes later, it had dropped to 40, and it finally ceased completely at the 12-minute mark.

Lunt erred slightly in calculating the drop but avoided the type of embarrassing, traumatic episode that had soured Hale on hanging. The rope cut into the flesh of Sullivan's neck but did not tear through the muscles. "The drop was six feet," noted the *Call* correspondent. "Had it been a trifle longer it would have severed the head from the body."[15]

While not yet widely known as San Quentin's hangman, Amos Lunt nonetheless received praise from the reporters who observed his work. *The San Francisco Examiner*'s man at the hanging wrote a glowing review. "The execution went through without any of the horrors too often attendant on such events. The rope was tied properly, the machinery worked perfectly, the executioners were not nervous or clumsy, and Sullivan never moved a muscle after he reached the end of his rope."[16]

*   *   *

Perhaps no one at San Quentin understood the stresses that came along with hanging a man more than Warden Hale. After each hanging, he gave Amos Lunt a few days off work. These short furloughs later provided fodder for Lunt's critics. F.F. Runyon, who wrote a series of articles in 1927 titled "In the Shadow of the Gallows: Prison Experiences," characterized Lunt as a "cold-blooded" mercenary. "An execution was just an incident to him. It meant a few days' vacation."[17]

Runyon, like other journalists who ventured behind San Quentin's walls, knew Lunt for his stoic façade and icy demeanor. He did not understand that even after just two hangings, the emotional strain, like white-caps slamming against the rocks below the prison walls, had already begun to pound Amos Lunt.

With two young children at home—11-year-old Lottie and her seven-year-old brother Arnold—Lunt may have refrained from talking about his duties with his family, and he most likely did not broach the subject at the prison, where he may have felt the need to maintain a granite countenance.[18]

Having once tied a noose himself, William Hale understood. He apparently believed that a few days' respite would help alleviate the stress.

* * *

After his case snaked through the courts, Anton Vital eventually arrived at San Quentin on August 11, 1894—four months after P.J. Collins dropped—with his hanging scheduled for Friday, October 12. Vital never kept his date with Lunt on the scaffold.

While Vital waited to climb the 13 steps of San Quentin's "stairway to Heaven," his extravagant claims of being able to control weather phenomena such as blizzards and cyclones eventually reached the ears of Governor Henry Harrison Markham. With lingering doubts about Vital's sanity, Markham commuted Vital's sentence to life imprisonment on October 10, just two days before his scheduled execution date.

Anton Vital managed to cheat the hangman, but fellow "dead man walking" Anthony Azoff, who arrived on July 4, 1894, would not be so lucky. Azoff's date with the hangman would take place in June 1895, when three men would mount the scaffold in the first triple hanging at San Quentin.[19]

* * *

With P.J. Sullivan dead and buried in the prison cemetery, Anton Vital off the hook for the death penalty, and Anthony Azoff sweating out his final months behind bars, Lunt returned to his everyday duties. For much of 1894, business as usual for Amos Lunt consisted of overseeing a crew of 100 prisoner laborers constructing a road leading to San Quentin.

In October, Lunt took a long-overdue vacation and returned to his old stomping grounds of Santa Cruz. The return of the former chief of police warranted a blurb in both local newspapers. "Amos Lunt, ex-Chief of Police of this city," gushed a writer for the *Santa Cruz Sentinel*, "is in town busy shaking hand[s] with his friends … this is his first vacation in four years, and he improved the opportunity by spending it here."[20]

12

The Triple Event

(Friday, June 7, 1895)

For Amos Lunt, 1895 would be the year when the public came to know him as the hangman of San Quentin.

The hangings of Sing and Sullivan provided on-the-job training for Amos Lunt, but during the following year, he would have the opportunity to perfect his art. Eight hangings would take place at San Quentin in 1895. In the span of 12 months, Amos Lunt would hang more men than most county sheriffs did during their entire careers.

The first three would take place on one day, Friday, June 7, 1895.

* * *

The year 1895 at San Quentin began with a minor scandal when guards Browning and Fitch—the Death Watchman who pinioned Sullivan—left prison service under a cloud. Rumors swirled that Warden Hale, who ran a tight ship, cashiered the pair for playing cards on duty and rebuked Amos Lunt for the same offense. The story eventually landed in the pages of the *San Francisco Examiner*.[1]

The trouble stemmed from a high-stakes poker game the previous month, in December 1894, when Lunt lost $22.50 to higher hands held by fellow guards Browning, Goodrich, and Fitch. Apparently a poor loser or a dupe—or both—Lunt told Warden Hale that the three guards had cheated him.

Hale issued all four men their walking papers and banned all prison employees from playing cards either on- or off-duty. The four poker players went to their political allies, who pressured Hale into revoking the firings. More than likely, Hale never intended to fire his hangman. Browning and Fitch, irritated with Lunt's betrayal and irked by Hale's heavy-handedness, decided to leave the prison service altogether.

Not one to shy away from controversy, Amos Lunt went on the defensive and whipped off a letter to his hometown rag, the *Santa Cruz Sentinel*.

I am satisfied you will allow me space to contradict a most willful falsehood that appeared in the Examiner. There never happened anything of the kind printed. Mr. Fitch and Mr. Browning, two good and tried guards, resigned their positions, and were given fine recommendations by Warden Hale. I deny the charge of playing cards, which is something I have not done in years. I have a family to support, and can't afford any of the natural luxury. I can't understand why the article was written, except for spite by some discharged guard or some ex-convict. A man holding a position connected in any way with politics expects shots, but if they would only tell the truth it would not be so bad. It being pretty near time for changes to be made we will expect to get a dose once in a while.[2]

* * *

In the earliest days of hangings at San Quentin, condemned convicts became objects of fascination to the reading public; they also became pawns in an all-out war to sell newspapers. Desperate to outsell their competitors, editors of competing newspaper editors sent reporters to San Quentin to interview the damned. The *Examiner* sent Annie Laurie to San Quentin; the *Call* sent Belle Dormer. Both women, pioneers in their field, visited with the men on death row in May 1895.

* * *

A fiery redhead with an effervescent personality, Annie Laurie was the pen name of 31-year-old Winifred Black. A native of Wisconsin, she began her writing career with the *Chicago Tribune*. In the early 1890s, Black relocated to San Francisco, where she went to work writing for Hearst's *Examiner*.

"I am not a 'sob-sister' or a 'special writer,'" she later said when summarizing her career in newsprint. "I'm just a plain, practical, all round newspaper woman. That's my profession, and that is my pride. I'd rather smell the printers' ink and hear the presses go 'round than to go to any grand opera in the world."[3]

In May 1895, Annie Laurie's "grand opera" took place behind the walls of the state prison, where she went to study the six men under sentences of death. She found four of the six working in the prison's rose garden. "Three of them were laughing, but the fourth man trembled like one with the ague," she later wrote, "and the others nudged each other, and made jokes at the palsy of his shaking hand."

"They are the condemned men," her guard-guide noted. "Azoff, Morasco, Smith and Garcia. There are three more, but Collins is saying his prayers in his cell all the time, and Fredericks is in the hospital in a strait-jacket; he's playing crazy, and has been reprieved until December."

Laurie did not name the guard in her article, but he may have been

Frank Arbogast or John Jones—two experienced Death Watch guards and as such familiar with the residents of Murderer's Row. He most likely was not the hangman himself; by mid–1895, Amos Lunt had become well known as the executioner, so Laurie would have noted this fact if she met him that spring day behind the prison walls. Besides, Lunt's typical duties at the prison did not include standing guard over death row inmates, and he later made several comments indicating that he spent as little time as possible with the condemned. The guard explained,

> They all talk, as every criminal I ever saw always talks, with an assumption that some malignant power is persecuting them just for the joy of persecution, and that the law is something devised for the torment of innocent and injured men.
>
> Three out of four of these men told the details of the hideous crimes of which they are convicted with perfect indifference. The fourth man trembles and crosses himself when he tells of the man he killed.

Each man was convicted and sentenced to die for a murder most foul: Anthony Azoff, for shooting a lawman during a foiled robbery at a train depot; Emilio Garcia, for beating an old man to death in an attempt to discover the whereabouts of his supposed gold cache; Patrick Collins, for knifing his wife in an alcohol-fueled rage; and Fremont Smith, for murdering two mates and dumping their bodies in the Sacramento River.

The guard sat down next to Laurie; he would remain by her side throughout the interviews.

One by one, each of the condemned men spoke with Laurie in the garden, which had acquired an ominous and sobering nickname. When transferred to the dreaded execution complex, doomed inmates crossed through the Garden of Death on their way.[4]

Anthony Azoff, whom the press had erroneously labeled a Russian, met with Laurie first. With a spring in his step and humming a tune, he strode toward the reporter and plopped down on a bench next to her. His demeanor stunned the reporter. He did not appear fazed in the least by his imminent journey through the Garden of Death.

Laurie described the diminutive bandit at this moment. "He is a little, proud man with a square face, big, empty eyes, a queer, twisted nose and a good-natured, foolish mouth. There was something so curiously young about him, for all his furrowed forehead, that he looked like a school boy, with lines painted on his face."

They chatted about the garden, the sun, and the daily routine at the prison.

"Does the time pass slowly to you?" Laurie asked.

"Slowly? Slowly? Ah, no; it goes pretty fast. You see, we have a pretty easy time of it; nothing to do but eat and sleep, and no worry or anything."

The cavalier response for a man about to go to the scaffold shocked Laurie. "No worry?"

"No," Azoff reiterated. "They treat us fine here; we're the star boarders, you know."

"The man was not talking for effect," Laurie concluded. "He was as simple and as unaffected as a child, and he meant just what he said."

Of his forthcoming fate, Azoff shrugged off the hanging as just a bad break. "Well," he said, "a poor man's got to have just so much trouble, and I 'spose I wasn't to escape."

Azoff described his death row neighbors. "[Patrick] Collins stays in his cell and prays all day. [Emilio] Garcia can't speak English … and [William] Fredericks is in the hospital playing crazy. He thinks he'll escape that way."

After describing Frederick's attempts to feign insanity, Azoff chuckled, wrote Laurie, "just as a mischievous schoolboy laughs at another who feigns illness to escape punishment." Laurie watched as Azoff, accompanied by a guard, waltzed back to his cell "with the same curious little spring in his walk that very, very happy children have."

Emilio Garcia, who spoke to Laurie through a translator, was the antithesis of the childlike Azoff. "He was lithe and sinewy, this man, with a quick turn of the body, and a curious way of looking over his shoulder at you—with eyes that were long and narrow and that gleamed like smoldering fires. His teeth were as white as the teeth of a gray wolf, and he showed them when he talked, in a strange way he had of lifting the corners of his lips in something that was meant for a smile."

Garcia had none of Azoff's nonchalance. He fidgeted and frequently looked over his shoulder as he spoke. Unlike Azoff, prison life did not agree with him, and he found that time passed very slowly on death row.

Laurie described Fremont Smith as "broad-shouldered and lean and powerful. His face was long and lean and marked with a network of evil lines…. His face was the face of the intelligent thief, or the clever schemer, yet he is going to be hanged because he murdered two fishermen to get a little bundle of old clothes and some tools."

Smith played the poverty card. "If I'd had money, they wouldn't have accused me of murder, much less hung me for it," he said with a howl that Laurie described as "a laugh which he meant to make satirical, and which was only wicked."

"But," the "broad-shouldered" murderer continued, "you know that as well as I do. You want to know what I do here and—say, I've read lots about condemned men. I'm a great reader, and I've read about men that the Indians caught and what they thought about when they were tied to the stake and the fire was being lit; but I don't have any of those lightning-flash ideas about my past life. Not one. I read and eat and sleep and take things easy, and that's all there is to it. I take things as they are, and not as they're going to be. Isn't that the sensible way to look at life, or at death, either, if you come to that?"

After a little more philosophizing, Smith returned to his cell.

The guard, who had listened to Laurie's interviews, chimed in as Smith trudged back to Murderer's Row.

"See here," he began in a tone sharp enough to warrant an exclamation mark in Laurie's article. Do you imagine that you can understand one of these men when he talks, or that he can understand you? They speak English, and so do you, but when you say white it means black to them, and when they say green you think they mean blue. Why, they live in a queer world of their own, these men. They ain't pretending when they try to act like martyrs. They think they are martyrs, that money idea they've got—well, some folks say there's more in that then there ought to be—but anyway, the idea that money's all there is on earth worth having is just what's made most of them kill somebody. They're just like children. They see something and they want it, and that's all there is to it to them."

"But their indifference," Laurie noted. "I couldn't bear to think when I looked at them of the awful day that is waiting for them—but they don't seem to mind much. They must affect that. Not a bit of it. If they felt the way they ought to feel about it they wouldn't have killed people."

Laurie ended her article—four columns in the May 12, 1895, edition—on a poignant note. After the interviews, she and the sketch artist who had accompanied her took a stroll on the beach nearby. "We went out on and walked on the seashore," she wrote, "and the artist quoted some German poetry, but I could not forget the four men who had just sat beside me and looked at the shadow that was like the gallows, and who had tried to explain the meaning of their queer, warped world to me."[5]

∗   ∗   ∗

The same day Laurie's piece appeared in the *Examiner*, the *Call* ran Belle Dormer's article about her desperate attempt to save the neck of Anthony Azoff.

Belle Dormer's odyssey to San Quentin began with a visit to Governor James Budd in the California Hotel. The journalist had come to believe that the childlike Anthony Azoff should not swing for his sins, whatever they happened to be. She detailed her logic in a feature article published the same day as Annie Laurie's interviews with four of the condemned men, including Anthony Azoff.

"Anthony Azoff, sentenced to be hanged on June 6 for the murder of Len Harris, is, I believe, an innocent man," Dormer wrote. "Some of the detectives set a trap to catch Azoff. Instead they caught their own man, Len Harris, and now have themselves and their miserable dupe to blame for it. Azoff had no money and that generally means no friends. Had Azoff's attorney put him on the stand to testify in his own behalf he would to-day be a free man."

Dormer, undeterred, brought her case to Governor Budd. Just a few weeks earlier, Budd had issued a reprieve. Dormer wanted the reprieve to become a commutation.

"If you please, Governor," she said, "I don't like to see Azoff hanged."

"Certainly not, madam," Budd responded. "That would be a most dreadful thing. Why, I wouldn't see Azoff or any other man hanged for anything." As women were not permitted to witness hangings at San Quentin, Budd likely meant his literal response as a jest, an evasive maneuver, or both.

After a series of interruptions, Budd shot straight from the hip. "Remember, madam, I had nothing whatever to do with the arrest, trial, conviction or sentence of this man, and I don't intend to have anything to do with the hanging. There are five of those men over at San Quentin who will hang the first week in June. Go over and tell Warden Hale that I said you were to interview every one of them if you want to, and when you come back let me know what you think of them, but remember that unless I change my mind, and I have no idea of doing so, the law must take its course with the whole five of them."

"Well, the next day," Dormer explained to her readers, "I went to San Quentin, and it is the loveliest place I ever saw in my life, and if the Warden will only promise not to turn the key on me, I will go there and stay the balance of my life—and I believe the turning of that same key is about the greatest objection that any of the Warden's guests have to this popular, all-the-year-round resort across the bay."

After waxing about the scenery and the "ample accommodations," the society reporter cleverly described the dress in vogue. "Black and white goods, in broad stripes, is the prevailing mode of dress worn by most of the guests at the Hotel de Hale—not, perhaps, so much for its beauty as for the durability of the cloth."

Patrick Collins refused to speak to female reporters. As he had done when Annie Laurie visited, he remained in his cell reading passages from his Bible. "Collins, the San Francisco wife-murderer," Dormer wrote, "declined to see lady reporters, feeling, no doubt, that such a sight would bring back his old desire to do a little carving. His wife was brutally slashed with a knife."

Azoff, Garcia, and Smith each spoke with the reporter, all of whom, Dormer said with her tongue planted firmly in her cheek, "are innocent—at least, they say so—and declare they can prove it if given a fair chance."

When it came to Azoff, however, Dormer was deadly serious. After listening to his side of the story, Belle Dormer believed more than ever that Governor Budd should intervene and commute his death sentence. "Fortified with the facts that Azoff has suggested for his defense," Dormer concluded in her story about the case, "I shall make another argument with Governor Budd.... If I can have another three minutes' talk with the Governor I think I can save Azoff's neck."[6]

No amount of pleading, despite Dormer's masterful use of rhetoric, would persuade James Budd to intercede on behalf of Anthony Azoff. The "little, proud man" would join Garcia and Collins on Friday, June 7, for a triple event.

* * *

Hangman's Friday, June 7, 1895, was going to be a quintuple event with five men scheduled to hang. Two days before, Governor Budd intervened on behalf of convicted slayers Fremont Smith and Rico Morosco. Doubts about Morosco's guilt remained, and ongoing microscopic tests on Smith's clothing had yet to determine if spots of blood came from a person or from a hog, as Smith claimed. When told of the temporary reprieve, Smith, who trashed his death house cell in an attempt to convince others of his insanity, danced a jig and said he felt like a 16-year-old again.[7] The governor's clemency came too late for Lunt, who had measured all five men and calculated the appropriate drops.

Emilio Garcia, Anthony Azoff, and Patrick Collins would hang as scheduled.

* * *

Emilio Garcia had heard rumors that James "Chicken Jim" Guilimot, an elderly resident of San Bernardino, had secreted a cache of gold on his property. Intoxicated by the possibility of instant wealth, Garcia and his accomplice, James Ferra, demanded the old man tell them where to find the gold. When Guilimot refused, Garcia stabbed him in the chest and then slashed his throat from ear to ear. Ferra received a 35-year sentence; Garcia, death by hanging.

On the night before he died, Emilio Garcia sat calmly and smoked a cigar, then fell asleep on his cot. He slept so soundly that the guards struggled to rouse him for his last meal. After breakfasting, Garcia took pen to paper and jotted a note addressed to Captain Edgar. Written in Spanish and enclosed in a envelope inscribed "I shall die very happy. Learn the reason and then you will know," the letter contained an enigmatic admission.

"Testament of my sorrow but it is of very little moment to me, because he who owes ten and more and pays one remains owning nine, and I have hoped to make up the dozen if God had given me license. And I am always

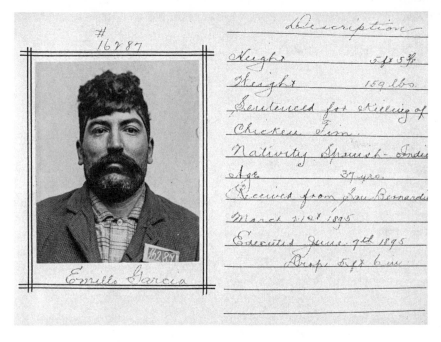

Emilio Garcia was the first of three hangings at San Quentin on June 7, 1895 (Anne T. Kent California Room, Marin County Free Library).

ready to give my life in payment for the past ten. If, as I have said, the debt is owing, and especially as I spoke of the last one, which was the only cause, it does not hurt me to pay when the thing is just."

The *Call,* in later publishing a translated version of Garcia's "confession," proclaimed that the rambling missive represented an admission of no fewer than ten murders and described Garcia as "one of the most cold-blooded and brutal criminals that ever faced a hangman's noose."[8]

* * *

Anthony Azoff's trip to the scaffold began on the Ides of May 1894, when he attempted to hold up a Southern Pacific Railway Company office at Boulder Creek in Santa Cruz County. Little did Azoff know that his confederate, George Sprague, had turned Judas and informed company officials about the upcoming robbery.

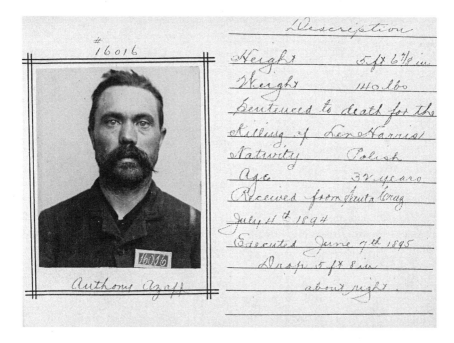

Annie Laurie described doomed slayer Anthony Azoff as "a little, proud man with a square face, big, empty eyes, a queer, twisted nose and a good-natured, foolish mouth. There was something so curiously young about him, for all his furrowed forehead, that he looked like a school boy, with lines painted on his face" (Anne T. Kent California Room, Marin County Free Library).

The Southern Pacific Railway sent a company detective, Len Harris, to foil the robbery and catch Azoff with his hands in the cookie jar. Hiding in freight cars across from the office, Harris and Sprague waited for Azoff to make his move. When Azoff shoved a revolver in the clerk's nose and demanded the money, Harris jumped out, ran toward the office, and ordered the bandit to surrender. Azoff fired at the detective, a slug tearing through Harris' groin and piercing his femoral artery. He collapsed onto the wooden planks and exsanguinated in minutes.

Following his conviction and death penalty, Azoff gave a partial confession that convinced many, including the *Call*'s Belle Dormer, that he did not kill Len Harris and did not deserve the rope. While he copped to robbing the train station agent at gunpoint, he claimed that George Sprague shot Harris—an accusation seemingly supported by the warm revolver with an empty chamber found on Sprague just after the shooting. Azoff alleged that Sprague had masterminded the set-up and planned all along to use him as a fall guy in a twisted ploy to curry favor with the railroad company and obtain a job.[9]

Azoff's 3,000-word statement convinced Belle Dormer, but it did not convince Governor Budd, who refused to commute the sentence.

When moved into the death cells, Azoff left behind in his cell on Murderer's Row three letters, including one to *Call* reporter Belle Dormer, and a smattering of art scribbled on the walls along with a few lines of verse:

> What need have I to fear so soon to die?
> 'Tis but a lifetime, and the end is nigh.[10]

Azoff, described as "a little Russian" with a "nervous temperament," grew increasingly perturbed as his execution date approached. He made several overtures about cheating the hangman, so Hale increased the number of men on the Death Watch; six guards watched him throughout the night of Thursday, June 6, much of which he spent waxing his mustache until the ends jutted out like poignards.

* * *

Residents of San Francisco experienced déjà vu on October 9, 1893, when Patrick Collins murdered his wife. About a year earlier, Patrick

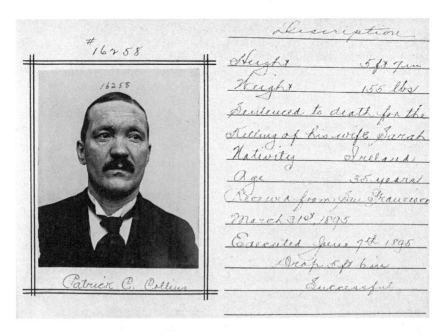

"I never knew of anything like his nerve," Lunt said of Patrick Collins, the third man to hang on June 7, 1895 (Anne T. Kent California Room, Marin County Free Library).

Sullivan had committed an eerily similar crime, which ended with his feet on the trap in 1894.

On October 9, 1893, Patrick Collins committed what the *Oakland Tribune* later described as one of the most brutal crimes ever committed in San Francisco when he stabbed his wife at least 30 times.[11]

An ironworker by trade, Collins abandoned his avocation and became a common laborer. Always heavy-handed with his wife Sarah, his abuse became physical whenever he took to the bottle. By 1893, browbeaten Sarah Collins had taken several jobs to support Patrick and her two children.

Meanwhile, Patrick Collins continued to tip the bottle. Whenever Sarah refused to give him drinking money, he beat her senseless. When she acquiesced and gave in, he beat her anyway. A mean drunk, he threatened to murder Sarah and during one binge attacked her with a straight razor, which earned him a six-month stint in the House of Corrections for assault.

Sarah Collins spent the six months eking out a hand-to-mouth existence in a small, one-room tenement that served as a home as well as a laundry for her side jobs washing clothes. "There is but a single cover on the bed, and that was ragged and threadbare," wrote a *San Francisco Examiner* reporter in an item about the crime. "There was the look and odor of abject poverty everywhere. It was more like a picture of wretchedness in London than a room in rich San Francisco."[12]

After emerging from the House of Correction, Collins stayed away from Sarah. He worked as an agricultural laborer picking grapes, but the meager pittance he earned did not go far in saloons, so he returned to San Francisco, where he harangued Sarah for money. With barely enough to support herself and two children, she did not have drinking money for Patrick.

On the morning of October 9, 1893, Collins trailed his wife to the kindergarten where she worked as a janitor. He cornered her in the hat room, stabbing her over 30 times in a frenzied attack that left the wooden paneling flecked with spots of blood.

With the knife embedded up to the hilt in her neck, she managed to stumble out of the room and fall into the arms of John Kelly, another janitor at the school.

"Oh my God!" the hysterical woman shrieked. "My man cut me!"

Kelly gently pulled the knife out of Sarah Collins' neck. "It's what he stabbed me with," she groaned.

"Who?" Kelly asked.

"My husband Collins."[13]

Sarah Collins died 30 minutes later in the Receiving Hospital.

Police collared Patrick Collins while he was on his knees in prayer at the St. Ignatius Church. He had changed shirts, but his underclothing and pants were speckled with the lifeblood of Sarah Collins. He denied killing his wife but provided no explanation for the blood on his clothes.

Like Azoff, Patrick Collins spent his last night in a state of frenzied panic. Prostrate with fear, he did not eat his last meal and devoted most of Friday morning to prayer. Of the three doomed murderers, Collins seemed the most remorseful.

*   *   *

The three men, while dissimilar in appearance, did not vary much in height and weight, which simplified Lunt's calculations. Of the trio to hang, Emilio Garcia weighed the most. At a height of 5'5⅜", he tilted the scales at 159 pounds. Patrick Collins stood 5'7" and weighed 155 pounds. Lunt calculated a five-foot drop for both men. Anthony Azoff, at 5'6" and 144 pounds, received the most rope with a drop set at 5'8".[14]

The triple event created a new wrinkle for Lunt. Unlike singular executions, the triple execution would require Lunt to use three ropes, changing each one in the interval between hangings. He had carefully measured all three ropes and tied the nooses the night before the hangings. He ran Garcia's rope over the crossbeam, the noose dangling in midair and waiting for the first of the trio, and he set Azoff's and Collins' ropes on the floor next to the scaffold.

*   *   *

The triple hanging brought a large crowd to the gates of San Quentin to witness morbid history in the making. Around 100 spectators arrived on the 7:40 a.m. train from San Francisco. One young man came to see his father's murderer swing. Jack Harris had blood in his eyes and reportedly asked Warden Hale if he could cut the cord that sent Anthony Azoff through the trap. A consummate professional, Hale rejected Harris' petition, instead giving him an invitation to attend the hanging.

At about the time the witnesses debarked, the condemned men finished their last meals. Warden Hale entered the death cells at eight sharp and read the death warrants to the three victims, who had already exchanged their prison uniforms for their funereal suits. Garcia listened as a guard translated the warden's words into Spanish. Then guards passed around a flask of whiskey. Both Azoff and Garcia took lengthy swigs, but Collins refused, apparently, like P.J. Sullivan, determined to go to the gallows sans bracer.

He passed the bottle back to one of the guards, who said, "It won't do those lads half so much good as it will me," and took a long pull on the flask. After finishing the bottle, the guard added, "The world looks brighter now. How do you feel, Collins?"

Patrick Collins tried to ignore the taunt and gripped the crucifix in his hands. "I'd like to go to the scaffold barefooted, for I don't see the use of wearing shoes."[15] Unlike Jose Gabriel, who wanted to die with his boots on, Collins preferred to go down without them.

For the next ten minutes, two Catholic priests from San Rafael prayed with the men while the Reverend Drahms stood by. Collins and Garcia were avowed Catholics; Azoff converted at the last minute and was baptized.

As the men said their final prayers, the spectators rode the elevator to the fourth floor and began to assemble in the gallows room. As the sun rose, an oppressive heat had enveloped the entire fourth floor, animating the crowd as the onlookers began to fan themselves and dab sweat beads from their foreheads while they waited for the first victim to appear.

At precisely 9 a.m., Hale returned to the death cells for Garcia, whose turn on the scaffold would come first. Hale, followed by the two chanting priests, led the somber procession to the gallows. Garcia, flanked by Amos Lunt and the Reverend Drahms, followed the priests.

Garcia appeared unfazed as he entered the gallows room, even when he spied the three coffins stacked against the wall. He smiled as he ascended the steps.

Once on the scaffold, Lunt made quick work of tightening the straps and placing the noose. As Lunt lowered the cap, Garcia uttered, "Good-bye…. Adios."

The fall produced the desired effect; Lunt's knot jerked back, dislocating Garcia's cervical vertebrae and crushing his spinal cord. Although he felt no pain, 13 minutes had elapsed before his pulse ceased altogether.

In the adjacent death cell, Anthony Azoff heard the thud. The sound further unnerved him, and he began to pace back and forth. "My God! What was that—the trap!" he yelped. "They do things quick out there."

In a vain attempt to calm the prisoner, the guard responded, "Oh, I guess that was the elevator."

"No, it was the trap," Azoff insisted.[16]

The sounds from the gallows did not appear to perturb Collins, who remained on his knees, praying.

Meanwhile, a contingent of prisoners, pressed into service, placed Garcia's body into one of the black-painted coffins, nailed the lid shut, and pinned a card with the name "Emilio Garcia" onto the side. They carried the coffin to an adjacent room and set it against the wall.

* * *

Fifteen minutes after the first hanging, with Garcia's body cut down and in the pine box, guards ushered the audience into an adjacent room, where they lounged in rocking chairs—remnants from the disused furniture factory—and puffed on cigars while Amos Lunt prepared for the next hanging.

The triple hanging created complications for Amos Lunt. After each hanging the rope was severed to lower the corpse, so Lunt had to install a new rope for the next victim, which involved measuring the drop and subtracting the appropriate length to compensate for the subject's height. Since all three men stood at 5'7" and their heights differed by just a little over an inch, this work would be more time-consuming than difficult. The three cords—one to release a trap and two connected to dummy sandbags—also had to be re-strung, and the trap mechanism tested to ensure that nothing, such as swelled wood from humidity or rusty hardware, would impede a clean fall.

The possibility of an error in measuring the drop was never greater than in these intra-hanging intervals on June 7, 1895. It would test Amos Lunt's acumen as a hangman and add to the emotional strain, the residue of which would accumulate in his psyche.

*   *   *

When guards ushered the witnesses back into the gallows room, Jack Harris made sure to find a spot as close to the scaffold as possible. He chuckled as Hale led Azoff to the scaffold at about 10 a.m. Harris, who one reporter described as "a sturdy young fellow with a high nose and a face on which was written most ruthless implacable hate," interested the newspapermen more than Azoff.[17]

Harris smiled as Amos Lunt mechanically repeated the well-practiced process of noosing and hooding Azoff, and when the trap opened and his father's murderer dropped like a sack of potatoes, he remarked, "Oh, I hope he strangles. I hope it didn't break his neck."

To Jack Harris' disappointment, Lunt had once again perfectly calculated the drop. Azoff's body hanged, motionless, as the doctors monitored his pulse. Jack Harris stood, his cheek pressed against one of the gibbet uprights, and stared at the motionless form of Anthony Azoff from about three feet away. He turned to another witness and asked, "Do you think there is any danger of them cutting him down before he is dead?"[18] If the hangman cut down Azoff's body prematurely, he could revive, putting prison officials in the awkward position of having to hang the man twice.

While Azoff's body dangled, Harris found Hale in the crowd and shook his hand as the journalists formed a circle around them and scribbled in their notebooks. "Now I'm satisfied," Harris said.

Fourteen minutes after Azoff dropped, the guards severed the rope and placed his corpse into one of the black-painted coffins. Hale presented Jack Harris with Azoff's noose. "He [Jack Harris] watched the next execution," noted the *Examiner*'s man on the scene, "and went away hugging a small coil of rope—the noose that had strangled Azoff."[19]

Once again, guards cleared the room, herding spectators to the waiting area, where they fell into the rocking chairs and chomped on cigars as they waited for the third act. Lunt, meanwhile, worked the third rope into place and carefully measured it for the calculated drop of 5'6" while the detail of prisoners carted Azoff's coffin out the room and stacked it on top of Garcia's.

* * *

Collins, prostrate with fear, turned to Father Hugh Lagan. "It's very soon now, father."

"Yes," Father Lagan responded, "but it will be a time of peace and rest."[20]

With Drahms on his left side and Lunt on his right, Patrick Collins slowly stepped toward the scaffold at 10:40 a.m. Too distraught to speak, Collins asked one of the Catholic priests to speak on his behalf.

While Collins stood on the trap and Lunt adjusted the straps, Father Lagan stepped to the rail and addressed the audience.

> This is an awful moment for the accused. He cannot be expected to express his thoughts. He comes here with a sincere heart and expresses his confidence in the future. He committed an awful crime while drunk and not responsible to God. He wished me to state that he believes he is forgiven for his sins and he forgives everybody on earth and asks forgiveness of all.[21]
>
> I take this opportunity from this pulpit of truth, where a man could not state a falsehood to thank the officers of this prison for their treatment of this unhappy man. Warden Hale, Captain Edgar, Captain Birlem, Captain Jamieson, have treated him like a brother. Better men never breathed. They have given us every opportunity to help these men and I now thank them. This unhappy man dies in the church. I only hope that all of you now present may die as well prepared as this poor man.[22]

Lunt positioned the noose and lowered the black cap. A few seconds later, Collins fell through the trap. Once again, Lunt's measurements proved fatally effective as the fall dislocated Collins' cervical vertebrae and crushed his spinal cord. A faint pulse lingered for 14 minutes before ceasing altogether.

As the spectators ambled out of the gallows room, the prison work crew placed Collins' body in the last of the three coffins and stacked it on top of Garcia and Azoff.

The "triple execution" was over.

* * *

Although Hale's role during the triple event amounted to signaling the drop by raising and lowering his arm, he nonetheless received the credit for a job well done. "The necks of all three men were broken," recalled the *Examiner*'s representative. "There was no blundering, and Warden Hale was congratulated on his performance of his trying duty."[23]

The Sullivan record creates some doubt about the efficiency of the drops. The page devoted to Collins describes his drop as "successful," but Azoff's is described as "about right" and Garcia's is given no designation at all. The absence of a description for Garcia's drop is provocative. Of the first 20 men hanged at San Quentin, only the entry pages for Garcia and John Miller, hanged in 1898, fail to record an outcome. From a hangman's perspective, Miller's execution was botched, which then suggests that the hangman also considered Emilio Garcia's execution as something less than ideal.

The "about right" designation for Azoff's drop is equally enigmatic. The vague phrase could denote either a success or a failure.[24] Although the exact definition behind the notation "success" in the Sullivan record remains obscure, a "successful" execution was likely one in which the hangman avoided either dreaded eventuality caused by a miscalculation in drop: a slow death by strangulation or a decapitation. Azoff's "about right," then, may represent a midpoint between these two extremes, evident in some outward manifestation such as slight writhing or trembling as his body dangled under the scaffold. Or that during the examination following Azoff's hanging, the doctors found no evidence of a broken neck.

A slow death by strangulation, which would occur if the drop failed to dislocate the cervical vertebrae, would create the unforgettable spectacle of violent thrashing—something not likely missed by the witnesses. None of the reporters at the hanging described such a scene, although the *Examiner*'s representative later described Jack Harris' trophy as "the noose that had strangled Azoff."[25]

* * *

Until the triple event, reporters did not mention the San Quentin hangman by name, creating the impression that some faceless phantom prepared the ropes or furthering the illusion that as the prison official in charge of hanging, Warden Hale tied the nooses himself. By June 1895, however, people began to identify the noose-tying phantom as Amos Lunt. The *Stockton Evening Record* reporter, in his day-after coverage of the triple hanging, remarked, "Lunt was the real executioner, for he affixed the appliances of death."[26] The other reporters on the scene added an epithet, referring to the hangman as "Amos Lunt, the executioner."[27]

This new notoriety would bring added psychological stress to Amos Lunt. As "hangman of San Quentin," he would become a curio and a target of journalists seeking sensational stories.

Lunt's new role would come at a tremendous risk of personal cost. Because his work would also become, in name only, the work of the official in charge of executions, Warden Hale. A slip-up, miscalculation, or error would embarrass not only Lunt but also his boss, which could affect his position at the prison. Therefore, his extra duties as hangman—for which he received no additional compensation other than a few days off work—could jeopardize his livelihood and the $600 per year salary that supported his family. And in communities employing an executioner, the hangman has long been reviled, not so much the person as much as what he represents.

13

"Tighten up the Rope"

(Friday, July 26, 1895)

The "stretching room" on the fourth floor of the former furniture factory—colloquially known as "hangman's hall"—contained, at all times, three ropes in the deadening process. After the triple hanging, Amos Lunt had to replenish his stock of "dead" ropes and began the process of preparing them for his next customers, slated for midsummer, when William Fredericks would go to the gallows.

Lunt, a *San Francisco Call* writer explained years after the hangman left the scaffold, preferred "a special twist made to order by the Tubbs Cordage Company" of three-quarter-inch thickness. William Hale's hanging of Sutton proved that the half-inch-thick rope could tear through a victim's neck if given too much of a drop. The thicker rope, on the other hand, provided a buffer should he err slightly in calculating the drop.

The directors of the Tubbs Cordage Company did not charge San Quentin for the manilas. "While corporations have no souls," the *Call* writer continued, "it seems that they have superstitions and for that reason the rope works, while willing to make the rope, steadily refuses to take any pay, believing that a 'hoodoo' would attach to money which had the taint of blood on it."[1]

When the new rope arrived in one, long coil, Lunt cut it into smaller lengths and proceeded to "deaden" them, or remove the springiness or elasticity, so that when the condemned dropped through the gallows trap, little or no recoil occurred. The drop, if calculated properly, would lead to a painless death, but a bounce could cause the noose to cut through the victim's neck and, in a worst-case scenario, yank his head off his shoulders.

Lunt referred to a properly stretched rope as "dead," which occurred after a lengthy process of suspending each one from a rafter with a box containing 300 pounds of bricks attached to one end.

With a rope stretched, Lunt next tied the noose in one end and installed the rope over the gallows trap with the exact amount of slack to create the desired drop. This process involved two calculations. He calculated the drop based on the subject's weight; the heavier the victim, the shorter the drop. For William Fredericks, who weighed 160 pounds, Lunt calculated the drop at 5'6"—the same drop he gave to Emilio Garcia, who weighed just one pound less at 159. This drop was measured from the gallows trap, so stringing the rope to account for the desired drop led to a second measurement; after measuring the distance from the crossbeam to the end of the drop, Lunt would measure the subject's height (5'9" for William Fredericks) and subtract that measurement from the rope.

Other biomechanical factors, such as an exceptionally thick neck, complicated what would appear to be a simple exercise in mathematics. Hanging, done properly to ensure a quick, painless death for the condemned, was equal parts science and art.

By Hangman's Friday, July 26, 1895, Lunt had a rope ready for the neck of William Fredericks.

* * *

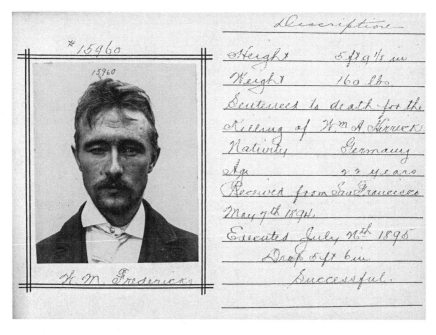

"I do not fear death," William Fredericks said on the eve of his execution. "Nothing matters really, and to a man in my position the strange part of it is that people make such a tremendous fuss over trifles" (Anne T. Kent California Room, Marin County Free Library).

"I do not fear death," William Fredericks said on the eve of his execution. "Nothing matters really, and to a man in my position the strange part of it is that people make such a tremendous fuss over trifles."[2] When Fredericks stepped onto the scaffold, however, the "trifles" of his hanging unnerved him and the death-house bravado he displayed to reporters the day before evaporated.

The *Chronicle* described Fredericks as a career criminal: "[he] had a long criminal record and had earned the death penalty in many cases before he was finally convicted."[3] The 22-year-old desperado spent most of his adult life behind bars.

Because he went by so many aliases, no one knew the real identity or true age of the man about to hang as "William Fredericks." By his own admission a member of the "Charles Evans" outlaw bandit gang, Fredericks left Northern California after he shot and killed two men, including Nevada County Sheriff William H. Pascoe.

He traveled to Butte, Montana, where he committed a string of highway robberies under the name "William Berrigan." While in Butte, he allegedly robbed and killed three Chinese men. As William Fredericks counted down his last days, his former roommate in Butte—August Barrenstein—came forward and identified him as "William Berrigan." While in Montana, "Berrigan" boasted to Barrenstein about his various misdeeds, including the murder of Sheriff Pascoe. He threatened to kill Barrenstein if he told anyone.

Fearful for his life, Barrenstein held his tongue until it became evident that the outlaw no longer posed a threat. When he finally came forward, he brought a photograph of "Berrigan" that left no doubt about his real identity as William Fredericks.

The crime that led Fredericks to San Quentin's gallows took place on March 23, 1894, when he shot teller W.A. Herrick during a robbery of San Francisco Savings Union branch at the corner of Market and Fell Streets. During the heist, a sliver of shattered glass pierced Frederick's right eye, scarring him for what little time remained of his life.

* * *

In the weeks leading up to his death, William Fredericks tried to wriggle his head out of the noose by feigning insanity. He went on a hunger strike, banged his head against the wall, and attempted to set fire to his cell. He spoke to the air, gesticulating wildly, his voice undulating with emotional outbursts. He tore shreds of cloth from the cot and wore them as leggings. Terrified of his cellmate Emilio Garcia, William Fredericks did not cross over the imaginary line that bifurcated their cell and demarcated their individual spheres. Supposedly, Garcia threatened to kill Fredericks if he wandered over the line.

As the date approached and Fredericks realized that he had failed to convince anyone, he dropped the insanity gambit and embraced Catholicism.

He appeared a man resigned to his fate when he sat with reporters on the afternoon of Thursday, July 25, 1895. He smoked a cigar as he fielded questions. Sniffing a juicy story, they asked him to set the record straight. He offered to sell his life story for $100 (he wanted to use the money for a headstone), but offended by the lowball offer of $20, he refused to talk about his crimes.

"That all belongs to the past," he said, his evasiveness chafing the writers, "as I will belong to the past tomorrow, and as I will be buried and forgotten, let what I did, whether good or bad, be forgotten. It doesn't matter. Nothing I can say now will change anything. I will not repair any injury that has been done me. I am to die tomorrow, and I am content." Fredericks spoke with a thick German accent. "I am past thinking of anything that belongs to this life. The talk of people outside is like voices from another planet. It is as if I was already dead."

Fredericks puffed on his cigar, exhaled, and watched the plume of smoke curl in the air, rise, and dissipate. "This life of ours is like that smoke, isn't it? It is warm and palpable for a moment and the next it has mixed with the elements. And, really, our life on this earth is of no more importance than that smoke, when it is done."

He responded to repeated questions about his crime with a morbid conclusion. "All there will be of Fredericks in this world will be a mound about six feet by two, and under that mound my story will be buried with me.... You might say I have read the last page and closed the book. There only remains to put out the light and then sleep."[4]

Fredericks' cigar went out as he spoke. Borrowing a match from one of the reporters, he relit it.

*   *   *

On his last night, Fredericks slept in intervals. At his request, the Death Watch roused him from a deep slumber at 1 a.m., and he spent the next two hours in prayer. He slept from 3 a.m. to 5 a.m. and then devoted the next four hours to the Good Book.

On schedule and following what had become standard operating procedure, William Hale came to the death cells at 9:55 a.m. to read the death warrant. Fredericks leaned against the cell wall and listened quietly. When Hale finished, he uttered, "I am ready."

Meanwhile, about a hundred spectators gathered in the gallows room, including three sons of the slain Sheriff Pascoe come to see their father's killer hanged. Hale began inviting victims' relatives at the hanging of

Anthony Azoff and continued the practice for this seventh, official hanging at San Quentin.

The procession formed with Warden Hale and Reverend Drahms in the front, followed by two priests, and bringing up the rear, Fredericks. According to a reporter from the *Alameda Daily Argus*, Lunt "half-supported" the pinioned man as he stepped toward the gallows.[5]

Charles Michelson, a longtime reporter and witness to many hangings, could not help but be impressed by the doomed bandito. The intrepid journalist characterized Fredericks as "the gamest man" he had ever seen hanged.

"My business has compelled me to attend at least a score of executions during the past ten years," Michelson wrote, "but among all these murderers there was not one who looked death in the face with as much unconcern as the undersized German lad whose body is now in the black box in the State Prison Morgue."[6]

Michelson remarked at how ashen-faced the others in the procession—Hale, Drahms, and Lunt—appeared as they stepped toward the gallows. "The warden of the prison was nervous lest some accident should make a horror of what turned out to be almost mechanical in its execution. The guard [Amos Lunt] who marched behind Fredericks was pallid and was obviously braced for a strain. The chaplain of the prison was ghastly pale and seemed ready to fall." The calmest person in the room, Michelson noted, was the man about to swing.[7]

Fredericks gave a brief speech that he had supposedly prepared the day before, although its striking similarity to another scaffold-sermon prompted journalists in the audience to conclude that the padres authored it. "Gentlemen," he began, "I heartily forgive all my enemies as I hope to be forgiven. The blindness of human justice will now be gratified, and I leave behind me the chains of slavery and the bonds of the flesh." Scanning the faces in the crowd, he lost his train of thought. He stared at the ceiling as he attempted to recall his speech and chuckled.

Father Lagan prompted Fredericks by feeding him cues.

"By the will of our omnipotent creator," Fredericks continued, "I die in the faith of Roman Catholic Church and cheerfully consign myself to the infinite justice and mercy of the one who is over and with and above all. Blessed is his name forever." The *Call* correspondent detected a tremor in Fredericks' voice when he said the word "die."

"Amen," Father Lagan said.

"Amen," Fredericks repeated.[8]

"Tighten up the rope," Fredericks commanded as Amos Lunt wiggled the noose to position the knot in the hollow behind Fredericks' left ear. They would be his last words.[9]

"Lunt held it [the noose] until the cap was adjusted," wrote the representative from the *Evening Bee*, "then gave it a lightning jerk, and raised his right hand."[10]

Fredericks fell through the trap at precisely 10:02 a.m., the drop snapping his neck. Lunt made quick work of adjusting the straps, fitting the noose, and lowering the cap. From the moment Fredericks had stepped on the gallows, just three minutes had elapsed.

"He fell about five feet," noted a *Chronicle* reporter, "and there were but a few convulsive movements of the body after it straightened. The execution was in every respect a successful one."[11]

Amos Lunt had become both an efficient and a skilled hangman.

During the 12½-minute interval while Fredericks' body dangled, his pulse fading with each second, a reporter overheard one of the Pascoe boys remark, "He lived like a brute and died like a brave man. I did not believe that he would die game, but he did, and he is entitled to that credit. We are certain he killed father, and we have naturally taken great interest in the case."[12]

Three condemned occupants of the death cells heard the thud signaling the last stand of bandit desperado William Fredericks. One of the men, Fremont Smith, had less than two weeks before he, too, made the long walk to San Quentin's gibbet.

* * *

The lengthy after-report by Charles Michelson, the seasoned *Examiner* correspondent, underscored the traumatic effects that hangings had not on the dead man walking but on the living. "It is not a pleasant thing to see a man hanged, and no one wonders as much at the spirit which prompts men to go to executions as those whose business or duty forces them to attend them. I never expect to attend another. Indeed, it was on a promise of the editor of this paper that I would not be required to again perform this unpleasant duty that I undertook the reporting of the execution of William Fredericks."[13]

Amos Lunt, the "pallid" guard who "braced for a strain" as he walked side-by-side with William Fredericks, had hanged his sixth man.

14

Hanging by a String

(Friday, August 9, 1895)

Amos Lunt most likely learned the art of tying a noose from Colonel McKenzie. He passed along the knowledge to at least two people: fellow guard and future hangman Frank Arbogast and a news reporter.[1]

The hangman's noose is not a difficult knot to tie, although the thickness of the rope that Lunt used—three-quarters of an inch—complicated the process. For Amos Lunt, the correct placement of the noose around the subject's neck was the most important consideration when it came to hanging a man. While English hangmen typically added a brass ring to their nooses, Lunt relied solely on the knot to dislocate the cervical vertebrae and crush the spinal cord, which made its placement a vital factor in a successful hanging. "I always take pains to place the knot closely under the left ear," Lunt later explained to a curious journalist.[2] He took pains so that his subject felt none.

By mid–1895, Amos Lunt had become a favorite of journalists. The hangman always had a good yarn, which was manna to writers looking for sensational stories. The hanging of Fremont Smith on August 9, 1895, would provide plenty of fodder for writers. For the first time as the hangman of San Quentin, Amos Lunt made an error in judgment.

Those who witnessed the execution of Fremont Smith on Friday, August 9, 1895, would emerge from the gallows room shaken. "His execution was so ghastly that it sickened even the most callous witnesses," the *Chronicle*'s man wrote.[3] His colleague at the *Examiner* remarked, "none who saw the body of the doomed man shoot through the trap will ever forget the scene of horror which followed."[4]

* * *

In December 1893, Fremont Smith went fishing in the mountains with two men known as Dolph and Charley who occupied a cabin on

110

"His execution was so ghastly that it sickened even the most callous witnesses," a *Chronicle* reporter wrote about the near decapitation of Fremont Smith (Anne T. Kent California Room, Marin County Free Library).

the Sacramento River. Dolph and Charley subsequently dropped out of sight, later to emerge when their bodies floated to the surface of the Sacramento River.

Smith had attacked the unsuspecting men at the cabin, felling one with an axe as he emerged from the outhouse and blowing the top of the other man's head off with a shotgun as he stood on the porch. He dumped both bodies into the river but neglected to clean up the cabin. Investigators found pools of blood, a portion of brain, and a skull fragment at the scene.

Smith made a fatal error in judgment in keeping the bloodstained overalls, which would tie him to the crime. Arrested in Collinsville, Smith said he knew nothing of the murders and claimed that the bloodstains on his clothing came from a hog he had slaughtered a few days earlier—a claim that influenced Governor Budd to stay the execution pending microscopic tests on the blood.

This temporary respite prolonged Smith's execution for two months, but when a team of scientists declared that the blood on his overalls likely came from a human, he was doomed. Originally scheduled for the June 7 extravaganza that sent Collins, Garcia, and Azoff to the scaffold, Smith's turn would come on August 9 instead.

*   *   *

Smith presented a bit of a challenge for the hangman.

At 220 pounds, Smith outweighed P.J. Sullivan by just five pounds, but Lunt opted to give him six more inches of drop at 5'6": the same drop that he gave to Patrick Collins and Emilio Garcia, who weighted 159 and 155, respectively.[5]

Name	Weight	Height	Drop
P.J. Sullivan (#15866)	215	5'7½"	5'0"
Patrick J. Collins (#16258)	155	5'7"	5'6"
Emilio Garcia (#16287)	159	5'5⅜"	5'6"
Fremont Smith (#15964)	220	5'9"	5'6"

San Quentin execution files contain weight, height, and drop but no other information that may have influenced Lunt to give a longer drop to a relatively heavy subject, but an article in the *San Francisco Call* provides a clue.

The article presents a description of Fremont Smith: "Smith is not a handsome man. His nose was broken in a fight at Willows twelve years ago, and remains bent and twisted. Since being in prison he has grown very fat, and weights probably 220 pounds. The arrangements for the execution have been all perfected, and the only concern now was hinted at in a remark this afternoon, 'Smith's got a big neck to break.'"[6]

The article does not name the speaker, but whoever voiced the big neck concern understood the dynamics of hanging, particularly how an anatomical feature such as a muscled neck may complicate things for the hangman.

A five-and-a-half-foot drop, Lunt apparently believed, would suffice in breaking Fremont Smith's "big neck."

Perhaps Smith knew something Lunt did not. Perhaps he just did not trust hangmen. Regardless, a remark he made the night before his execution proved eerily prescient. "I caught a glimpse of the rope," he said, "and I am not quite satisfied. They will never hold me up with that." And then he laughed so hard that "his sides shook," noted an *Examiner* correspondent.[7]

*   *   *

Smith professed his innocence to the end and reiterated his alibi from his death cell. "One of the men was shot, I believe, and the other's head crushed in with an ax," he said. "They were then thrown into the river. I was away traveling through the country on a backboard. I had gone two day's journey to Willows and Collinsville, where I was arrested. Yet the arrest took place forty-two hours, I think it was, after the death of those men."

Unlike his predecessors in the death cells, whose emotions ranged from unbridled remorse to apathy, Fremont Smith felt nothing but resentment. With a colorful vocabulary of oaths, he played the innocent man framed by circumstantial evidence. He berated the one ally he had—his lawyer, Edwin Swinford—whom he claimed sold him down the river.

> I never would have been convicted if that god-damned Swinford had not sold me out. He would sell his own mother for $50. He thinks less of a man's life than I think of a coyote, and that's damn little. He has been running to the Governor to do me up, too, else the Governor never would commit such cold-blooded murder as to hang me. Swinford has been slandering me, or else no man smart enough to be Governor could fail to see my innocence and let me hang.
>
> I'll die leaving my bitterest curse on all who have been connected with my murder and that of my mother.

He had concluded that his hanging amounted to no less than murder not just for himself but also for his 84-year-old mother, who surely would not survive the ordeal of knowing her son swung from the gibbet.[8] "Poor old mother," he lamented. "It's awfully hard on her. If it was not for her I wouldn't care a damn. For myself I don't care a cent, but mother—she'll not live a week after I'm hung." Tears formed in his eyes, but the emotion soon passed. "A moment later," wrote a reporter who witnessed the scene, "the condemned man was again the brutally jocose, hardened harlequin that he has been ever since his trial."[9]

On the night before his execution, the harlequin refused to see either priest or preacher, sending all away with the foulest of expletives. Instead of praying, he played cards with the Death Watch. Smith spent most of the night in intermittent sleep alternating with bouts of pacing and cursing.

"Where are the ham and eggs you promised me?" He barked when he woke about 6 a.m. on the morning of Friday, August 9. He gobbled down a plate of ham, eggs, a steak, and some fruit and then spent the rest of the morning pacing his cell and swearing about his unjust conviction.

* * *

Only about 35 spectators gathered around the gallows to witness Fremont Smith's execution, which was a blessing in disguise given the ghastly scene they would witness about five minutes after Warden Hale led the condemned man into the room at 10 a.m.

Smith carried his invective with him to the trap and made good on his promise to die leaving his "bitterest curse on all who have been connected" with his hanging.

"Gentlemen, I am as innocent as any man who ever stood on this trap, and I am ready to die," Smith declared in a steady, even tone unbroken by emotion. "I am not ashamed to be hanged, but I look at it the same as being murdered any other way. I have the distinction of being the first man in California to die this way without a particle of any evidence against him, and Governor Budd has the distinction of being the first Governor to commit a cold-blooded murder while in office." He paused before finishing his statement. "That is about all I have to say."[10]

Declarations of innocence from the scaffold put an enormous strain on the executioners. During the hanging of Patrick Collins, Father Lagan described the scaffold as a "pulpit of truth" from "where a man could not state a falsehood." Most people believed that a man about to meet his maker would not tell a lie at the last minute, before his ultimate judgment. As a result, Smith's final statement, despite emanating from an irascible individual seemingly incapable of remorse, created an added layer of anxiety for the personnel standing beside him at Lagan's penultimate moment of truth.

As Amos Lunt fitted the noose around Smith's neck, he said, "put it 'round tight." He repeated his demand three times.

Seconds later, Smith's body fell through the trap. As he feared, the rope did not hold his weight. Amos Lunt had overcompensated for Smith's "big neck" with the six inches of additional drop. The three-inch-thick noose tore through the muscles, sinews, tendons, and vertebrae of Smith's neck. The body, supported by a string of flesh, dangled as blood pouring from the carotid and jugular splashed against the floorboards of the factory floor. "The corpse hung," one witness later said, "with the head lolling over on the right shoulder and held to the body by a piece of flesh that was slowly giving away."[11]

Few accounts beat the *Call*'s graphic description of Smith's lifeless body hanging from the gallows. "Blood gushed from the wound, saturating the suit of black which had been intended for Smith's burial robe. The spectators stood as if struck suddenly dumb."[12]

The doctors ordered Smith's body cut down after six minutes to prevent gravity from tearing away the flesh that prevented a complete decapitation. The drop broke Smith's neck in two places; he did not feel a thing. The spectators, however, left the gruesome scene traumatized.

The *Call* reporter tried to downplay Lunt's error with fictitious mathematics. "The executioner, fearing such a mishap, had made the drop only five feet, whereas Fredericks had been dropped nearly seven feet, and

Warden Hale stated that never at San Quentin had more care been taken with an execution." In fact, both Fredericks and Smith fell exactly 5'6". The *Call* reporter characterized the near-decapitation as "unavoidable."[13]

The *Examiner*'s man at the scene was less forgiving. The bungled execution, he implied, had resulted from the hangman's error, but not in calculating the appropriate drop but in the noose, which Lunt had not drawn tight, despite Smith's repeated requests. "The knot in the noose slipped as the body dropped," he wrote, "and the rope became almost as keen as a knife. Had Smith fell [sic] three inches more his head would have been severed from his body."[14]

"Those who ought to know," the writer concluded, "declare that the drop through the trap could not have been shorter to insure death. The Warden, it is said, could not have prevented the horrifying scene."[15]

Although Hale did not measure the drop, prepare the rope, or tie the noose, he became the name associated with executions at San Quentin.

Hale was eager to correct the misimpression.

* * *

Six weeks after the Smith debacle, Hale and Lunt addressed hanging at San Quentin when they met with a reporter. Both men wanted to reassure the public about the civility and humaneness of executions, but Hale made an effort to disassociate himself from the behind-the-scenes work of the hangman. The Warden emphasized that his title of official executioner did not extend to anything beyond reading the death warrant, leading the procession to the scaffold, and signaling the cord-cutters. The hangman, Amos Lunt, made the preparations, including the calculation of the drop.

"I never do the mechanical portion of the hanging myself," Hale said, "but I make it my business to be present at all of our executions. As official hangman, I think it is my duty to do so. My chief deputy hangman, Mr. Lunt, makes and carries out all the arrangements, and to him is due the general success of the executions."

Hale defended capital punishment as a humane practice that functions as a "great preventative" of crime. "To a man who takes any pride in the proper performance of his duties a bungle is always regrettable," Hale said in an oblique reference to the Fremont Smith hanging.

In a subtle nod to the writers who criticized him for the Smith hanging, Hale suggested that strangulation would have been a worse outcome than the near-decapitation. "To a man who hangs men an unfinished execution is appalling. Some hangmen are content if they produce death by strangulation but, sentiment aside, death should be caused by a broken neck or the hanging is not properly done."

Lunt, whom the unnamed reporter characterized as "eminently

qualified for the unpleasant work," felt most comfortable behind the scenes. "He is a retiring nature," his interviewer suggested, "and did not like to force his claims as an expert hangman."

Nonetheless, Lunt discussed his work as the hangman of San Quentin for the first time publicly. Like Hale, he wanted to emphasize the civility of hanging. "I don't think the men feel the least pain after shooting through the trap," he said. "That is, providing the job is properly done."

In a clear reference to Fremont Smith, Lunt explained, "With an ordinary neck and well-stretched rope, death would be painless."

Then, like Hale, Lunt answered his critics, specifically the *Examiner* journalist who hinted that the deputy hangman had failed to pull the noose tight enough around Smith's neck. "I always take pains to place the knot closely under the left ear and see that everything is in proper shape before I motion to the man in the box to cut the three strings which spring the trap."

The interview came under the title "Placing Nooses on Necks" in the September 29, 1895, edition of the *San Francisco Examiner*.[16] Although Amos Lunt was the deputy hangman, with the publication of the article, Lunt became widely known as *the* hangman of San Quentin.

The article's subtext was clear: while Hale, as official executioner, would receive the lion's share of credit for successful hangings, Amos Lunt and Amos Lunt alone would shoulder the responsibility for botched ones.

15

"The Gallows Frame Rattled"

(Friday, October 18, 1895)

A contingent of three doctors attended hangings at San Quentin, but when two Federal prisoners went to the gallows on Friday, October 18, 1895, nine doctors stood at the base of the scaffold: three to monitor the ebbing pulse of the condemned man and six to monitor the racing pulse of United States Marshal Barry Baldwin.[1] The hanging of the two mutineers unnerved the marshal, who drank so much liquid courage that Amos Lunt had to help him to the scaffold.

For Amos Lunt, the Hansen and St. Clair executions would present a new challenge: hanging two men at the same time.

* * *

Dr. Mansfield would not join the contingent of physicians at the double hanging. Caught up in a scandal over $50 he received from a convict attempting to obtain a pardon, he resigned his position and returned to private practice. He would be replaced by Dr. William M. Lawlor. Dr. Lawlor came to San Quentin carrying some heavy baggage. His tenure as Superintendent of the County Hospital ended over a scandal involving fine wine. A connoisseur of champagne, Dr. Lawlor stood accused of using taxpayers' money to stock his personal wine cellar.

His subsequent posting also led to a scandal. As Quarantine Officer, he was responsible for administering a mandatory vaccine to each immigrant arriving in California, a service for which he charged a fee of $1 per head. This could be quite a lucrative venture for the physician; on some days, hundreds of Chinese immigrants arrived. Dr. Lawlor found himself scandalized by rumors that he gave immigrants injections of mucilage instead of the vaccine.[2]

On the same afternoon that Warden Hale accepted Dr. Mansfield's resignation, the death house cells received two more convicts. Shackled together by the ankles and wrists, Thomas St. Clair and Hans Hansen

Hans Hansen, whose romance with Emma Peterson made headlines, was buried with several of her love letters (Anne T. Kent California Room, Marin County Free Library).

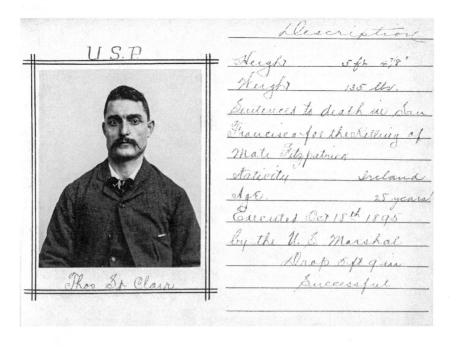

arrived from the San Jose County jail on Saturday, October 12. They would spend less than a week on death row before they went to the scaffold.

Marched to the office of the captain of the yard, the two traded their clothes for prison garb and sat for their final studio photographs: prison mug shots. After the two doomed men finished a late supper, the guards lodged them in separate cells on the fourth floor of the brick furniture factory, just a stone's throw from the gallows.

The capital crime of Thomas St. Clair and Hans Rasmus Hansen occurred on May 5, 1893. During an attempted mutiny aboard the *Hesper*, St. Clair buried an ax in the back of Second Mate Maurice Fitzgerald's head and with Hansen's help dumped his body overboard.[3] Originally, five men stood accused, but two turned state's evidence. Their testimony ultimately led to a death penalty for Thomas St. Clair, the unquestionable ringleader in a plot to murder the ship's officers and take control of the bark.

The joint trial of Hansen and Herman Sparf came after St. Clair's conviction. Jurors had a hard time determining the guilt of the pair, who claimed to know nothing about St. Clair's plan and merely helped dispose of the body and conceal the crime. They looked past allegations of Captain-Bligh-type abuse by the officers of the *Hesper*, allegations of perjured testimony by the two alleged conspirators who turned state's evidence, and repeated denials when they condemned the two sailors.

Sparf escaped the noose when his appeal resulted in an acquittal, leaving Hansen and St. Clair to pay the ultimate penalty for what occurred that day aboard the *Hesper*.

The two sailors differed in about every way possible. Twenty-six-year-old Hansen was a gentle soul who did everything he could to follow prison etiquette. His partner in crime, 46-year-old Thomas St. Clair, did everything he could to escape while in the San Jose County jail. Using scraps of tin, he fashioned a key to unlock his cell door and kept a shank made from a piece of clay pipe under his mattress in case anyone tried to stop him.

Few acquainted with the case felt sorry for the old sea dog, but Hans Hansen's saga was a sob story. He desperately hoped that a successful appeal or an 11th-hour commutation would unite him with his sweetheart, Emma Peterson.

Their romance was one seemingly torn out of the pages of a novel. Emma Peterson, a young Swedish girl who worked as a servant in the

Opposite bottom: An impatient man, Thomas St. Clair despised waiting for his date with the hangman. "It is not death which disturbs me, but this repeated preparation for death," he told a reporter. "That is becoming tiresome. I heard them testing the trap today. It is not a pleasant sound, is it, when you think that the next time that trap opens your body will shoot through it?" (Anne T. Kent California Room, Marin County Free Library).

sheriff's residence at the San Jose County Jail, recognized Hansen as a youngster she knew as a girl. Conversant in Danish, Peterson began visiting the prisoner. One thing led to another, and they agreed to exchange vows if Hans Hansen could beat the rap.

The failure of Hansen's final appeal and news that he would not receive a commutation destroyed his dream of a happily-forever-after with his Swedish nightingale. When the hack carrying the two condemned men pulled away from the San Jose County jail, Emma Peterson ran after it in a pathetic scene that moved guards to tears.

Where Hansen was repentant and pensive, Thomas St. Clair alternated between jocular and indignant. He joked with his guards one minute and carped about his unjust sentence another. In an invective-fueled rant, he verbalized what he had come to see as a raw deal. He indicted his lawyer, who represented three of the accused mutineers, and witnesses coached by the prosecution to spin testimony against him.

He even condemned the press for printing the false allegations. "The newspapers have fixed me; they had me convicted before I was tried," St. Clair barked at reporters who trailed him to San Quentin from San Jose. "Did I get a square trial? No; I don't think I did."

St. Clair stopped short of threatening his lawyer, unlike Fremont Smith, who once quipped that he would murder his lawyer if the guards would leave him alone with the man.

St. Clair appeared the dominant of the pair and often spoke on behalf of his young mate. When the reporters asked Hansen how he felt about the trial, St. Clair answered for him. "He feels about as I do," he snapped. In a rare display of self-assertion, Hansen contradicted the gruff sea dog. "I have had a just trial," he said, "and I am satisfied with my treatment."[4]

Less than a week later, the two convicted mutineers would walk the plank from their death cells to San Quentin's gallows, making them the first Federal prisoners executed in the state of California.

* * *

United States Marshal Barry Baldwin had no experience with hanging. St. Clair and Hansen represented the first Federal prisoners executed in California, and the prospect of taking an active role in the executions left Baldwin in a state of nervous prostration. Warden Hale, who did not expect to officiate over the executions, consulted with Baldwin and reassured him that other than reading the death warrants and signaling the drop, Baldwin would not have to do anything on the gallows; his master hangman, Amos Lunt, and the Death Watch would handle all of the dirty work.

Baldwin was terrified of a mistake. "Extraordinary precautions," noted the *Chronicle*, "have been taken by Marshal Baldwin to prevent the possibility of mishap."[5] He wanted both men to climb the scaffold together and to drop simultaneously.

Since the scaffold contained a single trap, it would need alteration for the dual hangings. Under Amos Lunt's direction, prison personnel engineered the new configuration to contain two traps and a device for dropping both men at the same time. A reporter who studied the new and improved scaffold described the curious device on the eve of the executions. "The scaffold has been enlarged to contain two traps," wrote a journalist for the *Examiner*, "which, with an electric apparatus, will be sprung simultaneously."[6]

A *Call* reporter described the newfangled "electrical apparatus" that would send the two condemned men hurtling into inner space. "As arrangements now stand there are to be three electric buttons pressed to work the drop, one man to each button, and no one is to know which completes the circuit that will start the current through the wires."[7]

With the gallows set, Amos Lunt measured and weighed both men to calculate the proper drop: 5'9" for St. Clair and 5'8" for Hansen. Both men weighed 135 pounds, but Lunt decided to give St. Clair a slightly longer drop, possibly due to some anatomical feature not recorded in either the Duffy or Sullivan records. The prison mug shots may provide a clue. St. Clair's tapered shoulders created a less distinct neckline than Hansen's, which may have influenced Lunt to add an inch. He may have also wanted to perfect on the "almost right" drop of Anthony Azoff, who received a 5'8" drop at a weight of 144.[8]

For Lunt, the most difficult aspect of the executions did not involve calculation of the drops—neither man presented an anatomical feature such as Fremont Smith's big neck that would complicate the mathematics—but the physical dynamics of hanging two men simultaneously. Unlike the triple event, which contained three separate hangings conducted one after the other in a sequence, the double hanging of Hansen and St. Clair would involve two men dropping at the same time. The gallows had been widened, a second trap added, and an electrical device replaced the three-cord system, but the complication had nothing to do with the layout of the scaffold but rather what took place on it in the moments before the floor dropped.

As Lunt and Hale knew, the less time involved in an execution, the better for all involved. A short interval between the walk and the drop drastically reduced the mental anguish suffered by the condemned as well as satisfying those officials and witnesses who simply wanted to get it over.

Lunt had become so adept with the scaffold work of adjusting straps and noosing his subjects that it took him less than a minute. The entire procedure from the entrance to the drop took less than five minutes, depending on the length of the condemned man's remarks.

With the St. Clair-Hansen hangings, Lunt would have to teach another guard how to place the knot, or he would have to noose one man and then as quickly as possible noose the other.[9]

*　*　*

On the day before the hanging, Emma Peterson managed to see something generally off-limits to the general public: the inside of a death cell. Hale acquiesced to the pleas of Peterson, who begged to say goodbye to her sweetheart, and Hans Hansen, who promised to go gently to the gallows if given the chance to say farewell. Peterson became "the first woman not attached to the penitentiary who ever entered it after nightfall."[10]

The two star-crossed lovers enacted a Romeo and Juliet-style scene on the evening of Thursday, October 17, in front of an *Examiner* journalist, who recorded the tender moment for posterity. The young woman, tears streaming down her checks and clutching the arm of Reverend Drahms, followed Captain Edgar to the fourth floor, where Hansen paced from one wall of his cell to the other in eager anticipation of his final moment with his would-be bride.

Her body heaved with sobbing as she crossed the courtyard and climbed the steps to the fourth floor. While Captain Edgar escorted her to a spot where he had positioned two rocking chairs six feet apart, Captain J.F. Birlem brought Hansen from his cell.

They had just five minutes together. Hans Hansen did all the talking. He told her about two letters he had written, one to her and another to his father. He also attempted to reassure her that he was innocent but had accepted his fate and would go to his death both a Christian and a brave man.

A pregnant pause followed the end of Hansen's monologue. Neither he nor Peterson appeared to know what to do or say. "Don't you wish to take her by the hand?" Captain Edgar asked.

Hansen took Edgar's advice and grasped Peterson's hands. "Good-bye and God bless you," he muttered. Drahms placed his hands on the sobbing woman's shoulders and led her away.[11]

With the scene played out, any unease evaporated in Hans Hansen. His face took on the look of tranquility, and he began to smile and joke with the Death Watch. "'Tis not so hard to die after all," he remarked. "One must die some time, why not now?"[12]

Hans Hansen wanted to die well, but just in case he faltered, he asked Baldwin to exclude the press from his hanging. Baldwin gladly honored the request, because like Hansen, he did not want his missteps recorded for all to read in the day's papers.

In fact, he had already decided to exclude reporters but not as a magnanimous gesture to a condemned man. Two days before the hanging—on October 16, 1895—Baldwin announced that he would bar the press from witnessing the double hanging. He had received a telegram from Washington, D.C., instructing him to make the affair as private as possible, which Baldwin interpreted to mean no reporters.

Stinging, the press corps came up with another reason for their exclusion. "It is known that he recently received a telegram from headquarters ordering him to conduct the execution with all the privacy possible," noted a *Call* reporter, "but it is said the message contained no word regarding press representatives and that Mr. Baldwin's interpretation of the telegram has been made to suit his own wishes. A number of Federal officers prefer to believe that Mr. Baldwin is not at all sure of being able to do the work properly and that his idea is to have as few witnesses as possible in case the hanging should be bungled."[13]

Hansen had another macabre request, which he relayed to Emma Peterson through his friends who visited him in his final hours. "I have a ring which was to be her wedding ring," he said. "I will wear it when I am hanged. When I am placed in my coffin I want the hand upon which that ring is placed to rest over my heart. I want my sweetheart to take the ring from my finger and wear it in remembrance of me."[14]

Like Hans Hansen, Thomas St. Clair appeared poised to assert his innocence to the end. He continued to blame witnesses whom, he alleged, had perjured themselves on the stand and offered nationalism as a defense: as the only other Irishman on board the *Hesper*, he would never have killed Fitzgerald.

Asked how he felt about the prospect of dying, Thomas St. Clair was equally philosophical but more voluminous in his comments. "One cannot fear when he knows that there is something even better than life," he said. "Do I feel nervous? I will bet that Marshal Baldwin feels worse than I do. He would give more not to be compelled to stand on the gallows than would I. I hate to see him around me. He comes and goes as if he were in misery. I always like to see him go away. He makes me feel worse than I should."[15]

Not even the sound of Lunt testing the trap upset St. Clair. "It is not death which disturbs me, but this repeated preparation for death," he said. "That is becoming tiresome. I heard them testing the trap today. It is not a pleasant sound, is it, when you think that the next time that trap opens your body will shoot through it? But I am getting used to it."[16]

Both men spent much of the night scribbling their final thoughts: Hansen wrote letters to both his father and Emma Peterson, while St. Clair wrote a lengthy statement, professing his innocence.[17]

Whereas St. Clair and Hansen became calmer as the hours passed, Marshal Barry Baldwin grew increasingly nervous. By Friday morning, his nerves had completely frayed. Those closest to the marshal wondered if he would withstand the strain.

*   *   *

After consulting Warden Hale, Baldwin decided that the executions should take place at 2 p.m., the later time allowing for a last-minute reprieve from Washington. As the fatal hour approached, a small group of 23 witnesses—none of them from the press—gathered on the fourth floor.

Hans Hansen spent most of his last morning speaking with the Reverend Drahms, while Thomas St. Clair nervously paced his cell. After he downed a bracer of sherry, he calmed down a bit. He chatted with the Death Watch until Father Lagan arrived from San Jose to hear his last confession.

In the next-door cell, Hansen received a letter from Emma Peterson, who had camped out outside the factory building to wait for Hansen's body. When her beau read the letter, which encouraged him to go to the gallows with bravery and dignity, his composure evaporated. He buried his face in his hands and his torso heaved with convulsive sobs. After a few minutes, he jotted a reply, which Drahms promptly took down to the first floor, where Peterson awaited the inevitable.

Hansen also jotted a partial confession on a scrap of paper and addressed it to the *Call*. In the short missive, he admitted to conspiring to beat up the second mate but denied entering into any plot to murder the first mate. "I know of no conspiracy whatever to kill him or take life," he wrote. "Whatever was planned or done in that direction was unknown to me and done without my knowledge or consent. Before I was aware of any such intent, I saw the fatal blow struck from behind. I was so unnerved thereby that I was unable to act."[18]

Thomas St. Clair maintained his innocence to the end, although Guard Frank Arbogast overheard him make a damning admission. "I don't want him [the priest, Father Lagan] to know that I am guilty," St. Clair said.[19]

Just before 2 p.m., Amos Lunt entered the death cells. A *Chronicle* reporter, barred from witnessing the hangings, described the ominous moment when the condemned eyed their executioner passing through into the gallows room. "Then the big iron doors at the entrance to the condemned room creaked ominously as it swung open to admit Hangman Amos Lunt. St. Clair saw him first and smiled meaningly as he returned his bow." According to the *Chronicle*'s article, "Guard Miller, who had been selected as the other hangman, came in a few minutes later. The two executioners passed on into the execution chamber and made a final inspection of the gallows."[20]

A few minutes later, Barry Baldwin wobbled into the death cells to take his prisoners on their final walk. His voice cracked as he informed them that their time had come. "From an inside pocket he drew forth the death warrant," a *Chronicle* reporter noted, "but he waived reading it for reasons best known to himself." He did not read the warrant because, on the edge of a nervous breakdown, he had administered to himself more than a few alcohol bracers and could not focus on the page.

"I am ready to die, Mr. Marshal," Hansen said. St. Clair just bowed his head in assent.[21]

Baldwin, with Hale, Lunt, Miller, and the clergy in tow, led the two doomed men to the gallows. Instead of ascending the scaffold as planned, he wobbled to a window and stood gazing outside while Hale took charge.

Once on the scaffold, Lunt and Miller made quick work of noosing Hansen, who remained steady in his final seconds, and St. Clair, whose legs began to buckle. Just 56 seconds had elapsed since the procession had first entered the room.[22]

Lunt had apparently apprenticed Miller in the fine art of noosing. Because newspapermen, barred from witnessing the hanging, relied on hearsay from eyewitnesses, their accounts came through highly prejudicial and, in some cases, emotional filters. As a result, stories about the effectiveness of this shared noosing vary greatly. While the *Chronicle* lauded the duo of Lunt and Miller for their rapid noosing, the *Call* was far less complementary.

"So far as can be learned," wrote a *Call* reporter with a hint of angst in his tone, "the condemned men were dropped into eternity without any shocking disaster; but one of them, with rope affixed and black cap drawn, was left to endure the mental torture of expectancy while clumsy hands prepared his companion for the fatal journey."[23] The "clumsy hands" undoubtedly belonged to Miller, whose nervousness may have transformed otherwise nimble hands into all thumbs.

At precisely 2:02 p.m., Lunt signaled the release of the trap, and both men dropped with a force that rattled the entire superstructure of the gallows. Baldwin's fears of a botched hanging did not materialize, and Lunt atoned for the bungled hanging of Fremont Smith; the fall broke the necks of both men. Hansen's body dangled, motionless, while St. Clair's body twitched and trembled with convulsions that abated after a few minutes. Their bodies hung while their heartbeats slowly ebbed until the contingent of doctors felt nothing but silence—at nine minutes for Hansen and 14 for St. Clair.[24]

Amos Lunt had orchestrated a painless execution for both the condemned men and the witnesses, while Barry Baldwin cowered in a corner gazing out of the window. "From the time he entered the execution-room until the corpses were cut down," wrote a *Chronicle* correspondent, "Baldwin was busy studying the contour of the hills along the eastern shoe of the bay. Only once did he turn his head toward the scaffold, and that was when Dr. Maltner pronounced Hansen dead. The instant he saw the gibbet with its dangling corpses his self-possession forsook him and he directed his attention again to the blue sky and sunshine without."[25]

Emma Peterson, wearing a black taffeta-and-lace mourning dress and a veil concealing her bloodshot eyes, accompanied her suitor's body to San Jose for burial. She did not accede to Hansen's final wish and left the gold band on his finger. He was buried with the ring and several of their love letters.

* * *

A profile sketch of Amos Lunt, under the title "Hangman Amos Lunt," appeared in the *Chronicle*'s day-after coverage of the St. Clair-Hansen hangings.[26] For the first time, the public had a chance to gaze upon the visage of the hangman of San Quentin, to put a face with the name that had become synonymous with executions in California.

The face became a symbol for the ongoing debate over capital punishment. For death penalty opponents, Lunt represented terrible retribution at the end of the rope and the finality that led to scenes such as the farewell between Hans Hansen

Hangman Amos Lunt -

The reading public's first glance of Hangman Amos Lunt came in the form of this profile sketch published in the *Chronicle* alongside a column detailing the sob story of the Hansen-Peterson romance.

and Emma Peterson. For death penalty proponents, Lunt represented the terrible yet swift sword that came down on the necks of the worst law-breakers in the state.

The press appeared ambivalent toward Amos Lunt. Placement of his image, his profile next to and facing the column describing the tragic Hansen-Peterson love saga, seemed like an editorial snipe at the hangman. At the same time, reporters lauded him for breaking necks in a fashion painless to both victims and spectators.

16

Tenth Man

(Friday, October 25, 1895)

A week later, Amos Lunt would hang his tenth man when William Young mounted the scaffold. At age 23, Young, ironically, would become the second-youngest man—behind 22-year-old William Fredericks—to go to the gallows during Lunt's tenure as hangman. It was to be the eighth and final execution in what had been a very busy year.[1]

* * *

Unlike the pair of salts Lunt hanged a week earlier, William Young admitted to shooting Pierre Latestere on March 22, 1894, although he said he committed the act while drunk. After waking from a deep slumber on his final night alive, he remarked, "It's all right. I killed him. Now let them hang me. I deserve it."[2]

A native of Germany, Young grew up with a heavy drinker of a father who became abusive when he tipped the bottle. He left home at age 15 and came to California. A drifter, Young moved from place to place, occasionally taking a short-term job as a ranch hand. In 1894, he turned up at a Monterey County ranch owned by an affluent San Francisco resident named E. Guittard and operated by foreman Pierre Latestere. Taking pity on the tramp, Latestere gave Young food and a bed.

When Young learned that Latestere had received a substantial sum of money, he cooked up a story of a fictitious sister arriving in nearby San Ardo by train and coaxed Latestere into taking him to meet her.

While the ranch manager hitched a horse to a buggy, Young tiptoed behind him and emptied one barrel of a shotgun into his back. The cluster of shot struck Latestere just below his right shoulder, tore away the lower part of his right lung, and perforated both his right kidney and liver. Latestere crumpled to the ground and passed out. Young rifled through the dying man's pockets and fled with $83 and change.

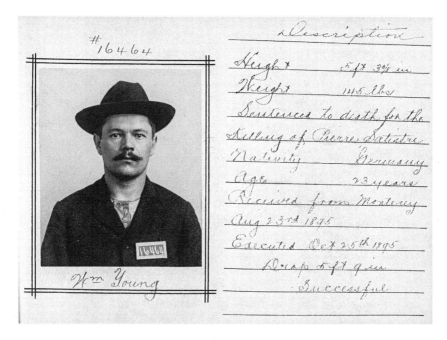

"He had the weakest nerve of any man I have executed," Amos Lunt said of William Young, "though St. Clair was nearly as bad" (Anne T. Kent California Room, Marin County Free Library).

Miraculously, Latestere regained consciousness and managed to crawl three-quarters of a mile to a neighboring house. Taken to a nearby hospital, he hovered on the edge of life and death as doctors fought desperately to save him.

Local law managed to collar Young within hours of the shooting and dragged him in front of his victim. "He's the man that shot me," Latestere insisted. He died of his wounds two days later.[3]

Now facing a possible death sentence, Young admitted to shooting Latestere although he attempted to lessen his culpability by claiming he was too drunk to know what he was doing. He also said that he did not take the bankroll from Latestere's pocket but found it lying on the ground next to his body.

Young's semantics did not sway the judge and jury. Tried, convicted, and sentenced to hang, he arrived at San Quentin on August 23, 1895.[4]

Three hours before his execution, Young made a partial confession, admitting his guilt in the shooting but describing the killing as an accidental rather than a premeditated murder. He explained that both he and Latestere had consumed a liberal amount of alcohol, so much in fact that his memory about the event remained hazy. As far as he could recall,

Latestere hopped onto the buggy and, eying the shotgun, said that they did not need it for their trip into town. He grabbed the firearm by the barrels and handed it to Young. When Young took the shotgun by the stock, it went off, the load of buckshot hitting his foreman at point-blank range.

"Where I made my great mistake," Young said while Amos Lunt tested the trap next door in preparation for the hanging, "was in taking the Frenchman's money after he was shot. I was so frightened and crazed from drink that I did not know what I was doing. I realized that I must get out of the vicinity as soon as possible, and I needed money in order to travel. Had I let that money alone I am satisfied that the jury would have believed my story and let me go."

Young spoke with a heavy German accent. "But," he concluded, "I killed the man and the law says I must die. I make no protest." Then he added a statement that hinted at a guilty conscience and undermined his accidental-shooting scenario. "I believe I should suffer for my crime."[5]

Lunt's job as hangman, however, was to ensure that he suffered as little as possible, both on and under the trap.

At just a hair over 5'3" tall, the "laundryman" from Monterey weighed 145 pounds but had a muscular neck, so Lunt gave him an inch more rope than he gave to Anthony Azoff, who weighed 144. William Young's drop would abruptly end 5'9" from the scaffold floor.

* * *

The procession leading William Young to the scaffold consisted of men who had played, or would play, key roles in the San Quentin execution machine. Hale headed the procession, followed by the Reverend Drahms—responsible for last-minute spiritual support—and the doomed man, who walked between Death Watch guards Miller, who noosed Thomas St. Clair, and Arbogast, destined to become a future hangman. Amos Lunt brought up the rear.

Young's nerves held until he eyed the noose hanging from the crossbar and the empty black coffin lying against the wall. He began to tremble, and his legs weakened. At the foot of the scaffold, his nerves gave way and his knees buckled. Each taking an arm, Miller and Arbogast walked him up the 13 steps to the platform, where Lunt waited with a black cap in his hands. Young swayed as the attendants tried to fasten the straps while keeping him upright.

Sensing an imminent collapse, Lunt quickly noosed and capped Young. It was all over in a matter of seconds. According to one account, only ten seconds had elapsed from the time William Young first stepped onto the scaffold.[6] Any of the 35 witnesses who blinked missed the young slayer's final moment. His knees gave way just as the trap opened.

Lunt had perfected hangings into a highly efficient and effective process. The entire procedure took less than a minute; a mere 40 seconds had passed from the time the death procession first entered the room.[7]

William Young's near-collapse bothered the hangman. "If he had had ten seconds more," Lunt commented after the hanging, "he would have fainted from fright. He had the weakest nerve of any man I have executed, though St. Clair was nearly as bad."[8] The fall, as planned, had snapped William Young's neck, but his pulse beat on for 17 minutes before the attending physicians gave the nod to cut down his body.[9]

* * *

With William Young dead and buried, life behind San Quentin's walls relapsed into the usual, timeworn routine for Amos Lunt and William Hale. Strict regimens dominated daily affairs at the prison, which sometimes led to the monotony that in turn created ennui for guards. Part of Amos Lunt's regimen involved walking the wall and toting a gun to guard against any escape attempts. In December, an interesting incident occurred that illustrated Lunt's demeanor while on duty.

An old acquaintance from Santa Cruz came to tour the prison and hoped that a fellow Santa Cruzan would show him the way. The man, whose name has escaped the historical record, entered the prison grounds and began searching for Lunt.

He found the hangman standing guard on the wall by one of the turrets, but instead of the warm welcome he expected, the visitor received a stentorian warning punctuated with a gun barrel pointed at his nose.

"Hello, Amos," he yelled when he spotted Lunt on the wall.

"Stand back!" Lunt ordered. He pointed his rifle at the man for emphasis.

Thinking himself a victim of a practical joke, the man continued to walk toward Lunt, who yelled, "Stand back, I tell you!"

Disgusted, the man turned to go when another guard approached him and asked him what he wanted. After a brief explanation, the guard went up onto the wall and took Lunt's place. When Amos Lunt recognized the man, he reached out with both hands, grasped his friend's right hand, and vigorously shook it.

For the next hour, Lunt gave his fellow Santa Cruzan a behind-the-scenes tour of the prison, including a glimpse at George Bullock, a notorious murderer from their hometown doing life for shooting C.O. Walker in 1893. Bullock was wearing a bright-red shirt, Lunt explained, because he was caught attempting to go over the wall. San Quentin's scarlet letter—the red shirt—served as a public shaming of the inmate but even more so made him easier to see should he attempt another escape attempt. The bright, blushing-red color made an excellent target even when moving.[10]

Amos Lunt may have appeared a bit paranoid to his guest, especially considering that escapes under William Hale's administration had slowed to a trickle, but within a few years, Lunt would be pointing his rifle at phantoms.

The Master and
the Apprentice

(Friday, December 11, 1896)

With eight hangings, 1895 was a busy year in San Quentin's death chamber. During his second year on the scaffold, Amos Lunt had hanged more men than most county sheriffs had in their entire careers. Lunt's third year was shaping up to be an even busier one. By March 1896, the number of prisoners awaiting their turn on the scaffold had swelled to nine.

Lunt jotted a note to his contact at the *Santa Cruz Sentinel*, who wrote a blurb that appeared in the March 26, 1896, edition. "Amos Lunt writes us that nine men are confined in San Quentin under sentence of death. The first one to be executed is Kid Thompson, the train wrecker, who will be hanged on May 22nd." The notorious train robber, however, would not keep his date with Amos Lunt. He escaped the scaffold when the appeals court reversed his conviction. Convicted a second time a year later, he went to Folsom for life.

Through the usual avenues of attrition—deaths, reprieves, commutations, and legal appeals—the number "confined under sentence of death" dwindled to just one. Although the ropes dangled in the stretching room, ready for action when called upon, over a year would pass before Lunt tied another noose, which he would place around the neck of Marshall J. Miller on Friday, December 11, 1896.

* * *

On May 1, 1895, Marshall J. Miller and his accomplice, Stewart A. Greene, attempted to rob Julius Pierre, an aged pawnbroker from Marysville. They tried to torture the pawnbroker into revealing his cache of gold, but Pierre took the secret hiding place of his stash with him to the grave when he asphyxiated on a dirty rag they shoved down his throat.

#16418

M. J. Miller

Description

Height   5 ft 6½ in

Weight   148 lbs

Sentenced to death for the Killing of Julius Pierr.

Nativity   England.

Age   50 yrs.

Received from Cuba July 5th 1895.

Executed Dec 11th 1896

Drop 5 ft 6 in

Very Successful

"Pull the rope tight," Marshall Miller said as Lunt fitted the noose around his neck. The hangman made quick work of Miller, who stood on the scaffold for less than a minute (Anne T. Kent California Room, Marin County Free Library).

Sheriff's deputies found a blood-drenched shirt in Pierre's outhouse and traced it to Greene, who had described the crime in detail to a prostitute when he begged her for money to leave town. Upon his arrest, Greene confessed to the murder and identified Miller as his accomplice.

The two thieves obtained separate trials. Greene, who came from an affluent family in Illinois, pled not guilty. His father traveled west and secured the best attorneys available for his son's defense. Powerless against overwhelming evidence of Greene's guilt, they nonetheless managed to convince the jury to send the younger offender to prison for life rather than to the hangman for death.

Miller did not have Greene's team of lawyers. Believing he would escape the gallows if he threw himself on the mercy of the court, Miller took the advice of his attorney and pled guilty, but the hanging judge gave him the death penalty anyway.

Appeals delayed the execution for over a year, but when it became evident that only a last-minute telegram from the governor would save Miller's neck, Warden Hale had him moved to the death cells a week before his "Hangman's Friday."[1]

*   *   *

Miller liked to talk but refused to talk to the press. He asked Hale to keep reporters out of the death house as he whiled away his final hours in prayer with Father Lagan. Hale honored the request, and Miller promised to make a final statement through his padre.

The 45-year-old Ohio native spit venom at Stewart Greene, his lawyers, and the courts in general. Poised to maintain the guise of a wronged man all the way to the gallows, Miller claimed that Greene plied him with drugged whiskey. As a result, he had no memory of what occurred in Julius Pierre's pawnshop. He later repeated this story when he penned an official statement that he passed to the press through his spiritual advisors. In his postmortem proclamation, he depicted himself as taking the fall, literally, for the real villain.[2]

*   *   *

While Miller said his final prayers in his death cell, Amos Lunt tutored Napa County Sheriff George S. MacKenzie in the fine art of hanging.

In less than a month, Sheriff MacKenzie would preside over the hanging of a shady villain whose crime took place in February 1891—before the law that made Hale the state's official executioner went into effect. The inexperienced executioner hoped to learn from the pre-eminent hangman in California.

With Miller's noose dangling from the crossbar directly over the trap, Lunt showed MacKenzie how to tie a proper noose, where to position the knot, and how to fit the black cap in a way that did not cause the noose to slip.

Using anecdotes from previous hangings, he emphasized the need for quick work on the scaffold. Time, Lunt explained, was the hangman's enemy. The William Young hanging provided an excellent exemplar of how every second counted.

One second more, and Young—whose knees buckled at the same time the trap was released—would have crumpled to the floorboards. If he had fallen onto his knees before the trap opened, the drop would have been shorter than calculated, and Young may have died a drawn-out and painful death by strangulation.

Miller, Lunt feared, might repeat William Young's near collapse at the end. While Miller feigned indifference and put on a devil-may-care façade, doctors monitoring him noticed an alarming jump in his respiration as the hour of his execution neared. With a quick wit and an uncanny ability to problem-solve, Lunt formulated a back-up plan. If, during the walk to the scaffold, Miller showed signs of an imminent implosion, Lunt would strap him to a board, which would prevent Miller's body from deflating on the trap like a pierced balloon.

The less time that elapsed while the condemned man stood on the trap, the less likely the hanging would devolve into the kind of melodrama that turned the stomachs of spectators. A hangman needed nimble hands to noose and cap his subject in a matter of seconds, and practice made perfect.

Sheriff MacKenzie would receive a form of on-the-job training. He would shadow Hale during the reading of the death warrant, join the procession to the gallows, and stand beside Amos Lunt as he made the final preparations before Miller's drop.

*   *   *

With Sheriff MacKenzie in tow, Warden Hale read the death warrant to Miller and, following the established routine, left him alone for a few solitary minutes before returning to take him on his final walk.

Miller wanted to address the spectators by giving a speech, but Father Lagan—fearful that the talkative man might let loose with a lengthy and caustic attack on those he felt had wronged him—discouraged him from causing what he considered an unnecessary delay in the routine. Instead, he offered to speak on Miller's behalf. "All right," Miller agreed, "just say that I am innocent."[3]

Once on the scaffold, Father Lagan stepped to the rail. Marshall Miller, he proclaimed, wanted to say three things: he died "not more guilty than others who had not to suffer the death penalty," a good Catholic, and ready to meet his Maker. Miller may have cringed upon hearing the priest's mistranslation of his dying declaration. He had not once wavered in maintaining his innocence and asked the priest to convey this idea, but Father Lagan apparently could not bring himself to follow this directive. The filtered version sounded more like an admission of guilt than a statement of innocence.[4]

Unlike William Young, Marshall Miller's nerve held. He did not sway or wobble as Lunt tugged on the straps binding his arms and legs, tightened the noose, and slid the cap over his visage. The last words he mumbled were directed at the hangman. "Pull the rope tight."

He dropped at precisely 10:12 a.m.[5]

Fifteen minutes later, a crew of inmates togged in striped garb cut down Miller's lifeless body and placed it in a plain, unadorned coffin. It was a lightning-fast execution, and according to the *San Francisco Call*, one for the books.

Said the *Call*'s representative at the hanging, "It was but a few seconds over a minute from the time Miller put his foot on the stairs leading up to the platform until he had been shot through the trap and the doctors had hold of his wrist counting the decreasing heart pulsations." Lunt's speed and efficiency made the Miller hanging "the quickest of the many executions in the State Prison."[6]

The next day, Bay Area newspapers ran stories of Miller's hanging, which included snippets of his final statement. In his latest and final rendition, he once again attempted to cast Stewart Green as the sole villain in the pawnbroker's murder.

According to Miller, Greene duped him into entering Pierre's shop on the pretense of visiting a bordello. To Miller's utter shock and horror, Greene attempted to pry the secret of the pawnbroker's cache by beating him senseless. When they failed to find the old man's stash, they left. Greene later returned and forced a rag down Julius Pierre's throat.

* * *

Hangman's Friday arrived at the Napa County Jail on January 15, 1897. A month after the Miller execution, Sheriff MacKenzie would put his training into effect by hanging William M. Roe, a sociopathic murderer who by his own admission committed 26 murders.

The crime Roe expiated was the murder of Lucinda Greenwood. The day before, Captain John Greenwood had sold a parcel of land for the princely sum of $5,000. When William Roe heard the news, he reasoned that Greenwood must have stashed the money somewhere in his ranch house. On the afternoon of February 9, 1891, Roe and his accomplice, Carl Schmidt, approached Greenwood as he worked in his yard. At gunpoint, they marched him into the house, where they hogtied him, forced him to swallow a dose of chloroform, and then gagged him.

When Greenwood's wife, Lucinda, returned from a neighbor's farm, they dragged her into the bedroom, tied her to a bedpost, and forced her to drink the same chloroform-spiked concoction. As the Greenwoods slumbered, Roe and Schmidt rifled through the house, searching for the cache. They never found the money, which Greenwood had deposited in the bank. Frustrated, they left.

A few hours later, Captain Greenwood recovered enough to stand and wobble into the bedroom, where he found his wife dead from an overdose of chloroform, her body still pinioned to the bedpost. According to some accounts, Greenwood found Lucinda lying on the bed, which may have been closer to an uncomfortable truth that the papers did not want to print.[7]

Greenwood remained at his dead wife's side until about 11 p.m., when Roe and Schmidt returned to continue their search for the fortune.

Noticing Greenwood in the bedroom, Roe and Schmidt mercilessly pummeled him. Roe put a bullet in Lucinda Greenwood's forehead, tied her husband to a stairway bannister and shot him in the jaw.

Miraculously, the bullet did not prove fatal. It tore through his mandible and knocked out several teeth, but Greenwood survived. He played possum until the two men left. The next morning at about 7 a.m., he managed to stand up. A neighbor noticed him near the front gate.

Schmidt, the less culpable of the duo, received a life sentence and, considered mentally unstable, ended up on San Quentin's "Crank's Alley." Roe, who reveled in telling tales of his criminal exploits that he said included no fewer than 26 murders, remained on the lam until September 1896. Nothing if not a braggart, his barstool boasts of murdering Mrs. Greenwood eventually reached the ears of Sheriff MacKenzie. Following a tip from a former sheriff-turned-saloon keeper, MacKenzie found Roe in San Fernando. His brief trial in November ended in a conviction and a death sentence.

Like a water tap frozen open, once Roe began talking, he found it difficult to stop. The *San Francisco Chronicle* sent a man to the county jail for an interview. "With that knowledge [of his execution] ever present he wasted the minutes in narratives of stage robbery upon the plains, murder in the dead of night, larceny in all its phases and the debaucher of women. He was the chief actor in all his recitals." Yet the *Chronicle* reporter remained incredulous and noted, "It is quite probable that Roe did not commit many of the murders to which he confessed."[8]

Sheriff MacKenzie, however, remained a true believer. In the desperado's waning days, he helped Roe pen an autobiography. He hired a stenographer to take down every lascivious tale and agreed to split the proceeds with his undersheriff and a deputy.

The hanging, which occurred in the yard of the Napa County Jail, attracted a great deal of attention. Around 400 people converged on the small plot to watch the execution of a villainous character whose notoriety had spread throughout the county and beyond. It would also be the last hanging any of them would likely see; by 1897, county hangings were essentially extinct, and those done behind the walls of San Quentin were closed to the general public.

Roe's hanging was a virtual repeat of Marshall Miller's. The scant information available about the event does not indicate if Amos Lunt traveled to Napa and watched, or even helped, MacKenzie with the preparations. If he did, he remained in the background. News accounts of the hanging named the participants on the scaffold, and Lunt's notoriety by early 1897 would have been something noted by reporters.

While MacKenzie duplicated the San Quentin procedure, he deviated in a few details, conducting the execution in a manner that would have made Lunt cringe.

While the San Quentin Death Watch routinely offered the condemned an alcohol bracer, Sheriff MacKenzie gave Roe access to an inexhaustible supply of whiskey throughout his last night. On the morning of the execution, he let Roe quaff more whiskey, and just before the death march, a doctor administered a hypodermic containing a full grain of morphine. Roe faced a greater risk of passing out on the trap than collapsing from nervousness.

Believing brevity the key to avoiding maudlin scenes and acutely aware that reporters from the "big three" (the *Call, Chronicle,* and *Examiner*) noted every detail, Hale discouraged scaffold speeches so Lunt could move through the final preparations with lightning speed.

MacKenzie, however, let Roe make a brief speech. "I haven't much to say," Roe said, speaking from the rail, "only my thanks for the way I have been treated. The Sheriff and all the officers have treated me well. I have got no creed nor kin nor anything like that. I think that is all."[9] The sheriff then allowed a brief delay so Roe could say a final prayer. Captain Greenwood, his jaw scarred from Roe's attempted coup de grace, watched the scene from the base of the scaffold.

As MacKenzie was drawing the black cap over the condemned man's face, Roe said he forgot about something and asked the sheriff to take a sealed envelope out of his pocket. It contained a letter addressed to the three men with an interest in his autobiography.

Roe dropped at 11:32 a.m. Seventeen minutes had elapsed from the time the procession first entered the jail yard at 11:15 a.m. The hanging itself went off without a hitch, the drop snapping Roe's neck. His body remained suspended for 15 minutes as his pulse dwindled.

A bit of a showman, the sheriff stood next to the hanging body and brandished a knife blade. "This knife was found on this gentleman," he said, "and it was used by one of the men for to cut the ropes. I propose to use it for to cut down the body." According to the *Chronicle* reporter, MacKenzie added a theatrical gesture by grabbing the dangling body and "swaying the corpse to emphasize his meaning."

The event had devolved into theater of the absurd. The *Chronicle* man described the sheriff's continuing theatrics. "Then he called for the official photographer, who posed his dead and alive subjects. McKenzie held the blade against the rope as if he were in the act of cutting."

Onlookers watched the spectacle with a mixture of shock and horror. Recognizing bewilderment in their expressions, MacKenzie offered an explanation. "He subsequently explained what many of the spectators called a 'somewhat theatrical proceeding' by stating that he wanted to secure illustrations to enhance the value of Roe's autobiography, soon to be published," wrote the *Chronicle* reporter.[10]

The sealed envelope, MacKenzie later said, contained a sensational account of nine additional murders that Roe allegedly committed in several other states. The sheriff believed every word. It would make good copy and surely sell a few more books.

The *Chronicle* reporter's account made it into print, occupying almost an entire page of the January 16, 1897, edition. MacKenzie's bizarre antics gave readers another reason to despise hangmen, and that meant Amos Lunt.

The circus at Napa also underscored the professionalism of Lunt's executions under the oversight of Warden Hale. Lunt would never have conducted a hanging that marred not just the dignity of the condemned but also the solemnity of the occasion.

18

Business Not as Usual

Chun Sing (Wednesday, February 17, 1897)

Business would not be quite as usual at San Quentin as 1896 passed into 1897. With his health failing, Warden Hale spent much of January at home in bed. On the advice of his physician, he and his wife traveled south and spent several weeks recuperating in the sun.

With Hale absent during the first execution of the year—the hanging of Chun Sing—Amos Lunt's role on the scaffold expanded to include signaling the drop. Lunt would continue to do the crucial job of positioning the noose, but to minimize the time that Sing stood on the trap, another guard would lower the black cap.

* * *

Chun Sing had the blood of three people on his hands, and it did not seem to bother him in the least.

Sing's crime occurred on October 2, 1895, when a feud between rival gangs in a Mono County mining camp evolved into a triple murder. Wielding a hatchet, Sing attacked an enemy named Ah Fook. After felling Fook, Sing darted after Fook's wife, who ran out of the cabin screaming, and buried the blade of the axe in her head. Fook survived the vicious barrage, but his wife died instantly.

With blood dripping from his axe blade, Sing raced to the house of Charley Tai, where an eerily similar scene occurred. A woman with Tai at the time escaped while Sing hacked his foe to pieces and beheaded the corpse. He then tracked down the woman and struck her several times with the hatchet.

Sentenced to death, the 40-year-old slayer arrived at San Quentin on December 19, 1896—about a week after Marshall Miller's execution.[1] He came with what a *Chronicle* reporter described as a "disdainful

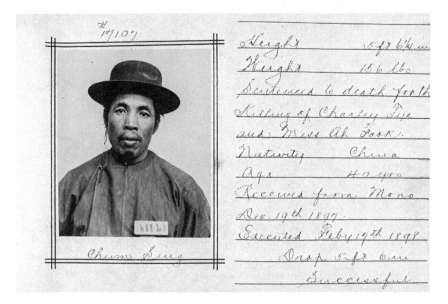

Height   5 ft 6¼ in
Weight   156 lbs.
Sentenced to death for the
killing of Charley Tye
and Miss Ah Fook.
Nativity   China
Age   40 yrs.
Received from Mono
Dec. 19th 1899.
Executed Feby 17th 1898
Drop 5 ft 6 in
Successful

Chun Sing, the silent axe-murderer (Anne T. Kent California Room, Marin County Free Library).

moroseness," a haughtiness evident in his prison mug shot. With head atilt, he gazed at the photographer with a slight grin.

Sing's head-and-shoulders mug shot also depicts the type of musculature—broad shoulders tapering to a heavily muscled neck—that could provide troublesome when calculating the drop. At 5'6¼" and 156 pounds, Chun Sing was an anatomical clone of P.J. Collins and Marshall Miller, so Lunt decided to give him the same 5'6" drop that proved effective in the earlier hangings.

Sing's execution date was set for Wednesday, February 17—the only hanging in Lunt's career that did not take place on a "Hangman's Friday."

* * *

In the three months Sing spent at San Quentin awaiting his date with the hangman, he never said a word to anyone. He did not speak with the Death Watch, and he refused to talk to Reverend Drahms or Father Lagan, both of whom attempted to provide spiritual counsel and comfort in his final days. When friends in San Francisco sent a messenger to find out where in China they should send Sing's bones after the hanging, he refused to speak to the messenger. He would not talk a reporter who attempted to pry a few words from his lips. Without a quote or two, the reporter had to rely on his powers of observation, describing Sing as "Morose and sullen, with a cynical self-sufficiency"[2]

For days on end, Chun Sing lay on the cot in his cell, curled into a fetal position, counting the days to his execution on his fingertips.

Time meant something different to each man on death row, but each one found his own, unique way to mark its passage. Sing counted time by tapping his fingertips together, a practice that amused the Death Watch. Somewhere along the way, Sing apparently lost track of time. On Monday, February 15, he broke his silence to ask a guard what day it was. The guard said it was Sunday, so Sing tapped out the three days to his execution date on his fingertips. The error—a mistake by the Death Watch, a cruel practical joke, or something lost in translation—led to the single moment when Sing showed any real sign of emotion while on death row.

At 9 a.m. on the morning of Wednesday, February 17, Captain Edgar came to Sing's cell to read the death warrant. Visibly surprised that Edgar had apparently come a day early, Sing suddenly realized the mistake. Apparently determined not to betray his flinty demeanor in the final hour, he showed no perceptible signs of nervousness.

"However," noted a *Chronicle* reporter who eavesdropped on the scene, "he soon began his devotions kneeling down in his cell and bowing his forehead to the floor repeating at the same time some formulary in his own tongue."[3]

At 10:30 a.m. sharp, Captain Edgar led Sing, flanked by Captain Jamieson and Amos Lunt, to the gallows. He did not falter as he climbed the 13 steps, but when he reached the top, he managed to place only one foot on the trap. As a small group of about 30 witnesses watched, Lunt gently moved Sing's other foot on the trap and then tightened the leather straps binding his legs.

"Good-by guards, alle samee me," Chun Sing uttered as Lunt fastened the noose around his neck.[4] He fell at 10:31 a.m., about a minute after he first entered the room.[5] Sing's neck broke at the bottom of the drop. He remained on the line while his pulse slowly ebbed, his final heartbeats ending around 15 minutes later.

The *Chronicle* reporter lauded Amos Lunt's 12th execution as flawless. "There was not a quiver of a muscle, nor, so well had the arrangements been made, was there any whirling motion given to the body as the rope sprang taut."[6]

* * *

One of the most infamous inmates to sit in San Quentin's death cells and Lunt's most notable subject, William Henry Theodore Durrant, arrived at the prison two months later, on April 10, 1897. As many as 250 people queued to see the criminal celebrity walk through the prison gates only to leave nine months later, feet-first, in a black pine box.

If San Francisco had a trial of the 19th century, it belonged to Durrant, a 24-year-old medical student convicted of strangling Blanche Lamont and leaving her nude body in the belfry of the Baptist Emmanuel Church on Bartlett Street. Gallons of ink went into reporting every minute facet of the trial, which captivated front pages when it began in 1895.

The attractive, 21-year-old Lamont went missing on April 3, 1895, after meeting Durrant—a friend and co-worker at Emmanuel Baptist Church—that afternoon. Ten days later, on April 12, another young churchgoer named Minnie Williams vanished after a heated discussion with a man later identified by an eyewitness as Durrant.

The next day—Saturday, April 13—ladies decorating the church for Easter Sunday stumbled upon the mutilated body of Williams tucked into a cabinet. A subsequent sweep of the church uncovered the body of Blanche Lamont stashed in the bell tower.

Arrested the next day, Durrant said he knew nothing about the murders and provided an alibi. Friends and relatives could not believe that the soft-spoken man of spotless character could have had a hand in the sordid crime, but the jury convicted him on circumstantial evidence. Although doubts about his guilt lingered, a summary of his case in the San Quentin death files contains the note, "The evidence against him was purely circumstantial but was undeniable."

With his appeals exhausted, Durrant began sweating out the final months to the date set for his execution in November 1897.[7] At San Quentin, Durrant's best friend was Lunt's next subject, Frank Cooney Kloss, set to hang on April 23, 1897.

19

Unlucky No. 13

(Friday, April 23, 1897)

Frank Cooney Kloss would be the 13th man hanged at San Quentin in a sequence that began with the inaugural drop of Jose Gabriel four years earlier in 1893. Thirteen would be an unlucky number for Amos Lunt, who would land at the center of a scandal caused by his own indiscretion. Trapped by a journalist probing for a yellow story, Lunt's loose lips almost cost him his job at the prison.

*   *   *

Kloss, a 27-year-old actor, would die for the senseless and seemingly motiveless murder of a San Francisco bartender on April 18, 1895.[1] Inebriated, Kloss went into a saloon at the corner of Hayes and Laguna Streets, where he spotted the barkeep, William F. Deady, fast asleep in a chair, his head tilted back, and his neck stretched. Kloss asked another bar patron to rouse Deady, but the man refused. He jabbed the slumbering man in the shoulder, and when Deady did not wake, he grabbed him by the shoulder and shook him. With more alcohol than water in his bloodstream, Deady slept the sleep of the dead and did not respond to Kloss' second, more forceful attempt.

The two men had had words the day before, the shots of whiskey blurring all inhibition and logic but not memory. Remembering not the content so much as the tone of Deady's words, Kloss recognized in Deady's exposed neck an opportunity to use his knife to right a wrong. "I will wake him up," he yelled. He unsheathed the dagger and jabbed the blade into the sleeping man's throat. Twice. When he heard a police whistle blow, he stabbed Deady a third time for good measure. Asked what he had done, Kloss bragged, "I wakened him; I fixed him; I killed the son of a bitch."[2]

At the trial, Kloss tried an insanity plea and claimed to suffer from epilepsy, but his "I came-I saw-I conquered" boast came back to haunt him. Sentenced to hang, he arrived at San Quentin in January and was

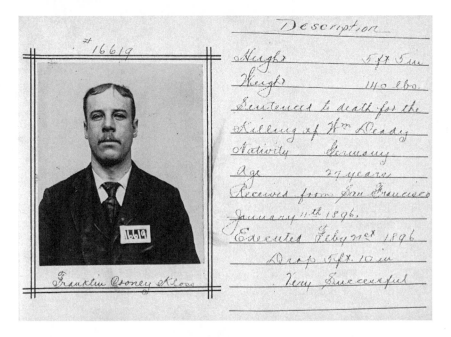

Frank Kloss was the thirteenth man hanged at San Quentin (Anne T. Kent California Room, Marin County Free Library).

lodged in the condemned cells ten days before his execution date, scheduled for Friday, April 23, 1897.

At 5'5" and 140 pounds, Frank Kloss was a slightly built man, which meant he would need to fall farther to achieve the neck-breaking velocity needed for a clean hanging. His physical characteristics translated to a drop of 5'10".

* * *

An *Examiner* correspondent sat with Frank Kloss on the eve of his execution. He described Kloss as "ignorant, brutal and even in small things vicious to the last degree. When his aged, crippled mother went to San Quentin a week ago to bid him good-by his curses and foul words shouted at her shocked the death watch as few incidents have power to do."[3]

The brutal and vicious character, however, said he had a bone to pick with Theodore Durrant, which would provide the reporter with a page-one scoop.

Kloss' animosity for Durrant began, he explained, when the two occupied adjoining cells in the county jail. They spoke often, chatting during exercise periods—called "walking days"—in the yard.[4] Kloss came to trust Durrant and shared with his fellow slayer plans he and a group of inmates had made for a mass breakout. It was a simple yet ingenious plan involving nothing more than red pepper and muscle.

The first-floor prisoners planned to throw red pepper into the eyes of Captain George Webb, overpower him, and steal his keys. Sheriff's deputies sniffed out the pepper plot and thwarted the escapees. Kloss said he believed that Durrant had ratted on him.

When the two ended up in San Quentin together, they renewed their friendship. Durrant knew nothing about Kloss' grudge. It was during one of their walks in the yard together, according to Kloss, when Durrant unburdened his conscience and confessed to murdering Blanche Lamont.

According to Kloss, Durrant's bombshell occurred through a slip of the tongue. In describing his crime to his walking partner during one of their many strolls together in the yard, Kloss attempted to justify his stabbing of Deady. "I killed my man when I was drunk, and I do not think I should be hanged," Kloss said. "But you, Durrant, you committed a frightful murder. There is no comparison between the two cases."

"Oh, well," Durrant responded, "we are both guilty men, and all we can do is to try to save ourselves. I am just as guilty as you are, I admit, but that has nothing to do with our efforts to save our lives."[5] Durrant did not name names or go into detail, but for Frank Kloss and his interviewer, the vague statement amounted to nothing less than a confession to murdering Blanche Lamont.

A close examination of Kloss' story raised some red flags. If he harbored such animosity against Durrant stemming from an incident in the county jail, then why did he resume their friendship—to all appearances a cordial, even warm acquaintance? Would Durrant, who never once waivered in proclaiming his innocence, make such a damning statement and to someone such as Frank Cooney Kloss?

Kloss must have realized that people would doubt the truth of his story, so he invoked a little death house logic. "I am about to die tomorrow, and this statement is true," he said. "I have nothing to gain by lying about it."

In weighing Kloss' statements, the *Examiner* reporter concluded, "It seems almost incredible that a man about to die would deliberately and gratuitously lie simply to injure another being who is already doomed to suffer the same fate as himself."[6] Durrant's confession-by-proxy, he inferred, must have been true.

In an attempt to verify Kloss' story, *Examiner* correspondents interviewed county employees who recounted details of the pepper plot. Chief Jailor Sattler, who would watch Kloss hang the next day, remembered the plot but knew nothing about Durrant turning Judas. He said they received a tip from a trustee named Brant.

Nonetheless, Sattler recalled Kloss' change in attitude toward his "walking day" partner. "As the story of it is recalled to my mind," said the jailor, "I remember that after the plot failed Kloss became very bitter toward Durrant. I have no doubt he believed that Durrant exposed the scheme, and I well remember how other prisoners acted afterward. They were evidently harboring some feelings against Durrant."[7]

Following Kloss' lead, the other county jail prisoners called Durrant "the traitor" and even hatched a plot to poison him. When Sattler heard whispers about the poisoning plot, he served Durrant food from the guards' table.

The pepper plot angle of Kloss' yarn checked out. That he believed Durrant betrayed him also appeared solidified by Sattler's statement. Durrant's confession, however, remained unverified and unverifiable. The entire story hinged on the word of a felon with a grudge, albeit one about to die.

Editors of the *Examiner* never let an issue like lack of credibility get in the way of a good story, and they ran Kloss' bombshell on the front page of the next day's edition. At about the time Frank Kloss mounted the scaffold, San Franciscans read all about the secret confession of the city's most infamous slayer.

The *Examiner* reporter scooped his competitors. His article occupied a full column on the front page, whereas the *Call* and the *Chronicle* each devoted a lone paragraph to Durrant's secret confession, left to the closing paragraph in their respective articles about the Kloss hanging.

* * *

The *Call* sent their own man, 20-year-old reporter Frederick F. Runyon, to interview Kloss. By 1897, Runyon already had eight years of newspapering under his belt. At the age of 12, he founded the *Mill Valley Times* with nothing but heart and a hand press.[8] Like his *Examiner* colleague, he would walk away from the prison with a scoop. His yellow story would not be about the condemned man but about the condemned man's executioner.

At about 11 p.m. on the evening of Thursday, April 23, Runyon stood at the gates chatting with "Big Kelley," the gatekeeper on duty, while he waited for Sergeant Ed Ellis to take him up to the death cells. Writing about the incident three decades later in a series entitled "In the Shadow of the Gallows," Runyon recalled the moment when he first met the hangman, Amos Lunt.

Lunt noticed Runyon standing at the front gate and asked, "Why up so late?"

"Going to have a talk with Frank Klose [*sic*]," Runyon replied. "This will be my first execution."

"Are you kind of nervous?"

"No, I'm not nervous, but it is a new sensation. I don't know how I will feel about it. How do you feel about it?" the reporter asked.

"Oh, I'm used to it," Lunt said. Runyon asked Lunt how he felt about the upcoming hanging of Durrant, his most infamous subject.

Lunt hesitated. According to Runyon, he acted like a man with something on his mind. "I saw Lunt rub his hands together nervously," the young reporter later wrote. "He walked up and down the narrow corridor in which we were standing, then stopped in front of me."

Then came a statement that Runyon never anticipated. "You know, I'd rather run him through with red hot irons."

Runyon smelled a page-one item. "Instantly," he recalled, "I sensed a big story—the man who was to hang Durrant would rather run him through with red hot irons."

The young reporter could not believe his ears or his luck. He called "Big Kelley" over to where he and Lunt stood. "What do you think Lunt says?" he asked Kelley.

"What?" the puzzled guard asked.

"You tell him, Lunt," Runyon said.

"I was just telling the kid that I would rather run red hot irons through Durrant than hang him," Lunt said.

At that moment, Ed Ellis appeared and led Runyon to the death cells, but anything he would hear from Kloss would pale in comparison to what he had just heard from the hangman.[9]

For Lunt, a consummate professional on the scaffold, his "red hot irons" statement was completely out of character. Runyon's reminiscences do not contain a description of Lunt's tone of voice or facial expression at this critical moment. The remark may have been an example of the deadpan gallows humor that reporters would later characterize, and misunderstand, as ill-timed jocularity, but Runyon's description of Lunt grinding his hands together implies a more serious undertone to the remark.

Lunt, it appears from Runyon's exposé, took a disliking to Theodore Durrant for some reason that has escaped the historical record. The murder of Blanche Lamont may have hit a little too close to home for the hangman, who saw in her a mirror image of his daughter Lottie. A few weeks after Kloss' hanging, Lottie would turn 14, and Amos Lunt would experience the angst of every teenage daughter's father: the reality that at some point she would bring a boy home to meet the parents.[10] Perhaps his worst nightmare materialized in the form of Durrant, who projected the image of an affable, church-going lad while inside hid, at least according to the jury, a fiendish slayer.

*   *   *

"I will try to die like a man in the morning," Frank Kloss said on the eve of his execution. "You see that I am not nervous or hysterical as has been said, and I no more fear hanging tomorrow than you do, and you are not doomed to die."[11]

Frank Kloss wanted to go to his death a brave man. He vowed to keep his composure and feigned indifference, although his last night hinted that behind the façade stood a frightened man. He went to bed at 11 p.m. but awoke around 3 a.m. and asked a guard to give him the time. "There isn't much time left now," he said. "I'm getting near to the end."[12]

He rolled around for another three hours, finally waking at 6 a.m. and spending much of the morning with Father Lagan, the San Raphael padre who provided some comfort to the condemned man. Perhaps to calm his own nerves as much as put on a show for J.D. Jones and John Miller, his Death Watch, he danced a jig. "I am all right, boys. Never felt better in my life. How is that for step?" he asked, referring to his dance. Then he jumped in the air and clicked his heels together.

Somewhat annoyed by the show, Jones said, "You won't be dancing that way at half-past ten." At 10 a.m., Hale would appear with death warrant in hand.

"Oh, yes, I will," Kloss retorted. "I will dance at half past ten, and I will dance tomorrow, too. I am not afraid of death."[13]

Then he repeated his allegation about Theodore Durrant. "I am about to die, and I would not die with a lie on my lips," he said. "I have only a few hours more to live, and in the face of all that, and as God is my judge, I again say that Durrant confessed to me that he was a guilty man."[14]

Warden Hale, who had fully recovered from his illness and had returned from Southern California, went to Kloss' cell to read the death warrant at approximately 10:20 a.m. Kloss waived his right to hear the warrant, and guards began to work the straps while Father Lagan whispered last-minute spiritual guidance. Kloss sucked on a cigar as he waited for the warden to begin the procession.

Some condemned men made deathbed confessions; Frank Kloss made one last attempt to disparage his enemy. Kloss said nothing about the murder of William Deady, but as the guards fitted the straps, he repeated Theodore Durrant's alleged confession. "Boys," he said, "Durrant told me he was a guilty man. I say this in the presence of death and it is as true as that I shall be hanged."[15]

Kloss apparently had no qualms about going to his death with a "lie on his lips." Reporters from rival papers mocked their *Examiner* colleague's gullibility by condemning the story as Kloss' attempt to get back at Durrant for some slight when they resided in the County Jail. Durrant, according to the cons who knew him, would never have confided in Frank Kloss.[16]

A small contingent of physicians, prison officials, and newspaper reporters gathered around the scaffold as the iron door separating the scaffold room from the death cells swung open and the death march entered the gallows room at 10:30 a.m.

True to his word, Frank Kloss did not crack. With a steady gait, albeit one hampered by the belt around his arms, he ascended the 13 steps. At the top, Amos Lunt took him by the arm and led him to the trap. As he had done for Fremont Smith, Father Lagan stepped forward and addressed the spectators on behalf of the condemned man.

In a few short sentences, the priest explained that Kloss wanted to clear the air about an allegation that he mistreated his mother when she visited him at the prison. The story had circulated in the San Francisco newspapers, and Kloss, through the priest, denied every word of it.[17] Father Lagan also challenged the reporters present to right the wrong done by their fellow scribes.

"In behalf of a dying man, and as his last request," Father Lagan began, "I wish to say a few words. It has been charged in the press that the condemned abused his mother and treated her unkindly when she came to see him. He denies this as an untruth, and I trust that the press of San Francisco will be magnanimous enough to give publication to his last words."[18]

Kloss remained stolid until he noticed a familiar face below. An eyewitness later described Kloss' reaction when he recognized Chief Jailer Sattler of the county jail. He smiled and nodded "as though he was passing a friend on the street."[19]

Lunt stepped forward and placed the noose around Kloss' neck. As Lunt positioned the knot, Kloss looked into his eyes and said, "Do a good job."[20] Lunt nodded and tightened the noose.

As he had done with the Chun Sing hanging, Lunt delegated the capping duties. This time, Captain Jamieson lowered the black hood while Lunt stepped back. He, and not Warden Hale, gave the signal sending Kloss shooting through the trap.

Once again, Amos Lunt had engineered an effective and painless hanging. "There was not a quiver of pain or the slightest struggle," wrote the *Oakland Tribune* representative. "The rope swayed for a moment and then the body hung like the pendulum of a clock stopped.... The physicians, all of whom have attended the previous executions at the prison, are unanimous that this was the most successful hanging of the series."[21]

Amos Lunt fitting the noose on Frank Kloss as drawn by *Examiner* artist Max Wilford Newberry.

The *Examiner* went a step further by crediting Lunt for the successful hanging. "Amos Lunt, the veteran executioner, was complimented on his work, and then the crowd disbursed"[22]

*   *   *

Frank Kloss' hanging made page one of the *Examiner*'s Saturday, April 24, edition, but not because of the jig he danced just before the death march. Upstaged by Durrant, Kloss became front-page news only as a conduit for Durrant's alleged admission.

Death Watch guards Jones and Miller, selected by Warden Hale to keep an eye on Kloss during his ten-day residency in the death cells, heard about Durrant's damning admission five days earlier. They promised to keep quiet until after his hanging. With Kloss dead and coffined, they repeated his story to the press. "I am satisfied that in the shadow of death he did not lie," Jones said. "I believe Durrant confessed to him that he killed Blanche Lamont. Kloss told the story to Miller and myself three times and I think it is true."[23]

Kloss managed to convince Jones, and although the substance of his story remained the same, the version he told to Jones and Miller differed in the details from the version he told to the *Examiner* correspondent. In the earlier version, Kloss heard Durrant sobbing in his cell. When Kloss asked Durrant why he was whimpering, Durrant explained that he had a guilty conscience. "Well," Kloss responded, "you are no worse off than I am. We are in the same boat."

"We are both guilty men," Durrant said, "but that is no reason why we should not try to save our lives."[24]

Yet Durrant had maintained his innocence all along, which left some wondering if Kloss had gone to his death with a "lie on his lips" and thus went out by playing a practical joke on the press. Perhaps he had a score to settle with a reporter or two as well.

*   *   *

F.F. Runyon recalled the reaction of the news editor at the *San Francisco Call* when he told him he had obtained an interesting story from San Quentin. "And then I told how the man who was to hang Durrant, the arch criminal of the century, had said the presence of a reliable witness that he would rather run red hot irons through the murderer than to hang him."

To Runyon's shock, the news editor responded, "Yesterday that would have been a good story but today we can't use it."

"What's the reason?" the shocked reporter asked.

"We are not going to run any more yellow stories. We are going to change the policy of the *Call* and cut out all the sensational stuff. I'm sorry, but we don't want the story."[25]

Perhaps feeling the sting of the so-called "Durrant confession," or sated by yellow journalism in general, the *Call* editor shied away from Runyon's "red hot irons" story.

Not one to take "no" for an answer, Runyon found a way to hoodwink his boss.

20

"With a red-hot iron"

(Friday, May 14, 1897)

A Hangman's Friday of a different sort arrived on May 14, 1897.

Determined that the *Call* should publish the "red hot irons" story, F.F. Runyon discovered a way around the news editor's rejection. He waited for the news editor's day off and then presented the story to the man left in charge. "The man on the desk pounced upon the copy like a vulture. He passed it on to the head writer. 'Play that up on page 1,' he said."[1]

The story broke in mid–May and appeared on page two of the *Call*. Half of the two-column article, under the subheading "Amos Lunt, the Guard, Would Torture Him with a Redhot [sic] Iron," was devoted to Lunt's provocative thoughts about Theodore Durrant.

"I believe that Theodore Durrant murdered both of those innocent girls in cold blood," Lunt was quoted as saying.

> His face to me is that of the fiendish and horrible criminal that I believe he is, and when I place the rope around his neck, as I expect to do on the 11th of next June, I will do it with the feeling that I am assisting in the hanging of a man who is meeting a death that he richly deserves.
>
> Hanging is too good for him. I could take him out on the road, run a red-hot iron into his flesh and hold it here until he fainted. I would repeat it as soon as he regained consciousness, and keep it up until he died a death of horrible agony. That is the way he should be treated. Think of the fiendish manner in which he hanged those girls! Hanging is too good.[2]

Perhaps concerned about alienating Warden Hale and jeopardizing future access to death row inmates, neither the *Chronicle* nor the *Examiner* ran parallel stories, but the *Oakland Tribune* printed a scathing criticism of the hangman.

Labeling Lunt's comments as "devilish," the *Tribune* characterized Lunt as an anachronism by comparing him to an Inquisitor. "Mr. Lunt has been born a little too late. He should have been a torturer in the days of the

Inquisition—that would have suited a man of his peculiar sensibilities to a nicety."[3]

Warden Hale tried to head off the criticism by dispelling any thoughts about his celebrated hangman heating up andirons until they glowed red. "He [Durrant] will be treated like any other prisoner under sentence of death. There will be no difference."[4] Barring a legal intervention, Hale emphasized, Theodore Durrant would hang by the neck until dead according to his sentence.

Hale tried to deflect the ire unleashed by the hangman's comments, but Lunt represented the prison, its warden, and in a broader sense, the concept of capital punishment in California. The public might dismiss Sheriff MacKenzie's behavior as a throwback to another time, but not that of the state's executioner.

Runyon described the fallout. "It started an investigation on the part of the board of prison directors to learn if Amos Lunt really had made such an assertion."

Lunt, predictably, tried to backpedal, but the reporter had cornered him with Kelley. Runyon gloated, "Lunt said he couldn't remember making any such 'crack' as that. But Big Kelley could remember and Lunt finally admitted that he might have had such an idea in his mind. And the prison board told him to be more discreet in the future, about what punishment he would like to inflict on condemned men. They told him they wanted him to hang them by the neck, not to run them through with red hot irons."[5]

Amos Lunt had reached a critical juncture. Had Hale shuffled the deck and replaced him with one of the Death Watch, such as Arbogast or Miller, he may have saved his hangman's life. Lunt, however, was simply too skilled an executioner. Except for the botched hanging of Fremont Smith, Lunt's skill in calculating drops was flawless.

William Hale needed Amos Lunt.

*   *   *

Despite Hale's attempts to run interference for his hangman, the "red-hot irons" comment did irreparable damage to Amos Lunt's reputation and became part of his biography. In a particularly scathing rebuke, one reporter suggested that Lunt had become desensitized by his duties.

"There is one official at San Quentin who ought to remain there just long enough to have his discharge papers made out," wrote an unnamed reporter for the small, Alameda-based *Daily Encinal*. "He is Amos Lunt, the hangman, who, judged by his own utterance, has become so utterly brutalized by his terrible and oft-repeated duties, that he has lost all sense of humanity not to say decency, both of which he has outraged by his published statements. If Lunt does not himself come to some bad end, it will be from sheer luck and not because of any redeeming elements in his own composition."[6]

This was more than a condemnation; it was a prophecy.

"The Criminal of the Century"

(Thursday, November 11, 1897)

Described as "the criminal of the century" by the *San Francisco Examiner*, Theodore Durrant began to prepare his mind for his execution as he entered San Quentin's death house on Thursday, November 11. He wanted to know what to expect on his "Hangman's Friday," and Captain Jamieson described each step in the sequence from Hale's reading the death warrant to the drop. Durrant listened intently and then made a list of last requests. "I have a request to make. It is my wish that the rope that will be used to hang me shall be destroyed after the execution, so that it cannot be cut up as mementoes. I do not care to have pieces of it hawked about the country by people who will say, 'This is a piece of the rope used in the execution of Theodore Durrant.' This I ask as a personal favor."[1]

He also did not want a postmortem conducted on his body, which Hale informed him would not be necessary if the drop broke his neck.

Durrant made these requests on Thursday,

This sketch of Amos Lunt appeared multiple times in both the *Chronicle* and the *Examiner*.

November 11—the night before the date scheduled for his execution. Subsequent court action delayed his execution. For a time, it appeared that the California Supreme Court might render a decision that would wipe away several death sentences and depopulate "Murderer's Row." Durrant's future depended on the fiery rhetoric of his lawyers.

Meanwhile, a rope with Durrant's name stretched from a rafter, ready for action, and Lunt measured and weighed his subject. At 140 pounds, Durrant weighed the same as Kloss and Harvey Allender (who was scheduled to hang in December) but stood slightly taller at 5'6⅛". He would have the shortest drop of the three at 5'8".[2]

More than ever, Lunt needed to avoid any mistakes in the planning of Durrant's execution. A botched hanging would amplify his comments about torturing Durrant and give critics more reason to condemn the practice as barbaric.

For the second time, the *Chronicle* published a portrait sketch of the San Quentin hangman along with the caption, "Amos Lunt, Who Will Be Durrant's Hangman."[3] The physical toll that the stress of 14 hangings had taken on Lunt was evident in his eyes, sunken behind a furrowed brow. Bags under his eyes hinted at sleepless nights, his rest disturbed by visits from the 13 men he had met on the scaffold.

22

The Rix Interview

(Saturday, November 20, 1897)

With Theodore Durrant's execution date looming, *Examiner* journalist Alice Rix interviewed the man who would tie his noose. Like her counterparts—Miriam Michelson at the *Chronicle*, "Annie Laurie" at the *Examiner*, and Belle Dormer at the *Call*—Rix broke the 19th-century mold for female journalists, who were typically confined to society pieces. Unlike the other female reporters, however, Rix was less interested in the condemned than in their executioner. In late November, Rix ventured behind the faux battlements of the prison, where she met Amos Lunt. The Rix interview presents a rare insight into the mind of the "San Quentin hangman."[1]

Impressed by her surroundings, Rix romanticized the moment she first eyed Amos Lunt as he approached from his spot on the wall near the Round Tower. "The Hangman's figure gloomed sinister against the sky," she wrote. "The length of a rough greatcoat swaddled him from neck to heels, and the breath of a slouch hat hid him from brow to chin."

As he stepped into Captain Edgar's office, the silhouette materialized into a five-foot-11-inch-tall figure whom Rix described as "a ruddy-faced man ... with keen, straight features, an easy, brilliant smile and clear, fearless, soldierly, blue eyes."

"I'm the hangman," Lunt said. He removed his hat and extended his hand. Rix gently shook his hand, which she said contained "nervous fingers and broad, honest thumb."

"Mine isn't much of a story," Lunt shrugged, "and it isn't the story they tell about me, either. Did you ever hear the story about me?" As the hangman of San Quentin, Lunt was used to wild and sometimes pernicious stories about him. People tended to confuse the man with the title of hangman.

"Yes," Rix responded, "but it doesn't matter."

"It matters to me—if it's the one I mean," Lunt retorted. "It's about hanging 'em all at twenty-five cents a head and running 'em through first with red-hot irons. Is that the story you heard? Is it? Well, that's the story that hurt me the worst way—hurt my feelings, I mean. Now I never said such a thing. What I did say was—well! It was something different." Lunt evidently wanted to clear the air about Runyon's story. He made it the first item of discussion during their interview.

"I'd no business to say anything in my position," Lunt said. "But what I've said I'll stick by. It was the day they brought Durrant over here and two or three of us were talking about those church murders, and I said that hanging was too good for the man that committed 'em, and that I could stand seeing him run through with a red-hot poker, and not pity him much."

"And could you?" Rix challenged.

"Well, may be when it came to looking on, I couldn't. I'm not much on looking on at unpleasant things."

"And when it comes to doing them?"

"Doing what?"

"Unpleasant things. I mean, when it comes to hanging men?"

"Oh! When you've got something to do, and when it's your work to do it, you've got no business, I take it, to be asking yourself whether it's unpleasant or pleasant. It's your business to get in and do it, and do it well, and do it quick." This line of questions made the hangman uncomfortable. According to Rix, he tightly gripped the brim of his slouch hat and twisted it.

"You must have some feeling, some personal feeling about it, though?" Rix asked.

"Of course I have a feeling. It's a hard feeling to describe. It's a kinder nervous feeling, a kinder dread—"

"A horror," Rix attempted to help Lunt find the right word.

"No, not that—it's more of a dread, a kinder nervous dread and a kinder hope with it—"

"A hope? Oh! A hope that something will happen at the last minute."

"No, no! A hope that it won't—that nothing will happen—that it'll go through all right."

Lunt's response caught Rix by surprise. Like her colleagues and their readers, she did not understand the intense pressure to make the hanging go smoothly and the intense embarrassment if it did not.

"You see," Lunt explained, "there's the dread that there will be a hitch and a hope that there won't. Do you see?"

Rix interpreted Lunt's answer for her readers. "Oh, it was easy enough to see," she wrote. "It was easy even to understand—the satisfaction in the terrible work well done. I saw across one of those chasms which divide the word of principles and convictions how a man who does the law's killing can come to his pride and pleasure in hanging men with neatness and dispatch."

"Is there ever a hitch?" Rix asked.

"There's never been one with me." Either Lunt did not want to admit error in the Fremont Smith execution, which nearly severed his subject's head, or he did not consider it a failure since the drop snapped the man's neck.

"How did you happen to go into this—er—profession?"

"I came here as Guard. I was Chief of Police in Santa Cruz before that. Yes, I came as a guard and the Warden he just picked on me." Lunt's word choice hinted that he felt "picked on" by Hale. "He says to me: 'Here, my man, here's something I want done. Now do you think you can do it?' And I says, 'Well, Warden, whatever you want done, I take it my duty to do.' And that's all there was to it. I've been hanging ever since." Lunt gave a very similar rendition during an earlier interview in 1895.[2] In all likelihood, Hale did not just "pick on" Lunt but saw something in his personality that convinced him he could hold up under the strain.

The hangman described his first subject. "Well, the first was a Chinaman, and I suppose nobody'd mind hanging a Chinaman. But the next one made me nervous—the kinder nervous dread I told you about. He was a young feller named Young, and I see when he comes from the condemned cell that he's pretty weak. The watch keeps a close hold on him, and as they pass me one of them says to me: 'My God! You've got to be quick.' That kinder nerved me to work and I had the rope on him before you could think, and I could feel his neck was like a piece of string, and I says to myself, 'Now I'll have to drop him before he drops himself' and it seems to be I never had such strength before in this arm—"

Amos Lunt had a bit of a theatrical bent. He pulled up his sleeve and balled his fist to show the "strength ... in this arm."

"It takes strength," Lunt continued, a grin spreading across his face, "and you've got to be quick. I must have been quick. It must have been quick that time, for a man down below, a reporter he is, a feller that knows me, he says to one of the guards: 'Where was Lunt today?' 'Lunt,' says the other feller, 'I never saw him!' It was just fifty-three seconds from the time he left the cell till he dropped. Of course it isn't much of a distance from the cell—but of course, you've seen a scaffold."

That Lunt knew the exact time from entrance to drop—53 seconds—illustrated the meticulous way in which he went about his duties.

Lunt asked Rix if she had ever seen a scaffold. When she said she hadn't, he contemplated taking her to the fourth floor to see the San Quentin gallows (Hale was absent from the prison) but decided instead to recreate the long walk using the furniture in Captain Edgar's office.

"These two chairs would be the cell," Lunt began his demonstration. "Well, the door opens and out comes the Priest. He walks first this way, chanting." Lunt crossed his arms over his chest and slowly walked in his best impression of Father Lagan.

"Then comes the man between the guards, the holding him one by each arm. Say these are the steps here…." He used another chair to represent the 13 steps. "The minute they're on the first step I'm after 'em and I keep close behind to the left of my man until he comes over the trap. Then I reach up and catch the noose and lip it over his neck so the knot comes here—"

The hangman made a motion toward the light fixture dangling over Captain Edgar's desk, which had now become a noose dangling from the crossbeam. He tugged at the imaginary rope and looped it over an imaginary subject's neck. To Rix, who called it a "ghastly movement," Lunt's demonstration looked all too real. She described the hangman at his moment as "bright and interested," as if engaged in a real hanging. "He saw none of these things in fancy, having seen them too often in fact," Rix noted.

"And then I draw it taut," Lunt said, tugging on his imaginary noose. "The man who works the black cap stands right behind and I never have to look at him. I can tell by the feel when he's got it ready, and I give my rope the last pull to be sure it won't slip. When the rope slips, it makes a poor job."

Lunt explained what happened when he raised his hand, how the three men cut the cords, one of which sent the condemned to oblivion. "Then I get down and out," Lunt explained. He did not want to stick around to see the aftermath of his handiwork. "I never want to see 'em after, and I never want to know 'em before. When their time comes then I'm ready to do my duty and I'm glad when it's over and thankful that it's gone off well."

This explanation clearly bothered Rix. "If you knew them, any one of them, would you feel differently?" she asked.

I wouldn't want to know 'em for more reasons than that. When a man's cut another human being to pieces or killed him brutally or in cold blood for a little miserable bit of money—and especially if he's killed a woman—to my mind, he's got a debt to pay and I'm not satisfied till he's paid it, and that's all I want to know about him. He's got to go, and he'd oughter go, and go by the rope, and if there's any other side to him I don't want to know it, as long as I know he's done that. I've had that feeling since I was a boy—an awful strong feeling against the taking of human life."

"Except," Rix added, "by hanging." By pointing out the double standard in Lunt's reasoning, she made Lunt squirm. "The Hangman fidgeted in his chair," she wrote.

"I take my orders from the Warden," Lunt said. "When I obey his orders I do my duty." Lunt's just-following-orders justification apparently did not satisfy the reporter, who continued her line of questions about his feelings toward killing.

"Do you think it the good way—when all is said?" she asked.

"Well, I may not be the one to judge, but I think it's the best way."

"Well, what good does it do?"

"When a man's killed," Lunt explained, "he can't do any more killing."

"Yes, but the rest of the world can, and it does, for all that you are ready with the rope—"

Lunt interrupted Rix. "Ah, yes. We're ready sooner than the murderers are, though, by a long way. There's these delays—that's what does the mischief. A desperate man will gamble on his chance to get off now at the last minute. I say when a man's convicted, of course he has a right to an appeal, but hurry it along, attend to business and if he's proved guilty let him come to the rope, and the quicker the better. What's got to be done ought to be done quick." After the William Young hanging, Lunt understood the importance of quickness. It would become even more evident with his next subject, Harvey Allender, scheduled to mount the scaffold in December.

"I can't say," Lunt continued, "that to hang a man phases the others [prisoners] much. It don't here in the prison. The convicts go in an out to their work and eat three meals the day of a hanging just the same as on other days but you've got to remember they're a pretty cool lot that comes here."

Lunt then presented his biography as a hangman. "I've hung twelve men and I never knew one to weaken—except that feller Young. The rest of 'em have been as cool and as nervy. That brute Sullivan—do you remember his case? He turned to me as cool as an icicle, and says he, 'Old man, I want you to make a good job of me!' and Collins—I never knew of anything like his nerve."

The hangman explained how he had made allowances for a knock-kneed subject on the verge of collapse. "The board," Lunt said, "is just a flat board a little shorter than the average man, made with one strap to go under the arms and another round the legs, so if he starts to drop the end of the board hits the floor and steadies him until we can get the rope on him."

He praised Collins as the bravest man he met on the scaffold. Collins took one look at the rope, shrugged, and remained motionless as Lunt went about his work. "That beats any of 'em for nerve," he said, "and I couldn't say that any I ever hung was what you'd call weak. They beat me! I know I'd have to be packed up."

"I beg pardon?" Rix said, confused by Lunt's last remark.

"Packed up the steps if I was going to be hung. Wouldn't you?"

"I—I never really thought much about the matter."

"No, I suppose not." Lunt, however, had apparently thought about it. Despite the disaffected attitude his displayed toward the men he hanged—"I never want to see 'em after, and I never want to know 'em before"—the hangman had literally walked in their path to the scaffold and envisioned himself in their shoes. Facing death in this way created a bond between executioner and victim, a horrible link that would haunt Lunt for the rest of his days.

"There's one thing breaks me up," Lunt leaned forward and spoke in hushed tones, as if he was about to spill a secret, "and that's talking on the scaffold. I can't stand it! Father Lagan, he's a great help to me in that way. He's a power on the scaffold, Father Lagan! He keeps 'em firm, and if a man starts talking he'll say to him, 'There, my son you've nothing more to worry about here. I'll talk for you.' And they listen to him every time. Then he gives me the word—not a word exactly, but a look that's sort of a tip, and the cap goes on and my hand goes up, and that finishes the thing properly."

"If you've got a man to hang you want to hang him quick," Lunt concluded. "That's the first thing you want to learn."

"And how did you learn?" Rix asked, curious about the hangman's antecedents.

"Well, I can't say as I ever learned hanging. I sorter took to it naturally."

Lunt concluded the interview by showing Alice Rix how to tie a noose.

The Rix interview, which occupied the entire fourth page of the November 21, 1897, edition, was the only one of its kind. None of the other Bay Area newspapers featured Lunt. The *Call*, which broke the

Lunt taught several journalists, including Alice Rix, how to tie a noose. This sketch accompanied Rix's profile of the hangman in the November 21, 1897, edition of the *Examiner*.

"red hot iron" scandal, avoided the hangman like the plague out of fear that his version would expose their reporter's story as yellow journalism. They so wanted to sanitize their pages of sensationalized news after the "red hot iron" story that they would not send a sketch artist to Durrant's execution.

The *Examiner* had no such qualms; their artist adorned Rix's piece with hangman's ropes, which framed the article's columns. Running along the bottom of the page, a pair of disembodied hands tied a noose above the caption "Lund [sic] shows Alice Rix how to tie a hangman's knot."[3]

23

Friday, the Thirteenth

(Friday, December 10, 1897)

Because Hans Hansen and Thomas St. Clair dropped at the same time, Amos Lunt considered Harvey Allender and not F.J. Kloss as his 13th execution. Unlucky number 13 bothered the hangman, and in some ways, unlucky number 13 would be the most troubling event in Lunt's career as a hangman.

* * *

Harvey Allender committed a crime passionnel when, on Sunday, August 9, 1896, he accosted his former girlfriend, Walberga "Wally" Fiener, and her beau, Venanzi Crosetti, as they strolled along Third Street in San Jose. When Fiener refused to speak to him, Allender pulled a pistol from his pocket and shot her in the neck. She crumpled, and Allender shot her a second time as she lay on the ground.

Crosetti lunged at Allender and attempted to wrench the firearm from his hands. As he reached for the pistol, Allender fired a third time, the slug tearing through Crosetti's stomach and liver. He wobbled across the street to the fire engine house, where he collapsed and died.

Allender then attempted to shoot himself by pointing the revolver at his head and pulling the trigger. He missed, the bullet passing through the brim of his hat and just grazing his scalp.

When asked why he would gun down the 25-year-old woman and her companion, Allender explained that he could not stand to see her with another man. After she rejected his marriage proposal and began seeing Crosetti, Allender snapped. He stalked the couple and sent them threatening letters covered with skull-and-crossbones graffiti. The couple avoided Allender if they could, but when he met them on the street that Sunday, they had nowhere to run. He tried to plead insanity but failed to make his case.

The felonious carpenter received three different death sentences. Following a guilty verdict in September 1896, the trial court sentenced him

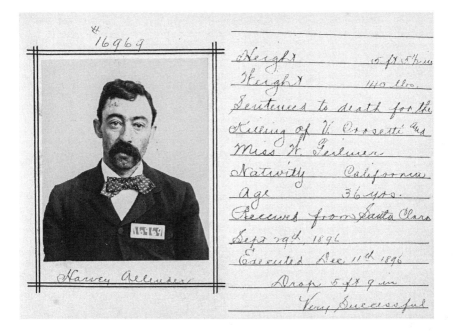

Lunt considered Harvey Allender his thirteenth subject. "I must say I was a little nervous today, and for one reason," Lunt remarked after the hanging. "This was the thirteenth man at whose execution I had assisted here, and I did not like the number" (Anne T. Kent California Room, Marin County Free Library).

hang. After finding no error in the lower court's decision, the California Supreme Court resentenced Allender to hang. A further appeal to the United States Supreme Court was dismissed on a motion by the attorney general, which led to a third death sentence.

Unlike Theodore Durrant, Allender made no attempt to deny his guilt. Instead, he expressed his remorse when he sat with a reporter on the night before his execution. He calmly puffed a cigarette as he discussed his crime and punishment.

> Well, after all, I do know I am sorry for killing the girl. I could not live and see another man marry her. Now that I am going to die, I feel as though there is a chance for me to meet my sweetheart in another land. Life was not worth living without that girl. I could not die alone and leave her behind. I am satisfied with my fate.[1]
>
> I am guilty of murder and deserve to die, but I would like to say to the public before they swing me off that I am not at heart a murderer or a criminal. The poor young fellow I killed, and the girl I loved and also killed, were victims of a moment's passion, and I only wish that my death would bring them back to life.

In what sounded like an attempt to steady his failing nerves, Allender concluded, "The scaffold hasn't got any terrors for me. I rather welcome it, and when I go up the steps tomorrow I will feel that I am going home. A man can only die once. My time has come, and I am content."[2] After three death sentences, Allender's "die once" comment thinly veiled the angst of a man tired of waiting.

As the night progressed, however, Harvey Allender was anything but "content."

*   *   *

Prior to each execution, Warden Hale drew up a list of attendees and send out formal invitations. These extremely exclusive lists typically included physicians, reporters, and lawmen involved in some way with the case. Although Hale shied away from creating the type of tawdry melodrama that might tarnish the solemnity of the event, in a few instances, he granted requests from victims' relatives to attend the hanging of their loved one's murderer.

One such request came from John Crosetti, Venanzi Crosetti's brother. When Allender heard about Crosetti's invitation, he asked Hale to rescind it. Not wanting to deny a condemned man's final wish, Hale recalled the invitation through Santa Clara County Sheriff James Hardy Lyndon.

Not to be denied, John Crosetti traveled to San Quentin on the morning of Allender's execution in hopes of sneaking into the gallows room with one of the reporters, but he never got past the front entrance.

*   *   *

Allender managed only about two hours of sleep the night before his execution, spending his last waking hours quietly reading his bible. The early hours of the morning passed slowly for Allender, who grew tired of waiting for the inevitable visit by Hale carrying the death warrant.

"I think that the execution ought to be earlier in the morning," he carped to the Death Watch, who had kept a steady eye on him throughout the night. "When the unfortunate man first awakens he is fresh, and ready for death. It is the suspense that unnerves him. I am ready to die this very minute and am only anxious to have it over with."[3]

By the time Hale did come with the death warrant, the suspense had turned Harvey Allender into a quavering mass. Allender was on his knees in prayer when he heard the electric bell signaling that the moment had come. Arbogast handed him a pink carnation he had requested the night before. Pinning it onto his lapel, he said, "That is in memory of the poor girl I loved and killed."[4]

*   *   *

As the clock struck 10 a.m., Amos Lunt was nervous. He worried about the drop.

For the hangman's purposes, Allender and Frank Cooney Kloss were anatomical twins. According to official San Quentin records, both men weighed 140 pounds and shared the same build. Only half an inch in height, with Allender taller by the width of a penny, separated them. Lunt calculated a drop of 5'9".[5]

Contemporary reports, however, state that Allender weighed 20 pounds less. A bundle of nerves in the ten days he spent in the death cells, Allender may not have eaten much during that interval, which would explain the rapid weight loss.

Lunt apparently feared that the length of rope might lead to a repeat of the Fremont Smith debacle. An *Evening News* correspondent described the hangman's concerns. "The condemned man's lightness, he weighed only 120 pounds, made it a question with the executioner, whether his neck would be broken. Executioner Lunt made the rope a foot longer than that used for heavy men. He took a chance in this, as the long drop might have cut the neck in two."[6]

The *Chronicle* also noted the longer-than-usual drop but erred in placing it at six feet. "Lunt will give his man a 'six-foot drop,' as he gruesomely expresses it, rather a longer distance than in ordinary cases, but Allender is a slim fellow, and carries very little flesh."[7]

Concern over the length of drop clearly rattled Lunt. He sweated out the final minutes before Allender's hanging by flitting about the scaffold, checking and rechecking the rope, the noose, the trap. "Lunt, the hangman," wrote the *Chronicle*'s reporter on the scene, "paced rapidly up and down the place in a condition of excitement that had the effect of making most of those who watched him as nervous as himself."[8]

*   *   *

Given Allender's near panic-state, Lunt attempted to quicken the pace of his final preparations. Allender mounted the scaffold at 10:31 a.m. and spent less than two minutes on the trap. It was a long two minutes.

The scene that ensued was almost too much for the hangman. Allender tottered and swayed. Reverend Drahms, who stood directly in front of him, tried to calm his nerves by whispering, "It's all right," but the doomed man sagged. Frank Arbogast and John Jones, the Death Watch guards, grabbed him just as his legs buckled. They held him upright as Lunt quickly placed and adjusted the noose.

"Some of the witnesses," noted the *San Francisco Examiner*'s representative, "think he had fainted before the trap opened."[9]

To Amos Lunt's relief, the drop did not tear Allender's head from his shoulders. While he died a quick, painless death, the hanging fell short of Lunt's standard. "[T]he execution was not as good as is usually performed in San Quentin," commented one witness.[10]

For the physicians present, however, Allender's hanging established a new record: his pulse ceased nine minutes after the drop, smashing the previous mark of 11 minutes. When the guards cut down his body and placed it in the coffin, the pink carnation was still in his lapel.

*   *   *

Allender's meltdown gnawed at Lunt, who expressed his distress after the hanging. He characterized Allender as the "weakest" man he met on the scaffold to date, weaker even than William Young. "Allender was as game a man as ever suffered the death penalty during my official career," Lunt said. "Up to the last moment was very courageous, and seemed anxious for the affair to be over as soon as possible." Then came the climactic moment on the scaffold, when Allender's gaminess evaporated.

"I had to hurry or he would have fallen," Lunt said in describing those critical final seconds. "The poor fellow tried hard to be brave and hold up. He was nothing but a bag of bones. He turned his head to look at me and said, 'Is it all right?'

"[I]t required the efforts of three of us to prevent his entire collapse," Lunt continued. "As the noose was adjusted around his neck, he endeavored to scream out, but was immediately cut short by the tightening of the noose, and without further delay I sprung the trap and all was over."

A superstitious hangman, Lunt also said that the number 13 hovered over him like a malignant succubus. "I must say I was a little nervous today, and for one reason," Lunt explained. "This was the thirteenth man at whose execution I had assisted here, and I did not like the number."[11]

In folklore, a succubus visits a man in his dreams and seduces him. Overtime, she causes her victim to have a mental and physical breakdown. Later accounts would indicate that the Allender hanging caused extreme emotional distress for Amos Lunt and may have begun a vortex from which he would not escape.

Lunt, however, looked forward to moving past unlucky number 13.

"Allender is the thirteenth man who I have had occasion to hang, and I fully believe that my next victim will be Durrant," whose hanging Lunt believed would take place on January 7. "This is but prophecy, however," he concluded, "and I fully believe that my surmise will be substantiated by facts."[12]

The year 1898 was shaping up to be the busiest yet for the hangman, with eight inmates of San Quentin under sentences of death.[13]

24

The Bat in the Belfry

(Friday, January 7, 1898)

During his time on death row, William Henry Theodore Durrant played three different yet related characters: the indignant, wrongfully convicted victim, the stoic martyr determined to die a valiant death, and the anguished son guilty not of murder but of breaking his mother's heart. All three made cameo appearances on Friday, January 17, 1898, but one of them in particular unhinged Amos Lunt.

* * *

Amos Lunt's prophecy came true. For months, Durrant's case snaked through various courts and involved complex legal concepts such as "bill of exception" and "writ of habeas corpus." With his appeals exhausted, and his attorneys even more exhausted, Theodore Durrant resigned himself to the fact that tomorrow—Friday, January 7, 1898—he would go to the scaffold. His last hope lay with his parents, whose attempt to obtain clemency from Governor Budd fell flat when he refused to see them.

On Thursday, Lunt made his preparations for the hanging that would define his career on the scaffold. He could not afford to fail, but on the eve of "Hangman's Friday," a general malaise left the hangman in a weakened physical state. Nonetheless, he personally checked the gallows apparatus.

"Amos Lunt, the hangman," noted one reporter, "visited Durrant's cell this afternoon for the purpose of taking his measure and determining the length of the drop. The machinery of the gallows was tested and everything found to work smoothly."[1]

Durrant's execution would play to an audience of about 150. The notoriety of the trial led to five times that number of requests, which Warden Hale culled down to a short list of invitees. The group of spectators—by far the largest in the short but storied history of hangings at the prison—would crowd into the gallows room and stand shoulder-to-shoulder as they watched the final episode of the "church belfry" case.

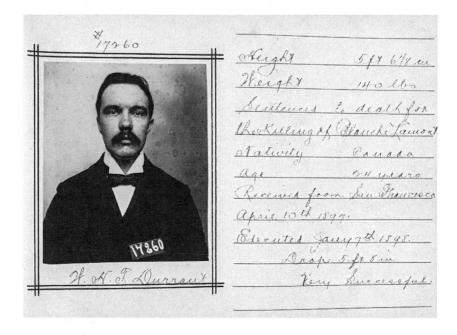

W.H.T. Durrant, the "Church Belfry Fiend," whose final words on the scaffold haunted Lunt for the rest of his life (Anne T. Kent California Room, Marin County Free Library).

The warden who steered clear of gallows drama uncharacteristically sent an invitation to a condemned man's relative—a first for San Quentin. Durrant's father William, against Hale's pleadings, insisted on attending his son's execution, which promised to add melodrama to the affair and give reporters a heart-wrenching headline.

*   *   *

A good indication of Durrant's infamy came in the copious newspaper coverage of his final night and his execution. Stories of hangings in San Quentin always merited a few columns, usually on page two or three, but news of Durrant's final night dominated the front pages of all three major Bay Area newspapers. The case occupied the entire front page of both the Friday and Saturday editions of the *Examiner*. Reporters from all three rags queued up to interview the doomed man, each hoping to hear a last-minute confession from the convict who continued to present himself as an innocent man.

They left Durrant's death cell disappointed. He continued to present himself as innocent, as a "martyr to the persecution of the courts," and declared that he would "die like a Durrant," whatever that meant.

The *Chronicle* reporter described the condemned man on his last day. "His eyelids were red and heavy with the weeping that comes at almost every mention of his family. His voice as he talked of himself was steady, but when he reverted to the parting that will come to-day his utterance was broken with sobs."[2]

The indefatigable Alice Rix also ventured into the death cells—a very rare instance of a woman permitted entrance into San Quentin's death house—to interview Durrant. Decked out in a black dress, a black plumed hat with veil drawn, and white gloves, she sat and spoke with the doomed man as his mother watched from the other side of the cell's wooden slats.

Rix sat with the convicted slayer in the 11th hour, literally making her the vessel for his final words to the press.

Rix began her interview with an eerie foreboding. "'Eleven o'clock and all is well.' The watch sounded the hour from post to post along the prison walls, and the man in the death chamber who will be hanged before another eleven hours have crossed the clock looked up and listened. 'Eleven,' he asked, quietly, 'or ten?'"

The hour mattered more to Durrant than anyone, yet he asked Rix the time with the nonchalance of a man enjoying a stroll through the park.

"I am extraordinarily happy," Durrant proclaimed, "so much at peace that I do not care to go over any of the old ground the long, long story which has been told so many times. The case is ended, and I am satisfied that everything has been done for me that could have been done by my lawyers. It would be weak and childish for me to say at this time that I have not had a fair trial. If I should make such a plea the public would reply, 'That is what they all say.'"

Yet Theodore Durrant just could not help himself. He pontificated about the errors made by the courts and added a dramatic coda. "I have been convicted of murder, and my hands are as clean as a child's. This is my last earthly interview, and this is my message to the people of California. Let the responsibility rest with them."[3]

Durrant scribbled a few lines on a scrap of paper and handed it to the reporter. "In conclusion," he wrote, "I will say that this is my last interview. That my hands are free, free from all stain of crime. I am glad to again proclaim, Alice Rix has heard, in this, my last interview to earthly mortals, my cry of innocence. This I strenuously and boldly proclaim."

He stood and said, "I will not see you again. I will say good-night."[4]

Not even Alice Rix, whose piercing line of questions caused Amos Lunt to disclose his feelings about hangings, could pry anything resembling an admission from Theodore Durrant.

Meanwhile, Durrant's parents gave Warden Hale conniptions. William Durrant begged Hale to let him take Theodore out of his cell for a photo shoot, then threatened to smash anyone he caught with a camera inside the death house. Feeling his authority undermined and perhaps usurped, Hale snapped at a reporter, "Don't talk to me of sympathy for these people…. They have been running the execution. They behave to me as if they were proud of all this."[5]

The *Chronicle* reporter, stung by the Durrants' attempt to turn the hanging into dollars, wrote a sharp rebuke. While Theodore counted down his last remaining hours, "the parents of Durrant were busy coining into dollars the last hours of their condemned son up in the death chamber. Durrant's mother Isabella interrupted an Associated Press man in the middle of a sentence to intimate broadly that a monetary consideration was expected.

"'Everything that Theo says now is worth a great deal,'" she said.[6]

*   *   *

Throughout Durrant's time in the death cells, veteran Death Watch guards Frank Arbogast and John Miller kept a close eye on their most infamous resident, who made overtures of cheating the hangman and once boasted that he could easily kill himself, despite the protective detail, if he really wanted to. To make sure that Durrant did not make good on his boast, Hale doubled the Death Watch by adding two additional guards, B.F. Merritt and Frank Davis. They moved his cot to the center of the cell, so they could see him from all sides. Two men remained in Durrant's cell at all times.

One of the extra detail, B.F. Merritt, could not help but admire Durrant's coolness. "He did not seem to fear death. Frequently he told me that his only regret was that he could not live to repay his parents for all their kindness to him," Merritt later recalled. "In all his talks with me Durrant never once referred to either Minnie Williams or Blanche Lamont by name, but always spoke indefinitely of 'these crimes.'"

Merritt remembered Durrant's odd reaction when hearing what they called him on the streets of San Francisco. "'They call me a monster,' and then, standing up before me he said: 'I don't look so much like a monster, do I?'"[7]

Durrant spent his last few waking hours on Thursday, January 6, rehearsing the speech he planned to give from the scaffold. He finally nodded off to sleep at about 1 a.m.

*   *   *

While Durrant gave his final interviews and practiced his speech, Amos Lunt made his final preparations. Along with J.A. Spencer, his counterpart at Folsom prison, he tested the rope and gallows apparatus.

Lunt had figured a drop of 5'8". After looping the rope over the crossbeam, he measured and then re-measured the distance the noose dropped from the point at which a man at a height of 5'6⅛" stood over the trap.[8]

The hangman took every precaution to avoid a bungled execution. He knew, perhaps better than anyone except Warden Hale, the consequences of a mistake in the most newsworthy execution at the prison to date.

In its January 7, 1898, edition, the *San Francisco Examiner* published a sketch depicting the moment when Lunt installed the rope. The drawing, which occupied a quarter of the page, came with a caption that noted, "Hangman Lunt has personally supervised every detail, to prevent the possibility of any mistakes."[9]

* * *

Men, with Hale's black-bordered invitation cards in hand, began arriving at dawn. County sheriffs arrived with prisoners, so their respective counties would pay the expenses of their trip to San Quentin. "The crowd looked more like an assemblage of Wyatt Earps than ever," wrote a reporter with a hint of irritation in his word choice.[10]

Warden Hale met the crowd of Earps at the gate and asked them to surrender their handguns or "shooting irons" by placing them in a large drawer. He also asked them to finish their cigars before they entered the prison. Each handed his black-fringed invitation to a guard as they walked through the gate.

Durrant was the only one involved with the hanging who slept much that night. Lunt fretted about the drop and Hale about the entire proceedings, but the condemned man slumbered from about 1 a.m. until he awoke at 6:20 a.m.

That Lunt's nerves bothered him became evident. As Durrant ate breakfast, "Above on the balcony, old Amos Lunt, the hangman, was keeping his regular watch and seeing spooks," wrote a *Chronicle* correspondent. The reporter's choice of words suggested that Lunt by this time had already begun receiving spectral visitors. He also noted, "Lunt began early to fortify himself for his grim ordeal, but not so Durrant. He did not taste a stimulant."[11] The comparison of Lunt's nerves to Durrant's coolness underscored the tension among those involved with the hanging and implied that the hangman may have downed a few shots of liquid courage to steel his nerves.

While Lunt steadied his nerves, Theodore Durrant prepared his soul. Alienated from Baptist church leaders he felt had betrayed him, Durrant summoned Father Lagan and converted into the Catholic faith 90 minutes before he went to the scaffold. He spent much of that time in religious contemplation with the priest, who heard his confession and then administered extreme unction. What Durrant said to the priest would remain a topic of idle gossip, but one of the Death Watch heard him say something about his innocence.

The retinue of newspaper reporters who followed Durrant's parents everywhere eavesdropped on an emotional, heart-wrenching scene when they said farewell to their son at 10:15 a.m. William Durrant, his eyes swollen with tears, gently grasped his son's hand. Too overcome to speak, he nodded as the tears streamed down his cheeks.

Isabella Durrant threw her arms around Theodore's neck and held him like a shipwrecked woman clinging to a piece of wreckage. "Theo, my Theo, my dear boy," she muttered. "Oh, my darling, may God comfort you and be with you all this day."[12] After she kissed him, he gently pulled her hands from his neck and placed them in his father's. "Good-bye," he stammered, his voice cracking. He tried to stifle the tears.

The Durrants embraced before parting. William Durrant moved into the gallows room while his wife went to Captain Edgar's office, where she would wait for guards to put "Theo" in his coffin. The hands of the clock indicated the time had reached 10:30 a.m. She would wait exactly 19 minutes.

*   *   *

A few minutes before 10:30 a.m., guards admitted the spectators, who flooded into the gallows room. A stampede ensued as several men rushed forward, eager for a front-row spot. Hale stood at the base of the scaffold and met the crowd. "Gentlemen," he said in a stentorian tone, reminding the throng that they were gentlemen, "you are limited to these four posts about the gallows. The guards will see that the spectators do not crowd in on the doctors. And, gentlemen, when Durrant is pronounced dead you will all leave the room at once."[13] There would be no attempt to take a strand of rope as a souvenir.

At 10:30 a.m., Amos Lunt would place the noose around the neck of a man that he said he would prefer to torture with "red hot irons" in front of an audience that included the doomed man's father. Fortunately for the hangman, reporters did not pay attention to that aspect of the drama about to unfold inside the fourth floor of the prison factory. They would, however, pay attention to every detail of Durrant's final moments, which meant that every step—and misstep—that the San Quentin hangman took would be scrutinized and reported in the next day's front pages.

All eyes turned as the iron door swung open and San Francisco's most infamous criminal walked into the room. A reporter described his hangman at this exact moment. "Amos Lunt, standing at the rear of the scaffold near the foot of the steps that lead to death, looked the hangman every inch. Schooled in the business as he is, Lunt was a shade paler than usual, and he seemed active almost to nervousness."[14] His cold may have contributed to his "paler than usual" appearance.

The *Call*'s man was more complementary in his description of the hangman, describing him as "Mild of aspect, with a frank face, a steely but gentle blue eye; not a cruel man, but firm."[15]

Writing for the *San Francisco Examiner*, E.H. Hamilton characterized both Lunt and Hale as nervous wrecks. According to the journalist, Hale took a "stimulant during the shuddery moments proceeding the drop," and the hangman "was forcing his nerves to the straining point."[16]

Unlike his executioners, Theodore Durrant kept his composure all the way to the scaffold. To prevent the type of last-minute collapse that happened with Allender, Lunt and the guards worked quickly. As soon as Durrant stepped onto the trap, John Jones knelt down and began tightening the straps while Lunt adjusted the noose.

Durrant turned to Lunt and grinned. "Don't put the rope on, my boy, until after I talk." Lunt ignored the command and fitted the knot behind Durrant's left ear. Realizing that his request had fallen on deaf ears, Durrant said, "Well, don't tighten it, then."[17]

Seven feet below, at the base of the scaffold, stood William Durrant. His emotions took control and he began an expletive-filled rant, railing against everyone involved in the execution, including Lunt. "William Durrant," noted the *Chronicle* reporter, "managed to inject a considerable amount of bitterness into the surroundings by a fit of uncontrollable rage directed against everybody connected with the execution."[18]

"Don't talk too long, my boy," warned Father Lagan, who stood in front of Durrant and blocked him from sight as Lunt adjusted the noose. The priest understood the importance of brevity on the scaffold. No one, especially Lunt, wanted to prolong this moment.

With his arms and legs pinioned and the noose fastened around his neck, Durrant made his final statement, which he had memorized and practiced during his final hours in the condemned cells.

In a calm voice unbroken with emotion, he began with a rhetorical question. "Do you wish me [to] say anything?" He knew the reporters in the room wanted nothing more than a deathbed confession.

After a dramatic pause, Durrant began. "Well, I would like to say this: I have no animosity against any one, nor even against those who have persecuted me and who have hounded me to my grave, innocent as I am. Forgive them all. They will receive their justice from the Holy God above, to whom I now go to receive my justice, which will be the justice given to an innocent boy who has not stained his hands with crimes that have been put upon him by the press of San Francisco; but I forgive them all." He tried to gesticulate for effect but, with the straps tightened, could do nothing more than wiggle.

E.H. Hamilton noted Amos Lunt's demeanor at this point. "Hangman Lunt leaned forward anxiously as the talk went on," he wrote. "He kept one hand on the rope and watched for signs of weakening. Once there was a slight quaver in the doomed man's voice, and the hangman moved his hand involuntarily toward the black cap. Evidently he intended to act speedily at the first sign of collapse."

Lunt gripped the black cap tightly as Durrant finished his remarks.

I do not hold anything against the reporters. I do not look upon them now as enemies. I forgive them as I expect to be forgiven for everything that I have done, but the fair name of California will forever be blackened with the crime of taking this innocent blood, and whether or no they ever discover the committers of this crime matters little to me now, for I, before the whole world, announce my innocence for the last time, and to those who have insinuated that I was going to spring a sensation of any kind, I must say there is no sensation other than that which I have said. Those who wish to consider it a sensation may do so, but I am innocent of the crimes charged to me before God, who knows the heart and can read the mind. I am innocent.[19]

The black cap came down quickly after the word "innocent," Lunt raised his hand, and Durrant dropped. Someone clocked the exact moment the trap was sprung: 10:38:02 a.m.

The fall broke Durrant's neck, and his body gently swayed with his head tilted to the right at an unnatural angle. The color of his hands changed from ecru to cyanotic purple to ash white as his pulse ebbed.

Most of the attendees had never witnessed a hanging. Some darted out of the room, nauseous. "Others, impelled by morbid curiosity," noted one spectator, "could not get close enough to the corpse, and watched eagerly every spasmodic movement of the swinging body."[20]

William Durrant, standing at the base of the scaffold, buried his face in the shoulder of a friend and did not look up until the physicians noted the final pulse, 11 minutes later.

During that 11-minute interval, the physicians took turns feeling Durrant's pulse through his wrist every 30 seconds, and Father Lagan continued to pray on the scaffold.

67–60–54–50–50–40

During the first few minutes after Durrant fell, the spectators remaining at the scaffold stood, silent, and studied the body. Father Lagan's prayers echoed through the spacious gallery.

50–55–56–70–40–45

After a few minutes, they began to chat in muted tones. Someone—a veteran of several public hangings—mentioned the possibility of reviving the victim if officials cut down the body before the pulse ceased.

This period must have proved particularly difficult for Amos Lunt, who was visibly agitated. He stepped down from the scaffold, his eyes wet with tears, and began pacing while the physicians counted down Durrant's dwindling pulse.

A prison trustee named Wilcox, who helped Lunt with various preparations such as stretching the ropes and as a result typically attended executions, congratulated the hangman on a job well done.

"That was the best job you ever done," he said.

Uncomfortable with praise at that particular moment, Lunt credited

Both the *Chronicle* and the *Examiner* sent artists to San Quentin in January 1898 to sketch the final scenes in the life of the "Church Belfry Fiend." These sketches also illustrate typical gallows procedures at the prison. In *Examiner* artist Mary Davison's sketch, Alice Rix interviews Durrant in the death cell on the eve of his execution.

While Rix visits with Durrant, Amos Lunt supervises a crew installing the rope and testing the trap in the adjacent room. The caption that accompanied this sketch by *Examiner* artist Deringer noted, "Hangman Lunt has personally supervised every detail to prevent the possibility of any mistakes."

Durrant's steel nerve for the success of his hanging. "He died the bravest of any man I've ever seen, and this is my fourteenth," Lunt said. "His legs were just as steady as they could be. All the others bent at the knees. I have never seen such nerve, and never do expect to see anything like it again. It

In this unsigned *Examiner* sketch, the Death Watch, Frank Arbogast and John D. Jones, join Captain Jamieson in fitting the straps on Durrant's arms while his father watches from the other side of the bars.

was Father Lagan who brought him through it so, and you can't give him too much praise."[21]

The physicians continued their macabre countdown.

$$36–60–40–42–22–20–30[22]$$

The day after the execution, the *Examiner* published this sketch of Durrant making his final speech from the scaffold while his father, distraught and overcome with emotion, clings to a friend.

A *Chronicle* artist drew this scene of Amos Lunt adjusting the rope. The accompanying caption preserved Durrant's final words. "As the rope went about Durrant's neck he turned to Lunt, and, in a tone that was audible to those who stood near, said: 'Don't put that rope on, my boy, until after I talk.' There was a shape of a smile on his face, and when he felt the rope on his neck, he added: 'Well, don't tighten it, then.'"

Dr. William M. Lawlor, the prison physician, declared Durrant dead. Upon hearing the announcement, Father Lagan stopped praying and stepped down from the scaffold, and the remaining spectators shuffled out of the room.

William Durrant reminded Warden Hale of his son's wish that the noose as well as the six-foot length of rope—the length of his drop—be burned. Durrant apparently feared that the hemp would be cut into pieces, distributed as souvenirs, and displayed as "part of the rope that hanged Theodore Durrant, the great California criminal." Upon Hale's order, prison guard Jack Savage cut the noose away from Durrant's neck and placed it in a white bag.

"What about the rope on the beam?" Durrant asked. Hale nodded, and Savage severed the rope and shoved it into the same bag.[23]

With the rope matter settled and the white bag taken to the furnace of the engine room, William Durrant followed the contingent of guards as they carried his son's coffined body into the next room. There they transplanted him into a fancier coffin provided by the family. While Captain Edgar escorted Isabella Durrant across the yard, William Durrant asked Dr. Lawlor to make his son more presentable.

A *Chronicle* artist's sketch of Dr. W. P. Lawlor and a team of physicians counting down Durrant's ebbing pulse.

Not an undertaker, there was little the prison physician could do, but he nonetheless tried.

Mr. and Mrs. Durrant looked upon their son's face as he lay in the coffin. While most of the reporters looked away, the *Call* reporter studied the face of Theodore Durrant. Reporters who attended hangings typically did not describe the bodies as they lay in their coffins, and Hale expressly forbid photography in his gallows room, so this description presented a rare glimpse at the physical damage done by the noose. "The black cap when taken off disclosed a shocking sight," he wrote. "The face was almost black: the eyes half protruding, and the lids half open. The jaws were firmly, rigorously set; the features distorted."[24]

Mrs. Durrant dropped to her knees. "My boy, my boy," she groaned. "My precious boy! They have murdered you!"[25] She kissed his lips while William Durrant stood over her, his hand on her shoulder. After a few minutes, he suggested they leave, but she refused. She stayed by her son's side for the next four hours, eventually staggering out of the building at 2:30 p.m. Those reporters who witnessed the strange scene commented on the mother's surreal poise.

"There's where the fellow got his nerves," a guard who eavesdropped on the moment said. "At least, that shows why he has no nerves. He was born without them."[26]

* * *

Warden Hale and Amos Lunt breathed a collective sigh of relief; the hanging had come off without a hitch. Both men were also relieved that the circus had left town with the carriage bringing Theodore Durrant's body home.

The *Chronicle* reporter praised their professionalism. "The machinery connected with the scaffold worked in a very satisfactory manner, and at no time from the moment that Durrant was brought from the condemned cell till he went down through the platform at the head of thirteen steps was there any hitch in the proceedings," wrote the *Chronicle*'s representative at the hanging.[27]

Drs. Frank Fitzgibbon and F. Stevens Cook—two in the retinue of physicians—praised the execution as perfectly engineered.

"Of all the executions I have witnesses the one of to-day seemed to me to be the most successful and perfect in every respect," Dr. Fitzgibbon declared. "The doomed man must have died without experiencing any pain. At the drop his neck was broken. One thing peculiar was that after the drop his respirations ceased. This very rarely occurs, as there are usually a few respiratory movements after."

His colleague Dr. Cook concurred. "I have witnessed a number of executions, and must say that for neatness of work and for exhibition of personal courage the one of today will take precedence. One peculiarity noticed from a physiological point of view was the absolute cessation of respiration, or attempts, from the instant of the drop.... The neck was broken and death took place instantaneously, there being little or no suffering; in my opinion none."[28]

That the Durrant execution occurred without cheap, tawdry melodrama was thanks to Warden Hale, still sick from what the papers called a "wasting illness." That Durrant died quickly and without feeling anything was the result of Lunt's acumen in measuring the drop.

Bulletins went out across the state to crowds that gathered around news offices eager to hear that the trap had sprung. On the streets of San Francisco, people rejoiced.

"It is hard to describe the feeling aroused in the city by the news that Durrant was really dead," wrote a *Chronicle* correspondent. "People, total strangers to one another, stopped and shook hands in the streets and together discussed the event. The bulletins of the 'Chronicle' office were surrounded by large crowds, and all day and evening the corner of Market and Kearny streets was blocked with people anxious to read over again and again the news of the murderer's taking off."[29]

Call journalist (and later novelist) Miriam Michelson authored a piece that neatly summarized the saga of the "Church Belfry Fiend." Written from the perspective of the noose speaking to the doomed man, "What the Noose Said to Durrant" represents a thought-provoking insight into late-19th-century attitudes toward hanging. The final three paragraphs in particular reflect the ideas that prejudiced the public toward the functionaries of the law, such as Amos Lunt.

> After all, the only shame in the death I administer is in what men have arbitrarily associated with me. Death is so great a fact that there can be no accessory to its awful majesty.
>
> To those, then, who still hold you human and love worthy, my power extends. The speedier, the surer you and I are in our union, the speedier, the surer is the healing of their wounds. Their suffering is in your suffering. What you have endured is as nothing compared to that which they have borne. Their cruelest pain is in knowing that they cannot suffer for you. With the knowledge that your agony is ended will begin their recovery from the long martyrdom.
>
> To them, as to you, my mission brings relief. Come.[30]

*   *   *

In an interview after the hanging, Warden Hale characterized Durrant as the coolest customer who ever occupied a death cell inside

San Quentin. "I have never before seen a condemned man meet his fate so calmly nor with less apparent fear," the warden said.[31]

Neither Hale's hangman nor his number one Death Watch guard, Frank Arbogast, shared Durrant's coolness. The hanging of San Francisco's most notorious criminal left both men on the verge of nervous prostration. Lunt already had demons, but the Durrant execution really bothered him.

Lunt and Arbogast were particularly haunted by Durrant's final moment on the scaffold.

"I was so unnerved by the coolness of that man and the manner in which he declared 'I am innocent,'" Arbogast told a reporter the next day, "that I have not since been able to do anything. All through the case I believed Durrant to be guilty and thought he would break down at the last, but the coolness he displayed on the gallows and the speech he made declaring his innocence, while the rope was dangling about his neck, fairly made me tremble."

If Durrant's final phrase made Arbogast tremble, it unnerved Lunt. He left the prison on Friday after the hanging and did not return until Sunday. The hours away failed to calm his nerves.

Still shaken as he resumed his guard post on the wall, Lunt's physical appearance had visibly changed. "He was restless," wrote a *Chronicle* reporter well acquainted with the hangman, "and his features had not resumed the placid look that is the hangman's normal expression."

Theodore Durrant represented the diametric opposite to Harvey Allender. Where one faltered, perhaps even fainted on the scaffold, the other remained cool and indignant to the end. Lunt told a reporter,

> In all my experience as a hangman, I have seen nothing that equaled the coolness of that man Durrant.
>
> When he stepped upon the trap he made no more impression on me than had other prisoners I have hanged before. After I had put the rope around his neck he asked me to allow him to speak. I thought he only wanted to declare his innocence, and did not remove the rope from about his neck. When he began in such a calm and deliberate manner to make a speech it sort of dazed me, and I felt somewhat nervous after it. It was enough to give any one a shock to hear him declare "I am innocent," as he stood there on the death trap with the noose about his neck, and as I already was sick it unnerved me a bit. Yes, he was the coolest man I ever saw on the scaffold.

The journalist's piece about the hangman appeared under the title "HANGMAN LUNT HAD NERVOUS PROSTRATION."

"[S]ince the church belfry criminal dropped through the trap of the scaffold," wrote the anonymous reporter, "the veteran hangman confesses to a creepy feeling in the vicinity of his spinal column … the remembrance of those last words of the doomed murderer causes Lunt to seek a quiet corner in which to quiet his unstrung nerves."[32]

Amos Lunt was a deeply disturbed individual, although in January 1898, no one knew just how disturbed. Beginning with Durrant's "I am innocent" remark, and probably much earlier than that, Lunt would begin down a dark path peopled by 14 souls who visited him at night, during his sleep.

25

Bloody Spring

(Friday, March 11, 1898)

Publicity before and during the Durrant execution, which included the "red hot iron" controversy and Rix's subsequent interview, made Amos Lunt a household name. An *Examiner* reporter gave a nod to the infamous hangman in an article about Frank Belew, who poisoned his younger brother and sister by spiking a teakettle with rat poison in November 1897.

"Frank Belew has decided that he does not want to make the official acquaintance of Amos Lunt, the hangman at San Quentin," wrote the *Examiner*'s correspondent. "He announced to-night that he will not plead guilty to the charge of murder and will make a fight for his life."[1]

Belew, who realized he could not undo the damning admissions he had made behind bars, ultimately threw himself on the mercy of the court by pleading guilty. He would meet the hangman, but not Amos Lunt; he hanged at Folsom instead.

Although Lunt would not tie a noose for Frank Belew, the spring of 1898 would be a busy one for the hangman, who would prepare ropes for three men, one execution scheduled for each of the months of March, April, and May.

*   *   *

Whoever followed Theodore Durrant to the scaffold was doomed to become a historical footnote but, coupled with the era's prevailing attitudes toward Chinese Americans, the hanging of Wee Tung went virtually unnoticed. News of Durrant's execution consumed four full pages, including the front page; Tung's fit in half a column on page four. The quiet, anticlimactic affair took place without the throng at the prison gate, the legions of reporters, and the hundreds of spectators crammed into the gallows room.

Tung's crime occurred during the same time that Durrant's appeals snaked through the courts. On September 2, 1897, he became embroiled

189

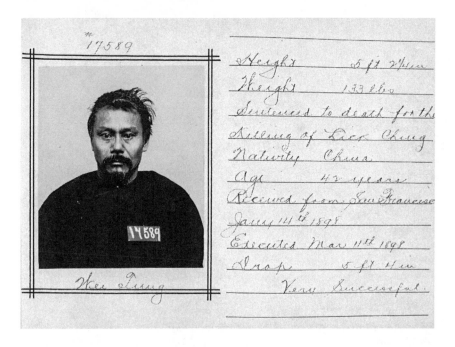

After the hanging of Wee Tung, a *Chronicle* reporter, noted, "Hangman Lunt says no one—not even Durrant—faced death with greater stoicism" (Anne T. Kent California Room, Marin County Free Library).

in an argument with his uncle, Wee Dick Chung, at the Globe Hotel in San Francisco's Chinatown.[2] He stormed out of the establishment and later returned with a handgun to finish the dispute, which he accomplished by shooting his uncle in the back. He turned himself in but offered no explanation for the murder other than that his uncle had "talked too much."

An interesting incident, which captures Tung's sense of fair play, occurred en route to the prison. The deputy in charge of Tung tipped the bottle one too many times and passed out. Tung did not seize on any one of numerous opportunities to slip away, instead remaining by the side of his captor. When they arrived at San Quentin, Tung helped the inebriated lawman to his feet.

*   *   *

At a weight of 133, Wee Tung would be the second-lightest man that Amos Lunt would hang in his tenure at San Quentin. Lunt had three reference points when figuring the drop: Lu Sing, who weighed 120, and Hans Hansen and Thomas St. Clair, both of whom weighed 135.

Name	Weight	Height	Drop
Lu Sing (#15372)	120	5'5¼"	6'0"
Hans Hansen	135	5'4½"	5'8"
Thomas St. Clair	135	5'4⅞"	5'9"
Wee Tung (#17589)	133	5'2¼"	5'9"

After making his calculations, Lunt settled on a drop of 5'9"— the 13-pound difference between Tung and Sing translated to a three-inch-shorter drop.[3]

* * *

Unlike the loquacious Durrant, whose collective statements from the death cell could fill an entire volume, the taciturn Tung had little to say. The night before his execution, he dismissed a few reporters with a string of expletives before refusing to say another word. When Chinese missionaries visited on the morning of his execution and attempted to provide spiritual guidance, he likewise cursed at them. Enraged, he rushed at the startled men, but the Death Watch managed to restrain him.

Frank Arbogast and John D. Jones, the Death Watch, told reporters that Tung had spoken only about a dozen words since he arrived, including a statement he made when he awoke on Friday morning. "Well," he muttered, "I will die like an American man."[4]

He even tried to shoo away Warden Hale when he came to read the death warrant at 10 a.m. on the morning of Friday, March 11. "Oh, go away!" Tung hissed. "Get out of here!"

"Do you understand English?" Hale asked, concerned that the prisoner might not comprehend the language of the order sending him to the scaffold.

"No," Tung responded, but he understood English perfectly.[5]

A select group of about two dozen men witnessed the Wee Tung execution. If any of them expected the type of drama that ensued at the Durrant hanging, they left disappointed. The execution took place in total silence. From the moment Tung entered the room at 10:30 a.m. until the drop, no one said a word. The condemned man made no final remarks, no last-minute assertion of innocence, no request to the hangman to tighten the noose.

"It was a strange scene that was enacted in the execution room," wrote the *Call* correspondent. "The entire performance did not occupy more than a minute's time." From the death march to the drop, the execution procedure took about 60 seconds.

Lunt worked the noose, paused to give Arbogast time to fit the black cap, and then raised his hand to signal the cord-cutters. The *Examiner*'s representative watched Wee Tung closely for any signs of his cool façade cracking. He saw none. "Tung faltered a moment, and with a smile slowly walked up the thirteen steps to the trap. He glanced at the crowd and shuffled his feet while Hangman Amos Lunt was adjusting the rope."[6]

Tung's fall stopped abruptly without recoil; the well-stretched rope had no play left in it. The contingent of physicians moved forward and checked Tung's respiration—only the second time since the Durrant execution they checked if the condemned took any breaths after the drop—and discovered that it had ceased the moment the noose had crushed his cervical vertebrae.

A rivulet of blood trickled from Tung's nose, so Dr. Lawlor inserted a cotton ball into his nostril to staunch the flow. His pulse lasted for 12½ minutes.

Tung's bravery in his final moments impressed his hangman. A *Chronicle* reporter wrote, "Hangman Lunt says no one—not even Durrant—faced death with greater stoicism."[7]

"It was a family affair and I killed her"

(Wednesday, April 6, 1898)

For convicted wife-slayer Benjamin L. Hill, Hangman's Friday came less than a month after Wee Tung's intrepid minute in the execution chamber.

Amos Lunt watched as Hill said his piece on the trap. Unlike

"I am getting my just punishment for a foul crime that I have committed and it is fair that I should suffer in this way," Ben Hill said just moments before he hanged (Anne T. Kent California Room, Marin County Free Library).

Theodore Durrant, Hill did not rehearse his speech, and unlike Durrant, he did not deny his guilt. "It is fitting I that I should tell you, gentlemen, before I am gone how I feel at this moment," Hill said as he stood on the trap moments before his hanging. He spoke with an eloquence and serenity that one witness likened to "the manner of a man standing on the platform for no other purpose than to deliver an exhortation."

> I am getting my just punishment for a foul crime that I have committed and it is fair that I should suffer in this way. Of course there is something horrifying to a man to know that death waits here for him, but what of that? I am going to meet my Maker and I am not afraid to go. For the last year and a half God has been my helper and has sustained me. It is the fact that I have found Christ and that my repentance is sincere that enables me to face this end with composure, and I think I am going to find peace. Good-by, my friends. When your time comes and eternity waits for you I hope you may feel as much with Him as I do now. Good-by.[1]

Hill smiled as Lunt raised his right hand.

* * *

Tung was one of Lunt's lightest victims; Hill, at 190 pounds, was one of his heaviest. Again, Lunt had two points of reference with which to calculate Hill's drop.

Name	Weight	Height	Drop
P.J. Sullivan (#15866)	215	5'7½"	5'0"
Fremont Smith (#15964)	220	5'9"	5'6"
Benjamin L. Hill (#17343)	190	5'7½"	5'2"

Yet Hill's physique complicated what would otherwise have been a simple calculation. Resigned to his fate, Hill ate heartily and exercised little during his ten-day tenure in the death cells, a possibly disastrous combination for the hangman. The surplus weight combined with the softening of muscles, particularly those in his neck, led to a worry that the rope would cut through Hill's neck muscles like a scythe through tall grass.

A *San Francisco Call* reporter described Hill as he waited in the death cells. "He sleeps well and eats everything that is placed before him. The approach of death has in no manner affected him in these respects, and he looks the picture of health. He weighs almost 200 pounds and his face is round and pleasing in its expression."[2]

This hanging weighed heavily on Lunt, whose error in calculating Smith's drop led to a bloody spectacle under the scaffold. For Hill, he evidently decided to err on the side of caution by settling on a drop just two inches longer than Sullivan's—fitting compensation for the 25-pound differential—but four inches shorter than Smith's.[3]

* * *

In some ways, Hill's story paralleled that of P.J. Sullivan, who hanged in 1894 for a remarkably similar crime. Like Sullivan, Hill had a contentious relationship with his wife Agnes. Heated arguments caused Hill to leave her and their son on occasion, but he always boomeranged after a brief sojourn away. On January 11, he returned to Oakland from Portland, Oregon, only to find that Agnes had changed addresses during his absence. He tracked her to a house on Eleventh Street near Kirkham and confronted her when she emerged. They walked together, squabbling, until they reached the intersection of Twelfth and Kirkham, where an ugly scene developed.

At some point during the fracas, Agnes slapped Benjamin. He pulled a handgun out of his pocket and squeezed off four shots. One missed and hit a nearby house, but the other three hit Agnes: one in the neck, one in the head, and one in the chest. She died before she hit the ground. The fatal bullets effectively orphaned their son, who went to live with Hill's brother and his wife.

While lodged in the local jail, Hill acted as if he did not have a care in the world. He showed absolutely no remorse for the murder. "At that time," Hill told a journalist, "I had no intention of killing her and as we walked up the street my mind was still free from murder. Just as we reached the corner she told me something; something that no man will know of his wife and let her live."

"And that was?" the reporter asked.

"That I will not tell. It was a family affair and I killed her."[4]

Hill made a play for temporary insanity on the basis that during the argument, Agnes admitted to infidelity, taunting him with scathing remarks about her liaisons. The jurors saw through Hill's transparent efforts to blame his victim and found him guilty of premeditated homicide, which meant the rope.

* * *

Reporters liked Benjamin Hill, who became a bit of a press darling. As a one-time professional baseball player, he was widely known throughout the Bay area. Unlike his death row peers, Hill was not a career criminal and did not worship at the area's shrines of substance use and prostitution.

Besides, as a *Call* writer pointed out in an exemplar of the prevailing belief in phrenology, "There is no appearance of the criminal in his features."[5] An *Examiner* writer described him as "a good-looking man—athletic, well-built, and thirty-seven years old."

Hill made the ideal death row inmate. He admitted his crime, appeared deeply repentant, treated his jailors with respect, did not resent his execution, and embraced his faith as his Hangman's Friday approached. He even organized a Bible class for his fellow condemned men and delivered sermons on Sundays. A natural orator with a compelling message for those awaiting their turn on the scaffold, Hill found an eager and enthusiastic audience for his preaching. When not passing on the Word, he spent his final hours reading from his Bible, on his knees in prayer with the Reverend Drahms, and writing letters to friends and family.

As with most men on death row, the waiting eroded Hill's verve and stoicism. To Frank Arbogast and John D. Jones, who had become fixtures as the Death Watch, Hill expressed his regret that he had tried an insanity plea, which only prolonged the inevitable; had he admitted his guilt at the outset of his trial and brushed aside appeals of his death sentence, he would have already met the hangman.

Still, he hoped for an 11th-hour reprieve, but when reporters brought word that Governor Budd refused to intervene, Hill remained steadfast in his desire to die a stoic.

"Well," Hill said upon hearing this crushing news, "I guess it cannot be helped. I will now trust in the Lord and He will take care of me."

Unlike Durrant, whose last word was literally "innocent," Hill admitted his guilt but still presented himself as a cuckold who only defended his honor. "It is true that I killed my wife," he told the cadre of newsmen in his death cell on the night before his execution. "The crime, although committed in a fit of passion, was justifiable. I never think of my wife or the crime—not even in my dreams."

Hill described one time when he received a visit from a ghostly Agnes in a death-house dream. "Once I dreamed of her before we were married. I thought she was young and pure and loved me. Then the scene changed and I imagined one of the events which led to my crime. I imaged that she was still alive, but unfaithful. I appealed to her and asked that she lead a better life."[6]

Then he penned a final statement.

I will sleep soundly to-night and when the morrow comes will be fully prepared for the worst. I do not fear the end, as I believe the Lord will be with me, and I will die like a brave man. My Maker has forgiven me and I now trust in him.

I will die to-morrow and cross the beautiful river. I only hope my sister-in-law will not worry, for the Lord will take care of me. I have made peace with all my enemies and I die knowing that the people of this State sympathize with me.[7]

* * *

When Hill finished dressing for his execution on the morning of Friday, April 6, he inserted a rose geranium into a buttonhole on his lapel. He pulled the sprig from a bunch of flowers that his son sent to him on Tuesday. He also placed a photograph of his family—Agnes, his son, and himself—in his breast pocket. Whatever the photograph and the sprig of flowers represented to Hill, he apparently planned to die with these tokens close to his heart.

"I say goodbye to you," Warden Hale said after presenting the death warrant. He extended his hand to one of the best prisoners to sit on Murderer's Row.

"I thank you, Warden, for your kindness to me. Goodbye."

When Dr. Lawlor offered Hill a bracer, he passed. "No, doctor," he said, "I am walking even now with God and will go like a Christian ought to."[8]

About 45 witnesses watched as the death march, with Reverend Drahms in the lead, entered the gallows room. One of the press corps in attendance described Hill at this moment in time. "He displayed no bravado, and his actions were gentle, instead of bold."[9]

After making a few brief remarks from the rail, Hill stepped back on the trap. He turned to Lunt and said, "I am ready." According to the *Chronicle*'s representative, Hill "gave Lunt a hearty handshake," although this would have been difficult with his hands pinned to his sides.[10]

As Lunt placed the noose, Hill leaned to the side and kissed the cheek of the Reverend Drahms, who held his hand. Captain George Reid of the Salvation Army, who had converted Hill to Christianity about a year earlier, held his other hand.

The deftness of the scaffold procedures impressed the *Examiner* correspondent. "Instantly the black cap went over the pleasant countenance," he wrote, "and with dexterity that told of experience, the guards pinioned the arms and feet. Not a full minute was occupied in the work."[11]

Drahms and Reid stepped back, Lunt gave the signal, and the guards severed the umbilical cords that kept Hill grounded on the trap.

Lunt's drop worked, snapping Hill's neck. The doctors detected three respirations, and his pulse lasted for about ten minutes, but he did not feel a thing.

27

"If I had been a good boy and obeyed my mother..."

(Friday, May 27, 1898)

The night before he died, Joseph Japhet Ebanks penned a lengthy statement to the press as well as a note to Dr. Lawlor.

> I will sleep soundly tonight at the foot the gallows, and when the morrow comes will be fully prepared for the worst. One cannot tell their feelings ahead of the time, but I hope and will try to die a brave man. I don't fear the end, as I believe the Lord will be with me. There is a place in heaven for me.
>
> I have heretofore been so often misquoted that I take this opportunity—the opportunity of a poor condemned convict—to state to the people of the outside world that I am innocent of the crime of murder. I can truthfully say that on the books of heaven not one stain of human blood appears against my name.

Ebanks went on to thank his jailors for their kindness and named Captain Edgar and his Death Watch, John Jones and Frank Arbogast, for treating him "like a brother rather than a condemned convict." He also thanked his spiritual advisors, Father Lagan and Sister Baptista, for their many kindnesses.[1]

These personages would represent the doomed man's only friends. During his time in San Quentin, only his attorneys visited him. Even the press lacked sympathy for the slayer, characterizing him as "grossly ignorant and physically a coward."[2]

The letter to Dr. Lawlor, which began "Mr. dear Sir," praised the Holy Ghost and "plenty of good whiskey."

> This is my personal experience. First, that there is nothing so good for the soul as the knowledge of the Holy Ghost. Second, there is nothing so good to brighten and keep in order the intellect of the person of man as plenty of good

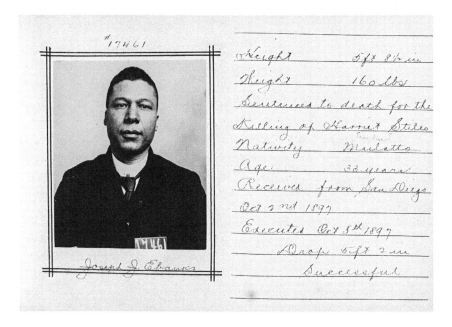

An *Examiner* reporter described Joseph Ebanks in the moments just before his death: "He spoke and acted in bewilderment, smiling now and then in a pitiable way. The horror of death had stunned him" (Anne T. Kent California Room, Marin County Free Library).

whiskey. But remember this must not be used to excess. For example, see the case of our Hon Admirable Dewey.

Yours very truly until tomorrow, J.J.E.

Perhaps Dr. Lawlor realized the value of whiskey to "brighten and keep in order the intellect"; perhaps, after sizing up Ebanks in his last hours of life, he recognized a man about to crack. Whatever the justification, the prison physician administered more than one bracer on the morning of Wednesday, April 27, 1898.

*   *   *

By the time Hangman's Friday arrived for Joseph J. Ebanks, Amos Lunt had hanged 18 men, which gave him a variety of precedents for figuring an appropriate drop. With regard to anatomy, Ebanks had two relevant predecessors on the scaffold—William Fredericks and Chung Sing, both of whom tipped the scales at about the same weight. Fredericks, at an identical weight and less than an inch taller, appeared to be the best model on which to calculate the drop for Ebanks. Since Fredericks plunged 5'6", a similar drop would appear apropos for Ebanks.

Name	Weight	Height	Drop
W.M. Fredericks (#15960)	160	5'9"	5'6"
Chung Sing (#17107)	156	5'6¼"	5'6"
Benjamin I. Hill (#17343)	190	5'7½"	5'2"
Joseph J. Ebanks (#17461)	160	5'8⅛"	5'2"

Instead, Lunt gave Ebanks the same 5'2" drop he gave to Benjamin Hill, who outweighed Ebanks by 30 pounds.[3] This shorter drop virtually eliminated the concern of an accidental decapitation but instead raised the specter of death by asphyxiation if the noose failed to dislocate the cervical vertebrae.

Lunt's reasons for giving such a short drop to Ebanks escaped the official records, but the relatively scant press coverage provides a clue. "Hangman Amos Lunt has tested the rope and, as Ebanks is a large man," noted a *Chronicle* reporter, "he will be given a very short drop."[4]

Ebanks' height and weight, as documented in the San Quentin Execution Book, do not suggest a particularly "large man" for the hangman's purposes. It is likely that Ebanks' weight, recorded at 160, ballooned during his time in the death cells. Writing on the eve of Hangman's Friday, an *Examiner* reporter described the condemned man as "stout and healthy. Prison life seems to agree with him, and he will tip the scales at 200 pounds."[5]

The sarcastic jibe, "prison life seems to agree with him," indicates that Ebanks ate well in the weeks leading up to his execution. If the prison clerk did not err when recording Ebanks' weight at 160, then he ate well enough to gain 40 pounds. For the hangman's purposes, this put his weight on par with that of Benjamin Hill's, which would explain the relatively short drop.

If a rapid weight gain occurred in tandem with a lack of exercise, the softening of his neck musculature may have led to a fear that a longer drop might pull Ebanks' head off his shoulders.

*   *   *

The crime that Ebanks said he did not perpetrate occurred on September 10, 1895, on a beach about 15 miles north of Oceanside in San Diego County. Leroy and Harriet Stiles, joined by Harriet's 85-year-old father John Borden, were enjoying a vacation camping out on the beach. On the morning of September 10, Stiles and Borden were fishing about a mile-and-a-half away when they noticed a figure approaching their campsite. Worrying about Harriet's safety, Borden returned to the tent while Stiles gathered up their fishing gear.

When Stiles returned to the tent, he found his wife and her father shot to death.[6]

About a month later, authorities arrested Ebanks. Despite his avowed innocence, several pieces of evidence appeared to tie him to the crime scene. Just two days before the murders, he stole a pair of .45 caliber handguns and a cartridge belt. Bullets from the belt matched those taken from the bodies of the victims. With evidence like that, prosecutors had little trouble convincing a jury, who sent Ebanks to the gallows.

Ebanks, whose mother, wife, and three children lived in the "West Indies," had no real friends in America and little money. Nevertheless, his lawyer managed to argue his case all the way to the United States Supreme Court in what the press characterized as "one of the most stubborn legal fights in the history of the State." The result was an unfortunate and agonizing series of delays that landed Ebanks in the same place he started: the San Quentin death cells. Despite the best efforts of his lawyer, Joseph Ebanks suffered the indignity of listening to the courts sentence him to death on four separate occasions.

When Ebanks first arrived at San Quentin, he did his best imitation of an insane inmate. When it became evident that his ruse had fooled no one, especially Warden Hale, and the courts would not reverse his death penalty, Ebanks dropped the act and joined fellow murderer Benjamin Hill's Bible class.

After Hill died on the scaffold, Ebanks warmed up to Father Lagan and the Sisters of Charity. On the Wednesday before his execution, he converted to the Catholic faith. Father Lagan baptized him and two days later administered the last sacraments.

Ebanks devoted most of his last night to reading the Bible while holding a crucifix and rocking in a wicker chair. His final comments, like those of many who went before him, reflected two common themes: he was innocent but would die a brave man. While he stopped short of anything resembling a confession, he did remark that he deserved his fate for not listening to "mother."

"If I had been a good boy and obeyed my mother," he said, "and remembered the lessons that I learned at her knee I would not have to die tomorrow."[7] One of the lessons, he hinted, was to mind his own business.

* * *

Ebanks' nerves started to fail him as the clock ticked away his final minutes. Sensing an imminent collapse, Dr. Lawlor gave the condemned man a few shots of whiskey so he could stand his ground on the scaffold.

As the ten o'clock hour approached, Ebanks stood on the verge of collapse, his poise glued together with bracers of whiskey. An *Examiner* reporter described him as "overcome by a stupor. He spoke and acted in bewilderment, smiling now and then in a pitiable way. The horror of death had stunned him."[8]

At 10:30 a.m., the metal door hinges groaned, and the death march entered the room. About 35 witnesses watched as Joseph Ebanks shuffled toward the gallows. On the scaffold, he attempted to make a final speech in which he planned to proclaim his innocence, but he only managed to stammer, "I cannot talk."

Recognizing the need to move through the final paces as quickly as possible, Amos Lunt slid the noose over Ebanks' head. As he adjusted the knot, Ebanks muttered, "Goodbye."

The drop snapped his neck, and his pulse finally died ten minutes and 30 seconds after the drop.

Once again, the hangman of San Quentin had engineered a painless hanging.

28

The Hunchback of San Quentin

(Friday, October 14, 1898)

By all accounts, the one execution that bothered Lunt more than any other was the hanging of John Miller on Friday, October 14, 1898. The newspapers dubbed it "the most ghastly execution ever witnessed in the State penitentiary."[1]

One witness likened the spectacle to the botched hanging of Nathan B. Sutton, when Sheriff (and later Warden) Hale gave the condemned man eight feet of rope. That revolting scene turned Hale away from hanging and would eventually lead to his appointment of Lunt as Lord High Executioner of San Quentin.

"Not since the execution of Nat. B. Sutton in the Alameda county jail-yard nearly ten years ago," wrote the *Examiner*'s man on the scene, "has there been in California a legal expiation so bathed in blood and so like the awful sights which come to unholy dreams."[2]

* * *

The subject of Amos Lunt's 19th hanging attempted to shoot the love of his life on the streets of San Francisco on November 18, 1896. The quasi-love story starred Miller and a widow named Nellie Ryan. The 41-year-old carpenter employed Ryan as a domestic. During their time together, he developed a deep crush on her. When she spurned his advances, Miller threatened to kill her. She called the police, filed a complaint against Miller for disturbing the peace, and moved out of the house.

Miller cooked up a ruse to see Nellie Ryan again. He went to the home of a mutual friend named Mrs. Burns, on Clementina Street, and asked her to send for Ryan on the pretext that he had money and real estate in Texas that he wished to give her. He also asked Burns to tell Ryan that he would not be present.

When Nellie Ryan arrived and realized that Miller was in the house,

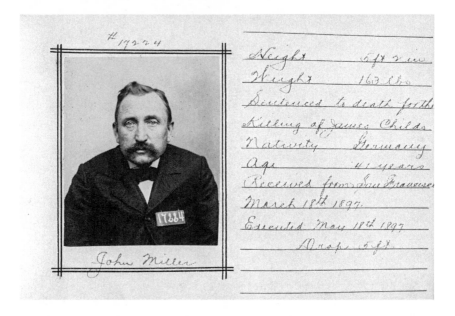

John Miller's physical deformity, evident in his mug shot, led to a miscalculation that ended in his near decapitation. One newspaper reporter called it "the most ghastly execution ever witnessed in the State penitentiary" (Anne T. Kent California Room, Marin County Free Library).

she ran out the front door. Miller pulled a revolver and ran after her, firing the pistol as he chased her down the street.

The terrified widow ran a few yards down the street and noticed a man standing at the top of the steps leading into a house. James F. Childs let Ryan through the front door and waited outside as Miller approached. When Miller tried to elbow his way past, Childs blocked him. Miller pointed his gun at Childs' head and shot him at point blank range. Childs crumpled to the pavement and rolled down the steps.

Miller fired a second time at Childs' inert body but missed. Then he pressed the barrel of the revolver against his own temple and squeezed the trigger. Unfortunately for Miller, he had fired the rest of his six rounds as he chased Ryan down Clementina.

He would not cheat the hangman.[3]

* * *

After a five-month reprieve from executions, Amos Lunt and his crew would prepare to hang two men within one week in October. As the first Hangman's Friday of October 14 approached, Lunt faced a vexing problem in calculating a drop for John Miller.

Name	Weight	Height	Drop
P. -J. Sullivan (#15866)	215	5'7½"	5'0"
W.M. Fredericks (#15960)	160	5'9"	5'6"
Benjamin I. Hill (#17343)	190	5'7½"	5'2"
Joseph J. Ebanks (#17461)	160 (200)	5'8⅛"	5'2"
John Miller (#17224)	163 (185–200)	5'2"	5'0"

San Quentin's Execution Book put John Miller's weight at 163 pounds, but like Joseph Ebanks, he apparently gained a significant amount of weight behind bars.[4] Contemporary news reports place him at a body-weight of 185–200, which if accurate, indicated that the 5'2" Miller carried a surplus of fat.[5]

Miller's short height combined with his excess body weight presented a new challenge for Lunt, who had hanged three men with a similar body weight but not body type. A physical abnormality further complicated the determination of the drop. Lunt once told a reporter that he preferred slender necks, but Miller did not have a neck at all. Referred to as a "hunchback," Miller's head appeared to rest flat on his shoulders. Inevitably, the papers linked Miller to Victor Hugo's Hunchback of Notre Dame. One reporter described him as "distorted as Quasimodo" and "fit for deeds of the realms of gloom."[6]

Hanging San Quentin's Quasimodo would be no mean feat for Amos Lunt, who faced the daunting task of positioning the noose knot.

"It had been expected by prison officials that Miller's neck would be slightly cut by the rope," noted a *Chronicle* reporter. "For several years he had had a stiff, crooked neck, in addition to his deformed back, and the muscles of the neck had become soft and tender from want of use. They had been rendered more tender by nearly two years of jail life, and this, added to Miller's weight of 185 pounds, made the matter of his execution a delicate problem to handle."[7]

The Execution Book records Miller's drop at 5'0", but contemporary news articles indicate that Lunt initially calculated a drop of six feet, the same drop he gave to Lu Sing, who weighed over 40 pounds less. He apparently believed that the added force would be needed to break Miller's non-existent neck.

Dr. Lawlor objected to Lunt's drop and suggested a reduction. "He had noted the weight and the flabbiness of Miller, and on his advice the length of the hangman's rope had been shortened, first six inches and then twelve, so as to decrease the 'drop' from six to five feet. Dr. Lawlor had feared that Miller's weight and soft condition would result in the severing of his head."[8]

The prison physician hoped that Miller's abnormality would help avert an absolute disaster. Miller's head tilted to the right, which suggested that the left side was tougher and more muscled. Since the noose knot would be positioned below the left ear and the rope yanked to the right at the bottom of the drop, Dr. Lawlor reasoned, if the rope cut into Miller's flesh at all, it would be on the side better suited to withstand a slight cut.

* * *

In a final statement to the world, which he inked on the night of Thursday, October 13, John Miller channeled Joseph Ebanks.

> I have little to say except that I was not properly defended. Regarding the end, I would say that now, with only fifteen hours to live, I believe that I will die like a brave man. I will walk up the stairs leading to the scaffold alone. I don't want to have a lot of humbugs along.
>
> Last, but not least, I wish to state that the jury system in San Francisco is corrupt. Thugs, ex-convicts and hired assassins composed my jury.[9]

By the morning of his execution, however, Miller had changed his tune. He expressed his regret for the murder to the Sisters of Charity, and welcomed Father Lagan to join him for his final moments on the scaffold.

Miller appeared to have kept his promise to die like a stoic. "Sharp at 10:30 o'clock the death procession began—that march to the scaffold during which all a murderer's misdeeds are supposed to haunt him, hissing in his ears, clutching at his conscience. Miller seemed unmoved ... there was not stumbling of his feet on the scaffold steps, no shuffling on the drop, no apparent shaking of the knees," recalled one witness.[10]

After he climbed the 13 steps, however, his demeanor changed. Miller's knees shook and his hands trembled as Amos Lunt affixed the noose. Unable to speak, he mouthed a "goodbye" to Father Lagan just before Captain Jamieson dropped the black cap.

"Grim old Amos Lunt, the hangman," wrote the *Examiner*'s witness, "fiddled some with the noose, because of the misshapen shoulders of the doomed."[11]

About 35 spectators gathered around the base of the scaffold to watch the hunchback hang. Unfortunately, they pressed forward in order to hear every word uttered from above them.

Miller's neck snapped at the bottom of the drop, but Dr. Lawlor had overestimated the development of the muscles on the right side. The noose ripped through the entire musculature, leaving the body dangling by a few sinews. A crimson rivulet ran down Miller's shirt and formed pools on the floor. The crowd collectively moved back, revolted by the sight of blood pouring from the black mask.

Lawlor had apparently anticipated this possibility and had a quantity of cotton batting at hand. He tried to staunch the flow of blood by stuffing the cotton into the gaping hole in Miller's neck, while a guard threw one blanket over the body and a second one over the mass of blood and clots on the floor below the body.

All three major Bay Area newspapers described, in explicit detail, what happened when Miller dropped through the trap. The *Examiner*'s representative offered the most graphic description. "Then it was found that the rope had cut through the right side of the neck to the spinal column, that this column was broken, and that but for a few of the neck muscles and tendons on the left side of the head would have been completely severed."[12]

The writer then identified the problem. "Had not the 'drop' been shortened, or had the murderer been slightly heavier, there would have been a decapitation." Another writer was more specific after discussing the debacle with Dr. Lawlor. Had the rope been just two inches longer, or Miller three pounds heavier, the noose would have separated his head from his body.[13] This discussion about drop represented both a criticism of Amos Lunt, who calculated a six-foot drop, and a compliment to the prison physician, who urged him to reduce it.

The *Evening Sentinel* writer praised Lunt's work despite the gaffe. "It is a wonder that his head was not pulled off, though Hangman Amos Lunt gave him but a five foot drop," he wrote. "His physical condition had been carefully considered and the death of the murderer without a struggle well attests the efficiency of Warden Hale and Hangman Lunt in such proceedings." Even as late as October 1898, when the *Sentinel* published this article, memories of lynch mobs and frontier justice—before the advent of a state executioner—were still vivid. Memories of amateurish proceedings during which untrained hands hanged men from tall trees with short ropes and no drop.

Although Miller died in a blood-drenched fiasco, he never felt a thing. As the *Evening Sentinel* pointed out, "The execution, from the hangman's point of view, was a success in every particular, and the poor murderer died almost instantly."[14] Few of the spectators who witnessed the near-decapitation, including the hangman, considered the hanging a success.

Fallout from the grisly spectacle reached across the state. Critics of the scaffold used Miller's hanging as an argument for replacing what they viewed as an outmoded punishment with the electric chair.

For Amos Lunt, what occurred under the scaffold that morning would have life-altering consequences. The *Examiner* writer called him "grim old Amos Lunt"; the strain of five years on the scaffold had become evident in his appearance and demeanor.

Perhaps no one was more unnerved than George W. Clark, who was in the death cells counting down the days before he too mounted the scaffold. Clark could not see the hanging but heard the chorus of gasps and could probably tell what had happened from the voices he overheard.

"George W. Clark, the St. Helena fratricide," noted a reporter, "is to be hanged from the same scaffold on Friday next. He heard the thud of the trap today, and turned to his Bible to steady his shaken nerves."[15]

The Final Noose

(Friday, October 21, 1898)

Eager to erase the stain of the Miller mess, Warden Hale had the scaffold painted to cover up John Miller's blood spatter. Meanwhile, Lunt went to work preparing for the hanging of George Willard Clark, which would take place on Friday, October 21.

* * *

George Clark, the "St. Helena Fratricide," was Amos Lunt's 20th and final victim (Anne T. Kent California Room, Marin County Free Library).

Clark's hanging would be the falling action in a drama that climaxed with the murder of his brother, which led to the epithet "The St. Helena Fratricide." *The Examiner* described the crime as "one of fiendish deliberation … fraught with a volume of sensational features." If the Clark case were a novel, it would be a real page-turner.

The tragedy began when Clark broke the ninth commandment, "Thou shalt not covet thy neighbor's wife." His neighbor's wife, in this case, was Lavina, married to his older brother William.

William A. Clark and Lavina Kneff grew up on neighboring farms in Clay County, Illinois. Geographical proximity and similar hardships of tilling the land in pioneer Illinois created a closeness between the Clark and Kneff families.[1]

In 1874, 22-year-old Lavina taught school in Clay County and boarded with the Clark family. Thirteen-year-old George Clark, whom Lavina knew since she first met him six weeks after his birth, was one of her students. At the same time that a bond formed between Lavina and the oldest Clark child William, his little brother George developed a crush on his teacher.

In December 1876, William, who was two years younger than his 25-year-old bride, wed Lavina. Now fifteen years old, George may have had already developed feelings for his sister-in-law by that time, feelings that intensified when he moved into William's farmhouse in 1883.[2] He would live with them on and off over the next four years.

According to the rendition that Lavina later recited in court, a 14-year-long affair de coeur began in 1884 between the then 23-year-old George Clark and his 32-year-old former teacher.[3] Certain comments she made suggest that the lovers carried on with the full knowledge and consent of William. "My husband knew of my acts here," Lavina said, "but said nothing. The children became aware of the dual life I was leading of late years. My husband never upbraided me because of the manner of life I was leading."

In April 1887, William Clark left for California, where he took a job with the railroad and began preparing a home for his family. Four months later, Lavina and four of their seven children, escorted by George, made the journey west. According to George, he and not William had fathered the youngest child, Georgie, who was born in 1893.

"I was intimate with George Clark for a year of two prior to my removal to California," Lavina explained during Clark's 1898 preliminary hearing. "These relations continued for several years in California, even though Lavina and William still lived together as husband and wife.

Almost as soon as they became intimate, George began to pressure Lavina about marriage and probably began thinking about removing the one obstacle he saw between the illicit couple and wedded bliss. "Probably he would say something to me every two or three months about liking to have me as his wife," she explained. "He would ask me if I would be his wife if things were so we could. I said yes. I would tell him not to talk about this thing, because it was not right. My husband's name was hardly ever mentioned; hardly anything said about him. He would say if Will was out of the way would I marry him."

Around the time of Georgie's birth, Lavina's willingness to continue the affair came to an end. The affair, however, did not.

"My relations with George Clark continued up to five or six years ago," Lavina said. "Yes, up to five or six years ago willingly on my part. There has been at times relations between myself and George W. Clark during the past six or seven years. I have not been a willing party to these relations during the past six or seven years."

In court, Lavina represented this part of her relationship with Clark as non-consensual, although she did not specify what she meant when she said she had not "been a willing party to these relations."

Undaunted, George continued to press for marriage, but in his mind, William still represented the sole obstacle in his way. Early on the morning of January 20, 1898, he walked up to William as he stood on his front porch and shot him in the head. Sheriff's deputies arrested both George and Lavina, whom they eyed as a possible accessory.

To the delight of Napa County Sheriff George S. MacKenzie, who arrested Clark, and William Randolph Hearst, who owned the newspaper, *Examiner* reporter John F. Connors managed to pry a full confession from the fratricide.

During an hour-long conversation with Connors, later repeated to the County D.A., Sheriff MacKenzie, and a stenographer, George Clark described his long-standing intimacy with Lavina Clark, his paternity of Georgie, and several attempts to poison his brother with strychnine so he could marry his brother's widow. Clark, however, insisted that Lavina had nothing to do with the plot.

Connors described the object of Clark's obsession: "It is the fat, full face of the country-bred woman of German origin (and to this Mrs. Clark confesses) and inferior refinement. Women of this type are seldom beautiful at forty-six. But there is a delicacy of profile; a certain weak sweetness still about the eyes, the nose and the lips of the woman that pleads for the faded prettiness of her youth. She has smooth, fine, sandy hair and the thin, easily scarred and roughened skin that goes with it, and the flaxen lashes and brows that weaken light eyes, and the peculiar, drawling, plaintiff voice that rises to the fret and sinks to whine, and belongs to this kind of woman and speaks out of her, of that feminine dependence, which to some men is so dear."⁴ "The country-bred woman of German origin" found herself on the hot seat during Clark's preliminary hearing, which played to a standing-room-only audience.

To the delight of the audience, Lavina had no trouble kissing-and-telling, although the press did have a problem reporting about it.

Under brutal cross-examination, the widow described an incriminating conversation that took place on their front porch the day before her husband's murder. "I said I was accused of that poison business and I said I knew I was innocent before God. He [George] said he was accused and it made him feel bad because he was accused by the folks at home. I said 'George, This seems to worry you. I would never marry you if such a thing happened, because I would prosecute such a man.' He says, 'Do you think I could do such a thing?' I said, 'Now, George, I do not think you could be so wicked at heart.'"⁵

District Attorney Theodore Bell believed Lavina had nothing to do with George Clark's machinations, and she managed to sidestep criminal charges. George would not be as lucky. After a brief trial and a quick conviction, he received a date with Amos Lunt.

*   *   *

The biodynamics of Clark's hanging presented a new challenge. A tall man with a pencil-thin frame, he stood 5'8" but weighed only 127 pounds, making him the second-lightest man hanged at San Quentin to date behind Lunt's first subject, Lu Sing.

Name	Weight	Height	Drop
Lu Sing (#15372)	120	5'5¼"	6'0"
Hans Hansen	135	5'4½"	5'8"
Thomas St. Clair	135	5'4⅞"	5'9"
Wee Tung (#17589)	133	5'2¼"	5'9"
Benjamin I. Hill (#17343)	190	5'7½"	5'2"
Joseph J. Ebanks (#17461)	160 (185–200)	5'8⅛"	5'2"
George W. Clark (#17687)	127	5'8"	5'3"

Reviewing the drops for men of a similar build, an anomaly becomes evident: Lunt gave Clark a very short drop of 5'3", more suitable for a much heavier man.⁶ Both Benjamin Hill and Joseph Ebanks, both of whom weighed around 200, dropped just an inch less.

The reason for such a relatively short drop was an idiosyncrasy in George Clark's anatomy. Unlike other subjects of similar weight—Sing,

Hansen, St. Clair, and Tung—Clark had a very long, slender neck. This stork-like feature is evident in both his prison mug shots and newspaper sketches of Clark in the death cells. Evidently, Lunt felt that it would not take any more rope to do the trick. "At the time of his execution," noted a *Chronicle* reporter familiar with the case, "Clark weighed only 135 pounds, yet he was given only a five-foot drop on account of his very slender neck."[7]

This short drop offered a fringe benefit for the hoary old hangman. Still reeling from Miller's near-decapitation less than a week earlier, Lunt decided to err on the side of caution and shorten Clark's rope. Such a short drop for such a slight customer virtually eliminated the possibility of a Miller-like debacle, but it created the possibility of an even more ominous outcome: if the noose did not dislocate Clark's neck, he could die a slow death by strangulation, which had yet to happen in San Quentin.

* * *

"I am a new man now," Clark declared the night before he met the hangman. "All my sins have been blotted out, and I will go into Heaven with a clean record. I wish to say that I myself plotted, planned and executed the murder for which I will pay the penalty. A shadow of suspicion has rested on Lavina Clark, my brother's widow. I now positively state that she was not implicated in the crime. I alone am guilty."[8]

On the eve of his execution, Clark slept like a baby, prompting his Death Watch—Frank Arbogast and John Jones—to note his remarkable serenity.[9]

* * *

Unlike Ebanks and Hill, Clark was popular, and requests to witness the final act in the tawdry drama flooded in to Warden Hale's office. Hale issued 40 black-bordered admittance tickets, and on the morning of Friday, October 21, the attendees gathered around the scaffold. According to the *Call*, about 75 people witnessed Clark's execution.[10]

Clark, at the center of a rood formed by the death procession, entered the room at 10:30 a.m. His knees did not wobble, but once he was on the trap, the gravity of the moment took hold of him, and he began to tremble. In a futile attempt to steady his nerves, Clark repeated the phrase "Bless the Lord" as Lunt tightened the straps and then looped the noose around his neck.

As Lunt began to drop the black cap, Clark asked, in a horse-whisper, if he could say a few parting words. Lunt removed the noose, but the condemned man could not bring himself to speak. He managed to mutter, "I am going home to glory." These were his last words.[11]

Recognizing a potential collapse, Lunt hastened to replace the noose, fitted the cap, and signaled the drop. Clark plunged into open space.

"His neck was broken by the fall," an eyewitness later wrote, "and the skin was slightly torn by the rope, allowing a little blood to trickle down his throat from under the black cap."[12]

After nine minutes, his pulse ceased. He left the building feet first in a black coffin headed to the prison cemetery.

George Willard Clark was the 20th man hanged by Amos Lunt. He would also be his last.

30

The End of the Line

(January 23–October 7, 1899)

Weary and perhaps already plagued by the dark figures who visited at night, Amos Lunt requesting a two-day leave for the second-to-last weekend in January. Warden Hale, who had no reason to question his hangman, signed off on the request with the understanding that Lunt would return to his prison duties on Monday, January 23. What Lunt did during that short furlough remains unclear, preserved only as scattered fragments in brief newspaper reports. According to some accounts, Lunt won $1,000 in a Louisiana Lottery and decided to resign his position.[1] According to others, he went on a weekend bender and painted San Francisco red.

Whatever the case, Monday, January 23, 1899, came and went without the familiar figure on the wall by the watchtower. When Lunt returned to duty on Tuesday morning, Hale dismissed him, in the words of one newspaperman, "because the Warden decided that he was not in a fit condition for duty."[2] Lunt's eight-year career at San Quentin, a tenure that included the hanging of 20 men, thus ignominiously came to close over less than 24 hours of absence without leave.

On the surface, it seems illogical that Hale, who stood by his hangman during the "red hot iron" controversy, would fire Lunt for simply missing a shift, especially given Lunt's skill in conducting executions. In all likelihood, Hale had mixed motives for the dismissal. The "not in a fit condition for duty" comment hints that Lunt may have tipped the bottle over his weekend in the city and returned to the prison with the smell of whiskey on his breath. Hale ran a tight ship, but at the same time, he needed Lunt as a hangman, so he may have recognized something in Lunt's visage that convinced him he was on the verge of collapse.

Amos Lunt had become a magnet for reporters, who recognized a headline in his dismissal. The *Examiner*'s editors ran the least inflammatory headline: "AMOS LUNT, FORMER HANGMAN AT SAN QUENTIN."

The *Los Angeles Record*'s editors made a sarcastic comment on the dismissal with the headline "NOTED HANGMAN'S RETIREMENT."

The *Call*'s editors dispensed with a headline story and instead ran a single, sympathetic blurb that may have best reflected Amos Lunt's attitude toward his own firing: "Hangman Lunt may console himself with the thought that while he has lost his job, it was not a particularly pleasant job, anyhow."[3]

Once news of Lunt's "retirement" hit the streets, applications to take his place on the scaffold poured into Hale's office. Most came from ne'er-do-wells who knew nothing about the dynamics of executions behind the brick and mortar of San Quentin's death factory. Hale chose Frank Arbogast, a long-time Death Watch guard and a fixture at executions.[4]

Another Hangman's Friday would not arrive at San Quentin until late April, and Frank Arbogast would end up tying the noose.

*   *   *

Two months after his dismissal, Amos Lunt briefly re-entered the stage as San Quentin's hangman when he testified at the Brandes murder trial in March. William A. Brandes stood accused of strangling his young daughter, Lillian, and then tying her to a bedpost in an attempt to create the appearance that the girl had hanged herself with an apron.

The noose and the marks it had created on Lillian's neck became the key element at Brandes' trial, which consumed most of March. To the delight of the jurors and press alike, who had cloyed on seemingly endless medical testimony from contentious physicians, defense attorney J.E. Bennett called the state's preeminent noose-tier to the stand as an expert witness for the defense.

Bennett hoped that the testimony of Lunt and a guard named D.S. Brown, who had helped lower the bodies of three men into their coffins, would show the difference in the physical effects of a judicial hanging and a suicidal hanging. If Bennett could establish that men hanged on San Quentin's gallows displayed certain characteristic rope marks, and that these marks did not appear on Lillian Brandes' neck, then the jury would conclude that girl had committed suicide.

When Amos Lunt strode to the witness box, the color drained from William Brandes' face. "That his sudden appearance in court had a harrowing effect upon the accused," wrote a *Call* reporter, "was evidenced by the extreme pallor of Brandes. Once only did the accused murderer glance at the ex-hangman during his narrative."

"Have you observed whether there is blood on the ropes after hanging murderers?" Bennett asked.

Deputy Chief District Attorney Harry Melvin objected to Bennett's question and was allowed to probe Lunt's expertise on the aftermath of his hangings. "Before dropping the subject you put on a black cap, don't you?" he asked.

Lunt nodded but explained that the cap does not cover the subject's neck. "You can see the bare neck where the rope is."

"Do you remain with the body after the execution," Melvin asked.

"Oh, no," Lunt explained, "the only object I'm there for is to get them on to the trap. That done, I've nothing more to do. The doctors take charge."

Satisfied with Lunt's responses, Melvin sat down, and Bennett resumed with this line of questions. Lunt explained that only twice had he ever seen blood on the rope, and both times occurred when an overly long drop nearly decapitated the subject (Fremont Smith in 1895 and John Miller in 1898).

"With the usual drop and ordinary abrasions on the neck would you expect to find blood on the rope?" Bennett asked.

> In all my experience, I have never expected or found blood excepting in the two cases mentioned. One was a man named [Fremont] Smith, who weighed about 300 pounds. He was dropped too far and the rope nearly tore his head off. The other was a hunchback [John Miller] who had a stiff neck. Of course the rope was bloody after the hanging in each of these cases.
>
> I always examine the ropes carefully before and after an execution. I take the rope down from over the beam and carefully inspect it. When I get through and replace the rope I don't expect anyone to go there till I go up with the man. My ambition and anxiety is to have everything right, and that when the time comes there will be no slip.
>
> When the man comes all I have to do is to take the noose, place it firmly on his neck and throw up my right hand and that settles it.

Brandes, who apparently worried that at the end of his trial, the court would give him a date with the hangman, briefly glanced at Lunt and then, as the *Call* reporter noted, "as quickly glanced at the floor again, with an apparent shudder."

"In the case of Smith," Lunt explained, "I did not arrange the drop. He weighed about 300 pounds and was dropped five feet six. Four feet eight would have been about right."[5]

Guard D.S. Brown followed Lunt to the stand. Where Lunt's job ended, Brown's began. After three executions, including that of Theodore Durrant, Brown took charge of the bodies immediately after the hanging, which gave him a unique insight into the physical aftermath of the rope.

"When the rope is removed," Brown explained, "I usually found it leaves a reddish mark on the neck. In one particular case, four hours after the execution, the mark assumed a still redder color at the edges, with purple in the center, and finally it becomes a copper color. I also examined the ropes after hanging and never found on them any blood."

"In the latter case [Durrant] and in that of Harvey Allender," Brown testified to an audience of spellbound court-goers,

> I found abrasions on the side of the neck opposite to that on which the knot was fastened. On Durrant's neck there was an abrasion on the right side, but no blood, and no abrasion on the left side. The knot is usually under the left ear.
>
> The mark on Durrant's neck first assumed a red color, then grew darker, and when the body was removed the mark was quite purple. The mark is usually more distinct on the sides of the neck than in front. Durrant's eyes protruded and on his mouth appeared blood-tinted mucus. Two hours after death Durrant's face had the appearance of a man in sleep. He had not moved a muscle when the trap dropped and he fell dead, like a log.
>
> Allender was a smaller man, and after he dropped he drew up his shoulders and heaved his chest. He dropped over six feet. There was no abrasion about the neck or froth at the mouth. In both cases the features at first were horribly distorted. In some cases the eyes do not bulge or protrude.[6]

Lillian Brandes' eyes did not bulge, which the defense attorney hoped the jury would see as physical evidence of a suicide.

Recalled to the stand, Deputy Chief District Attorney Melvin's cross-examination of Lunt led to an interesting and provocative episode.

"How thick is the rope used at executions?" Melvin asked.

"Well," Lunt responded, "at first it is about an inch in diameter, but when it is ready for the victim it is about seven-eighths of an inch. You see, we stretch and harden it before we attach it to the gallows. A thin neck is the easiest to break by hanging. It is hard to hang a man with a short, fat neck and make a neat job of it."

"How do you gauge the distance of the drop?"

"Well, it all depends on the height of the victim." Lunt eyed the Assistant District Attorney. "Now, you are a big man, six feet in height and weigh over 200 pounds. If I was hanging you I would give you about a five-foot-eight drop."

According to the *Examiner*'s reporter, "everyone laughed except Brandes."

The *Examiner*'s man in court, however, did not find the incident amusing, and prefaced his description of the scene with a caustic comment. "He [Lunt] apparently takes a hanging as a joke."[7]

The reporter considered Lunt's sizing-up of Melvin as an overly glib and flippant sentiment considering the gravity of the situation and the seriousness of the hangman's official position, but he did not understand his subject. After seven years on the job, measuring and re-measuring the rope for "victims"—many of whom never made it to the scaffold—Lunt had become accustomed to analyzing men in this manner.

When author Charles Duff interviewed the legendary English hangman John Ellis, he experienced the same eerie sensation as Melvin. Ellis, who hanged over 20 "victims" in over two decades as England's Lord High Executioner, took mental measurements of his interviewer. "Whenever he spoke of hanging," Duff wrote in *A Handbook on Hanging*, "he would run his tongue round his lower lip as if he could taste the flavor of it, and once he paused to look me up and down as if mentally taking my weight and measure for a drop."[8]

Reporters reveled in the subplot of Lunt's testimony in the Brandes case, and editors were quick to capitalize on the story with provocative headlines.

Oakland Tribune: "State Hangman Gives Expert Evidence at the Trial."

San Francisco Call: "Accused Murderer Brandes Listens to Grewsome [*sic*] Testimony Given by Amos Lunt."

San Francisco Examiner: "BRANDES FACES THE HANGMAN. Some Expert Opinions on the Art of Breaking Necks."[9]

Despite Amos Lunt's headline-producing turn in the witness box, the jury remained convinced that William Brandes had beaten and strangled his little girl and then staged the apron-suicide. Convicted of second-degree murder after a trial that lasted over 50 days, he did manage to avoid the hangman when he received a life sentence in San Quentin instead. Two of the jurors reportedly voted for hanging.[10] Etta Brandes, also charged with murder, avoided time when the District Attorney dismissed the charges due to a lack of evidence.[11]

Such publicity would dog Amos Lunt. Fifty-two years old and unemployed, every time he mentioned his name, people invariably linked him with his former role at the state prison. "Hangman" had become a life sentence.

* * *

Following the dismissal, work for the former hangman was spotty and periodic. He sometimes aided local law enforcement when they needed an extra hand. In May, he took part in a raid led by Marin County Sheriff William Taylor.

Under Taylor's direction, Amos Lunt led a squad of detectives on a raid of two Sausalito pool halls that had become headquarters for illegal bookmaking operations. The contingent of lawmen waited for an opportune moment to strike and decided on Saturday, May 27, 1899, when a throng of men crowded into the halls to hear the returns of three races at the Brooklyn Track.

With handfuls of "John Doe" warrants, Lunt and company burst into a swarm of men as they clustered around a "caller" who relayed race results by reading from the telegraph. After gathering evidence in the form of betting tickets, they rounded up the proprietors, marched them to the depot, where they boarded a train to San Rafael, and escorted them into Justice Court.[12]

For Lunt, who stood guard over the most dangerous criminals in the state and who stood toe-to-toe with the condemned on the scaffold, the arrest of relatively minor offenders in Sausalito must have seemed anticlimactic.

* * *

The first Lunt-less execution at San Quentin occurred about a month after Lunt testified in the Brandes trial.

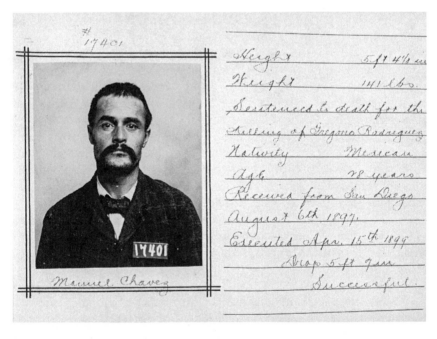

Manuel Chavez, the first man hanged by Amos Lunt's replacement, Frank Arbogast, whose 18-year-career would last until 1913. It was not a smooth beginning. "Frank Arbogast, acting as hangman in place of Amos Lunt," reported the *Chronicle*, "had been very careful with his preparations, but though death was almost instantaneous the victim's neck was not broken by the fall. It is the general opinion of the medical men present that Chaves [sic] died of strangulation" (Anne T. Kent California Room, Marin County Free Library).

William Hale, whose term was scheduled to end in April, remained warden until July 1. The board of prison directors decided to extend his service for two months in order to oversee the complicated business of the prison's jute mill at high season. As a result, Hale presided over the prison during the first execution in the post–Lunt era and the first execution of 1899.

To replace his celebrated hangman, Hale tapped Frank Arbogast, who began preparing for two executions scheduled for consecutive weeks in April. The first—the hanging of Manual Chavez, who murdered his mistress in San Diego—took place on Saturday, April 15.

Speaking almost 15 years later, Arbogast recalled his terror as the date of Chavez's execution neared. In the days leading up the hanging, he slept very little and suffered more, he believed, than the condemned man.[13]

Whoever measured the drop—Arbogast, Hale, Captain Jamieson, Dr. Lawlor, or a combination—should have given Chavez a longer rope. Lunt had hanged three men of comparable dimensions. At a bodyweight of 141 and standing just a few hairs short of 5'5", Chavez should have been given a drop of 5'9" or more.

Name	Weight	Height	Drop
Frank Cooney Kloss (#16619)	140	5'5"	5'10"
Harvey Allender (#16969)	140	5'5½"	5'9"
William H.T. Durrant (#17260)	140	5'6⅛"	5'8"
Manuel Chavez (#17401)	141	5'4⅛"	5'7"

Instead, Chavez dropped 5'7".[14] During Lunt's tenure, the head nearly came off two of his subjects, but all 20 men died quick, painless deaths. Because of the relatively short rope, the drop failed to break Chavez's neck, and although he apparently did not suffer, he died by strangulation.

Unlike the previous executions, Chavez's hanging virtually escaped notice by the press. It was almost as if interest in the San Quentin death factory evaporated with the exit of Amos Lunt. This lack of interested caused Hale to take an unprecedented step. He had to ask reporters to attend the hanging just so he could meet the legal quota of witnesses.[15]

A few very brief accounts of Chavez's hanging made it into the papers. "Frank Arbogast, acting as hangman in place of Amos Lunt," wrote a journalist for the *Chronicle*, "had been very careful with his preparations, but though death was almost instantaneous the victim's neck was not broken by the fall. It is the general opinion of the medical men present that Chaves [sic] died of strangulation. The pulsations of the swinging body were very peculiar. In the middle of the fifth minute after the trap had been sprung the pulse measured 48. It immediately jumped to 55, and then together with the respiration, ceased altogether."[16]

While the reporter was careful to emphasize the fact that "death was almost instantaneous," the next line of his report, in which he referred to the "swinging body," suggests that either Chavez did not die immediately or that Arbogast failed to stretch the rope adequately.

According to another account, "After the drop the body trembled and the knees were drawn up in faint convulsive movements."[17]

George Owens, the second man set to swing in April, heard everything that happened because the Death Watch guards failed to close the heavy iron door separating the death cells from the gallows room.

*   *   *

Less than a week later—on Friday, April 20—Owens mounted the scaffold. His execution took place with considerably more fanfare, all of the area's major news organizations sending representatives.

Owens, who had murdered his wife and daughter in Modesto, gave a few brief remarks from the scaffold. "Gentlemen," he began with a

"It is the most remarkable case I ever witnessed," prison physician William M. Lawlor said of Arbogast's second subject, George Owens. "There was not pulsation after the first half of the third minute. Then the heart fluttered for an instant, but that was all" (Anne T. Kent California Room, Marin County Free Library).

whiskey-induced calmness that shocked eyewitnesses, "I am about to face my everlasting God. Before I did I wish to say a few words. I killed my wife. I loved her madly. I loved her with my whole heart and soul, as I love her now. When I killed her I was not in my right mind. I was not responsible for my actions, and I pray God will have mercy on me. Good-by."

This time, the drop—calculated at 5'4" for the 170-pound wife-slayer—worked.[18]

Dr. Lawlor gushed about the effectiveness of the execution. "It is the most remarkable case I ever witnessed," he said. "There was no pulsation after the first half of the third minute. Then the heart fluttered for an instant, but that was all."

The Arbogast era, however, appeared to be as doomed as Manual Chavez and George Owens. Influenced by Frank Arbogast's reluctance and Lunt's know-how, incoming warden Martin Aguirre asked Lunt to resume his duties. According to the short piece "LUNT AGAIN THE HANG-MAN" in the *Examiner* of October 7, 1899, it was Lunt's experience that mattered. "Warden Aguirre concluded that he must have some one familiar with the work to perform the duty, so Lunt was sent for and this evening assumed his old position."[19]

Lunt appeared delighted with his reinstatement. "Amos likes his job," wrote a Santa Cruz reporter familiar with the old sheriff, "and sought restoration thereto not in vain."[20]

Unknown to the reporter and Warden Aguirre, Amos Lunt dreaded the possibility of standing on the scaffold and slipping a noose over the head of another condemned man. The possibility gnawed at him until he became a nervous wreck. Sleep came only in brief increments that grew shorter as the next Hangman's Friday approached.

31

Descent

(October 23, 1899–September 20, 1901)

While the ropes stretched in preparation for the next hanging, Amos Lunt's nerves frayed. Although happy to be back on the wall at San Quentin, Lunt dreaded going back on the scaffold. He lived in fear of the next Hangman's Friday, and that fear materialized in the shape of ghosts.

Although the seeds of Amos Lunt's downfall were planted months and perhaps even years earlier, contemporary newspapers pinpoint the exact date when they broke through the surface: Monday, October 23, 1899.

In the two weeks since Aguirre reinstated the old hangman, Amos Lunt's deteriorating mental state began to manifest in unsettling ways. While on duty at the front gate, he raised his rifle and pointed it at figures who existed only in his mind. He refused to turn on the lamp in his quarters or light a fire, apparently fearful that someone or something might find him. "They are after me, Frank," he complained to Frank Arbogast. "There are several under the bed now. A convict is assisting them, and it's only a matter of time until they get me."[1]

The press had little trouble identifying "them" as vengeful souls of the 20 men Lunt had noosed.

These night terrors kept Lunt awake, and as October progressed, lengthy periods of sleeplessness left him with bloodshot eyes and a glazed-over expression. He refused to eat breakfast and began to lose weight at an alarming rate.

By Monday, October 23, his behavior had grown so erratic that Warden Aguirre summoned Laura Lunt to the prison. According to Mrs. Lunt, Amos began to show signs of a mental break six months earlier, at about the time he lost his job at the prison. She also said that he had gone with almost no sleep for the previous 12 days. During the meeting, they agreed to send the troubled guard to Dr. J. Henry Barbette in San Francisco. They hoped that a period of rest would rejuvenate Amos Lunt and keep him from a hearing with the state lunacy commission.[2]

While Dr. Barbette treated Amos Lunt, the press had a field day with one, final "yellow" story courtesy of the San Quentin hangman. They promoted the romantic version that had Lunt haunted by the demonic spirits of the men he had hanged. The *Call*'s editors reveled in the irony, as evidenced by a headline proclaiming, "HAUNTED BY THE GHOSTS OF THE MEN HE HANGED; Amos Lunt, Formerly Executioner of San Quentin Prison, Becomes a Maniac." The *Chronicle*'s headline teased, LUNT'S MIND IS GIVING WAY: SAN QUENTIN'S FAMOUS HANGMAN BREAKS DOWN.[3]

According to Laura Lunt, it was the title of "hangman" that haunted Amos Lunt and not the ghosts of the men he had hanged. She later explained that her husband's mental anguish began the previous January when he lost his job at the prison and tried to find employment, at which point those newspaper stories about his exploits on the scaffold came back to haunt him. The mere mention of his name triggered a predictable response: "Amos Lunt! Oh, yes! You were the hangman."[4]

Lunt's hometown paper, the *Santa Cruz Sentinel*, ran a four-sentence blurb about the hangman's breakdown. Compared to coverage in the San Francisco dailies, it was relatively sympathetic. "Amos Lunt, formerly Chief of Police of Santa Cruz, is reported to be mentally unbalanced. We do not wonder, for any man who assists in as many executions as Lunt has is bound to have his nerves shattered and be haunted by visions. His duty as hangman was the most unpleasant in the State. Most sensitive men would go insane at the thought of being a State executioner."[5]

In a subsequent piece, the *Sentinel* presented a less forgiving portrait of the hangman and with it an alternate reason for his breakdown. It wasn't his duties as a hangman that haunted Lunt; it was the residue of a hedonistic lifestyle. Years of tipping the bottle had had a deleterious effect on Lunt's mental and physical health.

Because Frank Arbogast "quickly sickened" of the work and Lunt promised to stay away from liquor, the *Sentinel* noted, Aguirre reinstated him, "but his work, and his want of employment and income while idle, added to the ravages his constitution had suffered from his periods of alcoholism, were too much for a constitution never robust."[6]

Two weeks of rest and recuperation in a private sanitarium under the guidance of Dr. Barbette did nothing to calm the restive mind of the former hangman. His weight plummeted, and he took on a hollow, cadaverous appearance.[7]

Barbette, two of his colleagues, and Laura Lunt all testified to Lunt's "melancholia" at a hearing in front of the Lunacy Commission. At the end of the proceeding, Judge Bahrs signed an order of commitment sending Amos Lunt to the Napa State Hospital for the Insane.

Of all the Bay Area newspapers, the *Call* provided the most coverage of Lunt's breakdown. Continuing with the haunting theme, the paper ran a piece in the October 31 edition. Under the headline "MADHOUSE CLAIMS NOTED AMOS LUNT, THE HANGMAN," an unnamed writer described Lunt as "palsied wreck of humanity, afraid of his own shadow," dogged by the 20 men he helped usher into the netherworld, from the depths of which they reached out to him at night. "The weird shadows of the night to his distorted vision transform themselves into a myriad of vengeful devils, each reaching forth a pair of claw-like hands to clutch his throat, while fiendish leers of triumph distort their already hideous faces. With daylight the ginning demons come to him in different form, but always the same faces, the faces of the executed murderers who perished by his official hand on the prison gallows. The priceless boon of sleep is denied him, and his poor specter-racked brain knows no rest or respite from the horrible nightmare."

Lunt's pitiable condition deeply impressed the *Call* writer, who characterized the hangman as suffering from a worse fate than the 20 men he had dispatched. In a nod to Lunt's effectiveness with the rope, the writer described Lunt's "torture" as worse than that of the men whom he hanged and suggested that none of them would have wished this fate upon "the innocent instrument of their taking off."

"No murderer among the long array of those around whose guilty necks Amos Lunt placed the deadly hangman's noose ever suffered such torture as is being inflicted by an inscrutable Providence on the innocent instrument of their taking off and probably not one among them would, even in his most vengeful moments, have wished such a fate to befall his executioner."[8]

With Lunt in Napa, Frank Arbogast resumed his duties on the scaffold. In January 1900, he hanged Go See, convicted of murdering a rival and torching his body. The Sullivan record characterized the execution as "successful." So began a run of hangings that would end 18 years later when Arbogast left the prison service.[9]

*   *   *

William Hale, long afflicted by stomach ailments that ravaged his body, had retired to a quiet life in San Francisco. His golden years ended abruptly after a dinner during which he experienced crippling stomach pains. He died later that night at the age of 58.

Hale's final moments may have been spent writhing in agony, but reporters let the former sheriff and warden rest in peace. Although Hale would be forever linked with Lunt, who was at the time writhing in agony in Napa, reporters missed a golden opportunity for a provocative news item linking the fates of the two men. Instead, their coverage of Hale's passing was polite, respectful, and brief. His obituaries did not mention his role as a hangman either before or after he became warden of the state prison at San Quentin.

*   *   *

As the new century dawned, it appeared that Amos Lunt would recover his senses, but his brief rebound did not last. As the months progressed, his physical health further deteriorated.

Dr. R.W. Hill, a Los Angeles–based physician, stumbled across Lunt during a visit to the asylum. "The hangman is now dying of softening of the brain and his mental sufferings are horrible to see," Hill later recalled about his chance encounter with Lunt. "He is constantly crying out to the victims of his noose. He fancies that the spirit of Durrant and the eighteen other men he had hanged are hovering about him all the while, reproaching him for their taking off."

Dr. Hill also noticed something peculiar. In his ravings, Lunt described the ghost of Warden Hale tormenting him. "Sometimes he thinks he sees the spirit of Warden Hale," Dr. Hill noted. "In his shrieks of agony he calls out that he had sprung the trap only by express order of Warden Hale. He would put all the blame upon the warden. His agony is something terrible to see."

Hill ended his description of his brief visit with a sort of explanation for Lunt's ghosts. Like other readers, Hill had known the hangman only from descriptions in the papers, and those descriptions almost invariably described Lunt as a man of iron nerve. After meeting the man in the flesh, however, Hill discovered that behind the façade was hiding a highly sensitive man who struggled with his duties. "I learn a new side to the character of hangman Lunt. The public has been led to believe him a man of wonderful nerve. I learn that whenever he had a job to perform he always filled up on alcohol stimulants before executing his man and would remain drunk for days afterward to keep down the blues."[10]

Lunt's rantings, which sometimes morphed into violent episodes, reached the ears of reporters who carried on with the theme of haunting in their coverage. Mini-biographies of the hangman began to dot newspapers across California. One story attributed Lunt's breakdown to the specter of future hangings. "Some months ago he returned to the position and resumed his duties as hangman, although the prospect of arranging the rope on another man seemed to appall him. He constantly talked about it and brooded over it, and suddenly one morning the iron nerve snapped and he became a hopeless madman."

The writer ended with a prescient conclusion by stating, "it is feared that only a few days remain before Lunt, the hangman, will face that same hereafter to which he has sent so many before him."[11]

This new spate of news attention climaxed in mid–September, when a full-page article detailing Lunt's career on the scaffold appeared in the *Call*. "The Haunting of Amos Lunt" came with a sketch of skeletal hands clawing at a terrified figure, the entire tableau encircled by a rope with a noose tied at one end.

The article ended with a sobering thought. "There is many a man in California who can show you a bit of rope an inch or so long which was taken from the necks of one of the hanged men above referred to, and those bits of rope will soon take another value in the eyes of their possessors, for Lunt himself will soon have passed away."[12]

Less than a week after the *Call* ran "The Haunting of Amos Lunt," the writer's prediction came true.

32

Hangman's Friday

(Friday, September 20, 1901)

As befitting a story that one newsman characterized as a "ghastly romance," Amos Lunt's end came on a Friday, the same day of the week traditionally reserved for the hangings he officiated.[1]

The final Hangman's Friday for Amos Lunt came on September 20, 1901, when he died in the Napa State Hospital for the Insane. His funeral took place three days later at the Odd Fellows Hall in Santa Cruz. It was a quiet affair. Reporters who had hounded Lunt as a source for yellow stories kept their distance.

A quintet sang two hymns, "Nearer, My God, to Thee" and "Rock of Ages" while Laura, Arnold, and Lottie said their farewells to the family patriarch. After the short ceremony, a small group gathered at the cemetery, where Chaplain E.D. McCreary and contingent of the G.A.R. saw to the burial of their comrade.[2]

As Amos had done after his father's passing, Laura Lunt placed an article in the local paper thanking all those who helped with the funeral. "We desire to thank all of our friends who so kindly assisted at the last sad rites of our beloved husband and father, Amos Lunt, especially the Workmen, Grand Army and the choir." The note was signed "MRS. LAURA J. LUNT AND CHILDREN."[3]

* * *

Following her husband's passing, Laura Lunt attempted a little postmortem spin control. Although she did not command the media attention her husband did, she spoke to enough reporters that eventually one of them—a reporter from one of her hometown newspapers—wrote an item detailing her side of Lunt's breakdown. She blasted the San Francisco papers for churning out rumor-fueled sensationalism designed to sell papers rather than tell the truth.

Amos Lunt, she said, did not crack because of his duties as a hangman.

He did not even consider himself as a hangman; although he did make the necessary preparations and fitted the noose, he did not release the trap. He did not take part in the Death Watch or visit with the condemned.

Laura Lunt did not mention Dr. Hill, but in an oblique criticism of the physician's comments, she insisted that her husband did not drink before, during, or after executions. Instead, Lunt's pre-execution Friday routine included a breakfast of ham and eggs washed down with a strong cup of black coffee.

He did not see phantoms of the men he hanged; instead, his breakdown resulted from a sense of worthlessness emanating from his lack of employability in the days after Hale dismissed him from the prison service.

Except for a small piece published in a local Santa Cruz paper under the title "The Late Amos Lunt," Laura Lunt's efforts to protect her late husband's image went ignored by the press. Newspapermen, and their readers, much preferred the romantic image of a hangman haunted by his subjects.[4]

The old noose-tier of San Quentin had been strangled by his own legend.

Fates of the
Major Characters

The Hangmen

Amos Lunt

Lunt's notoriety died a slow death. In the years after his passing, his name occasionally arose in connection with some aspect of the fine art of hanging. In 1901, when a mob of 13 men lynched a man and his two sons near Lookout, Justice of the Peace J.R. Myers had tied the nooses. "He ... did the work with surprising skill for a man nearly blind," noted a local journalist, who gave Myers a little street credibility by making a comparison quickly recognized by his readers. "Amos Lunt, the expert hangman, could not have tied a better noose."[1]

* * *

Reporters continued to tap Amos Lunt for stories for years after his death.

The hangman had left a deep impression on those who came to know him, particularly Pete Dotz and F.F. Runyon, two young journalists who later wrote feature articles about their experience interviewing Lunt.

In a 1912 piece titled "Amos Lunt, The Hangsman of San Quentin Penitentiary, and His Fate," Pete Dotz said of Lunt, "Probably in all my newspaper experience, I have never met a person that so quite impressed me as Amos Lunt, the hangsman of San Quentin."

Dotz, who saw Lunt as a source of "a hundred thrilling yellow stories," became entranced by the hangman's charisma. "He held me in a strange fascination," the reporter recalled.

Like most writers who chronicled the life and times of Amos Lunt, Dotz devoted the bulk of his article not to the "hangsman" but to the men he had hanged. Even in death, San Quentin's hangman could not escape the ghosts of the men he had dropped. "One of the last acts he did before his mind commenced to fail," Dotz noted at the end of his article, "was to teach me to tie a hangsman's knot."[2]

Like Pete Dotz, Frederick F. Runyon's work on occasion took him to the prison gate, where he met Amos Lunt. Unlike Dotz, however, Runyon formed a distinctly negative impression of the hangman, whom he described in a series of articles about his experiences chasing stories inside the walls of San Quentin. "Lunt was a cold-blooded fellow," Runyon wrote, "He apparently had no feeling. An execution was just an incident to him. It meant a few days' vacation." Runyon had apparently missed, or decided to look past, the spectrum of emotions noticed by his colleagues, particularly the "nervous prostration" Lunt displayed after the Durrant execution.

Disdain aside, Runyon relied on Lunt as a fountain for sensational stories. "A hangsman was an object of some interest to me, then a young newspaper man," Runyon begrudgingly admitted. "He would tell of executions where he had officiated. Grewsome [sic], to be sure, but intensely fascinating."

Runyon added, "He showed me how to tie a hangsman's knot."[3]

The noose was Lunt's stock-in-trade, and he was proud to display his art.

William Hale

It seemed as though the fates of William Hale and Amos Lunt were forever linked after 1891.

William Hale and Amos Lunt came into prominence together, one as a warden and the other as his hangman; and they went out together, one as a result of deteriorating physical health and other as the result of deteriorating mental health. While Lunt fought specters that attacked him in his nightmares, Hale retired to a quiet life with his wife at their residence on Twelfth Street.

On July 11, 1900—about a year after he left San Quentin—Hale experienced a sudden fit of cramps at dinner and died later that night from "acute inflammation of the stomach."[4] His brief obituaries noted key events in the life of the "prominent Californian," including his tenure as Alameda County sheriff and warden of the state prison at San Quentin. They did not, however, mention his role as "Lord High Executioner" of California. That dubious honor was bestowed on the guard he hired a few months after becoming warden in 1891.

Even in death, Hale could not escape the orbit of his most infamous employee. Over the next year, he would make a postmortem appearance or two in news stories about Lunt's breakdown. The press made much of the idea that spirits of condemned men haunted Lunt, but according to Dr. R.W. Hill, the restless spirit of William Hale also visited the afflicted hangman.[5]

Frank Arbogast

The Death Watch guard and Amos Lunt's successor on the scaffold, Arbogast served as San Quentin's hangman until 1913, when he left the prison service under a cloud. Warden James A. Johnston discharged him for "unsatisfactory conduct" arising out of his duties as a prison steward.

During his 13-year career as an executioner, Arbogast hanged over twice as many men—46—as his predecessor. Unlike Lunt, he received more than two days of furlough for every man who dropped. "And for this duty, 'extra' duty, I always called it," Arbogast explained during an interview after his discharge, "I got $25. The state allows $50, but the rest of it, I believe, goes for rope and other appliances."

In an oblique reference to Amos Lunt's breakdown, the reporter asked Arbogast what he thought about the widely held belief that the stresses of executions cause hangmen to snap.

The ex-hangman laughed. "I have heard hundreds of tales of that import, but my conscience is as tender as that of any man and I feel no effects from the experience. I don't believe the stories, for this reason: If men are likely to feel the effects of this business they quit after the first experience; if they go through a second one, every succeeding one affects them less." Each hanging, according to Arbogast, deepened the callous on a hangman's psyche.

Arbogast said that he did not discuss gallows business with his wife, comments that provide possible insight into the dynamics of Lunt's relationship with Laura. "Yes, she knows all about it, of course," Arbogast said, "but we never speak of it. I do not know her opinion of capital punishment, and as for mine, I have simply done my duty and left the question of whether it was right or wrong to the powers above me."[6]

Arbogast managed to avoid the type of magnetic notoriety that stuck to his predecessor, perhaps the result of several factors, including his personality, his acumen in avoiding the press, the atrophy of yellow journalism, and the public's satiation with stories about executions. By the time Arbogast began tying nooses, hangings at San Quentin had lost their novelty factor.

Frank Arbogast died of colon cancer in 1934 at the age of 73.

Colonel John W. McKenzie

The first official noose-tier of San Quentin, Colonel John W. McKenzie predeceased his successor by less than a year, dying a few days before Christmas in 1900. His obituaries chronicled his career in the military and glorified his derring-do during the Mexican War but said nothing about his experiences as a hangman.[7]

McKenzie's role as the first official hangman of San Quentin remains a lost footnote in the history of law and order in California.

The Supporting Players

Laura J. Lunt

Amos Lunt's family members remained on the periphery of his infamy, seldom occupying more than a mere mention in the occasional news item. After Lunt's passing in 1901, they would continue to make cameo appearances in local society news.

In the years after her husband's passing, Laura J. Lunt made ends meet as a seamstress, advertising her services as "Dressmaking and plain sewing by Mrs. Amos Lunt," which included "plain sewing, summer dresses, shirt waists, children's clothes and mending."[8] The hangman's widow, however, never entirely escaped the orbit of the California penal system. In 1940, she lived at the Preston Industrial School alongside her daughter Lottie, who worked as an officer at the reform school.[9]

Laura J. Lunt died in 1944 at the age of 87.

Captain John C. Edgar

John C. Edgar continued to serve as deputy warden of San Quentin until 1906, when he became warden. In July 1907, a severe case of diabetes cut short his tenure and ended his 28-year career in the prison service. The former Yuba County sheriff died on January 30, 1908, at the age of 74.[10]

The Reverend August Drahms

Drahms ministered to the spiritual needs of San Quentin inmates for 18 years, a position that required him to provide spiritual counsel to the condemned and stand next to them on the scaffold. Based on his experiences at the prison, he authored *The Criminal: His Personnel and Environment, a Scientific Study*. Considered a groundbreaking study at the time of publication, Drahm's book became a mainstay in the study of criminology.[11]

After he left the prison service, Drahms ventured further west and became pastor of the First Congregational Church in Hilo, Hawaii. Upon retiring, he returned to California, where he devoted his time and energies to Grand Army of the Republic affairs and writing poetry.

He died in Los Angeles in 1927 at the age of 77.[12]

Father Hugh Lagan

The man who ministered to condemned Catholics at San Quentin, Father Hugh Lagan, went from his parish at San Rafael to helm the Sacred Heart Church on Fillmore Street in San Francisco. Upon returning from a trip to his native Ireland in November 1904, the beloved pastor became afflicted with a painful ailment diagnosed as spinal meningitis. He underwent surgery but died of complications on December 23, 1904, at the age of 52.

The *Examiner* noted Father Lagan's omnipresence at San Quentin executions. "During this time [in San Rafael] he officiated at nearly all of the hangings at San Quentin, and by his kindly ways became endeared to all of the convicts in the prison."

Even in death, the kindly rector could not escape the gravity of publicity black hole Theodore Durrant. "He was the priest who converted Theodore Durrant, the murderer, to the Catholic faith, and was with him on the scaffold."[13]

Dr. Isaac L.R. Mansfield

Following his resignation from the prison service, Dr. Isaac L.R. Mansfield returned to private practice and quickly acquired a reputation as an expert in pulmonary disease. After several years in San Francisco, he relocated to Wyandotte, where he died on April 27, 1922, at the age of 73.

Of his prison service, the *Oroville Daily Register* noted, "Under his regime as physician for San Quentin the sanitary condition was much improved, and the death rate was reduced from 40 percent to 18 per cent during the second year of his incumbency."[14]

Dr. William M. Lawlor

The beneficiary of political patronage, Dr. William M. Lawlor became health officer when his fellow Republican, Governor Henry Gage, appointed him to the spot in 1899. A few years later, he was named superintendent of the Home for the Care and Training of Feeble Minded Children despite a complete lack of qualifications. His tenure lasted less than a year; Gage dismissed him in July 1902 after an investigation revealed what the *Call* characterized as "the most disgusting, inhuman and brutal practices."

During an interview with an *Examiner* reporter, Dr. Lawlor admitted using draconian measures—confining inmates to solitary confinement in the "dungeon," chaining them to rings embedded in the floor, and restricting them to diets of bread and water—to enforce the Home's rules.[15]

"It is difficult to conceive," a *Call* reporter concluded, "how a man can get so low as to punish weak-minded and irresponsible children by methods that would disgrace an Apache."[16]

The embattled physician died in October 1907 at the age of 61.

The Writers

Alice Rix

The pioneering female journalist who profiled San Quentin's notorious hangman in 1897, Alice Rix continued to pen feature stories for the *Examiner* until 1905. After her home and personal library went up in a blaze, she moved to Surrey, England, where she died in 1930 at the age of 64.[17]

Fellow scribe Annie Laurie wrote of her groundbreaking colleague and the witty-bordering-on-sassy tone she sometimes adopted when covering people who took themselves a little too seriously: "And how she put out that saucy little foot of hers and tripped up the rich and great, and laughed like a rogue when she did it."[18]

Annie Laurie

Annie Laurie's career writing both columns and feature stories for the *Examiner* and other Hearst newspapers lasted nearly half a century and came to close in 1936—41 years after she visited with Anthony Azoff and his fellow dead-men-walking.

Six years after writing her emotional, heartfelt farewell to Alice Rix, Mrs. Winifred Black Bonfils, aka "Annie Laurie," passed away at the age of 72. Millions of readers mourned the loss of an intrepid reporter whose five decades on the beat took her to places few writers dared venture, such as behind the walls of San Quentin to interview the men on death row.

Thousands shuffled past her coffin as she lay in state in the rotunda at City Hall and paid their respects to a columnist whose words sometimes moved them to tears and sometimes to laughter and sometimes to both.

Her obituary appeared in newspapers from coast to coast. The *Detroit Times* called her "America's best loved woman journalist."[19]

Her male colleagues characterized her as a "great newspaperman," an epithet that would have made Annie Laurie smile.[20]

Belle Dormer

Call journalist Belle Dormer, who once tried in vain to save the life of doomed murderer Anthony Azoff, loved adventure and seemed to have a nose for the action.

In 1900, Dormer left California for Alaska, where she took a job as a columnist writing about the local social scene for the *Klondike Nugget*. Dormer followed the rush to Rawhide, Nevada, after gold and silver were discovered there in 1906. She invested heavily in real estate, opened the Dormer Hotel—billed as "one of the best structures in Rawhide"—and tried to cash in on the crowd that quickly grew from 500 when she arrived to 10,000.[21]

The journalist, adventurer, and real estate scion died in Santa Cruz on December 20, 1937, at the age of 83.

Charles Michelson

Covering hangings had traumatized *Examiner* journalist Charles Michelson, who only agreed to attend the 1895 execution of William Fredericks if his editor promised never to send him to another.[22]

After years of writing feature articles for the *Examiner*, Michelson became editor in 1906. He followed that with editing posts at the *Chicago Examiner, Chicago Post,* and *New York World*.

Michelson turned to politics in 1929 when he became the publicity chief of the Democratic Party, a post he held until 1942. During his tenure, he scribed speeches for such party luminaries as President Franklin D. Roosevelt.

Although he spent his last four decades away from California, he always considered San Francisco his home and returned often to visit his sister, fellow author Miriam Michelson. The political spin master died of heart failure in 1948 at the age of 79.

Frederick R. Runyon

The 20-year-old journalist who broke the "red hot irons" story after interviewing the hangman of San Quentin, Frederick F. Runyon evolved from writer to editor, eventually helming the *Nevada State Journal*. He returned to California in 1920 to help media mogul F.W. Kellogg establish the *Pasadena Post*—the first of 16 dailies he would help organize. His news career, which began 55-years earlier when he founded the *Mill Valley Times* at age 12, ended abruptly when he died of a heart attack in 1944 at the age of 67.

34

Twenty-One Ghosts

The Man Behind the Myth

Two Faces of the Hangman

On Sunday, September 15, 1901—less than a week before Amos Lunt died—the *San Francisco Call* ran a full-page feature entitled "The Haunting of Amos Lunt." The article, which consumed the entirety of page five and included the sketch of a wide-eyed, gaping-mouthed man encircled by a rope, detailed the hangman's career.

The bulk of the article is devoted to gallows procedures at San Quentin and the men Lunt hanged. The unnamed author provides very little detail about the hangman other than to describe him as a "mild-mannered Massachusetts boy." This is typical of news coverage about San Quentin's first hangman. He became synonymous with the men he helped dispatch and the rope he used to dispatch them. In a way, even the author acknowledges this association when he concludes, "There is many a man in California who can show you a bit of rope an inch or so long which was taken from the necks of one of the hanged men above referred to, and those bits of rope will soon take another value in the eyes of their possessors, for Lunt himself will soon have passed away."[1]

For the reading public, Amos Lunt and the noose became one and the same. Yet behind the image projected by the media was a real man whose essence has become obscured by time and mythologizing. While it is impossible to conduct a séance and raise the spirit of a dead hangman from the scant information available, news articles provide a few provocative clues about the man behind the myth.

Behind the Curtain

The reading public preferred the image of a strong figure standing on the scaffold, noose in hand, ready to dispatch the worst criminals in the west, to a trembling, quivering mental and emotional wreck unhinged by his duties as hangman. Most of the time, the press acquiesced and presented the former, possibly because Amos Lunt himself promoted this image. He adopted an almost cavalier, devil-may-care attitude during his interview with Alice Rix and a flippant tone during the Brandes trial, when he eyed the prosecutor for the best drop. In both instances, he projected a sense of pride bordering on hubris about his work as a hangman.

The press reported that after the triple event in 1895, when Lunt presided over three consecutive hangings, he "sauntered from the execution room smoking a cigarette." Such statements typified how reporters presented Amos Lunt to their readers.

"But despite his apparent utter indifference as a man-killer," noted another reporter who managed to pull back the curtain to reveal the true face of Amos Lunt, "it was known by many of his intimate friends that in secret he brooded over it."[2]

It was during the Durrant execution, when the limelight shone most brightly on the San Quentin scaffold, that the hangman's ambivalence was the most evident. "On this occasion [the hanging of Durrant] Lunt was reported as being the coolest man in the room, with the possible exception of the condemned man himself," a reporter later recalled.[3]

As good as Lunt was at concealing the maelstrom of emotions he experienced in hanging a man—a storm he may have attempted to calm with a few doses of whiskey—evidence of the man behind the façade occasionally seeped through the surface and even made it into news coverage. An intuitive *Chronicle* reporter noticed that "the coolest man in the room" wasn't so cool after all and concluded that his nerves came from the fact that he believed in Durrant's innocence. This reflected a common heartstring tugged on by the press, that the state of California was about to execute an innocent man. And if Lunt showed any outward signs of nervousness, as he had during the Durrant execution, the press invariably reported that this show of emotion suggested that the hangman believed in the condemned man's innocence.

"Hangman Amos Lunt is evidently too susceptible for his trade," the *Chronicle* reporter noted. "He was actually impressed with the apparent sincerity of Durrant's declaration of innocence on the gallows. The traditional hangman is always cynical and this type of man would have rated Durrant's gallows speech as a clever bit of spectacular work and nothing more. To believe it in the face of the evidence in the case required rare credulity."[4]

Durrant's gallant speech from the scaffold, during which he steadfastly maintained his innocence in the murders of Blanche Lamont and Minnie Williams, may not have unnerved Lunt as much as the time he took to make it. By this point, Lunt understood the need to move quickly through the procedures to avoid a last-minute collapse of the condemned. But the condemned wanted to speak, the public expected it, and Lunt was left waiting with noose in hand, watching Durrant's knees for signs that he might collapse. Lunt expressed his dislike of gallows speeches in his November 1897 interview with *Examiner* journalist Alice Rix. "There's one thing breaks me up," Lunt said, "and that's talking on the scaffold. I can't stand it!"

Other factors certainly contributed to Lunt's emotional reaction: the size of the public spotlight; the fear of a botched execution for all the world to see (or read about); the pathetic scene of a young man's story ending on the scaffold; or of his mother waiting for her beloved son to emerge from the room feet-first.

Of these factors, one—the fear of a botched hanging—may have put the greatest strain on Lunt, who was known for his meticulous planning. "My ambition and anxiety is to have everything right," Lunt said during the Brandes trial, "and that when the time comes there will be no slip."[5] He expressed this fear in a similar statement to Alice Rix, referring to the source of his fears as a "hitch."

Never was the pressure greater than during the hanging of Durrant, billed as the final act in the crime of the century. Any slip, whether of Lunt's doing or not, would have become a headline story and ammunition for death penalty critics. The "red hot iron" story only increased the pressure.

Whatever the cause or causes, Durrant's hanging unnerved Lunt. "Lunt, the hangman," wrote the *Chronicle*'s reporter on the scene, "paced rapidly up and down the place in a condition of excitement that had the effect of making most of those who watched him as nervous as himself."[6]

That such incidents haunted Lunt became apparent by the ghosts that supposedly visited him in his last days. Three ghosts, in particular, hounded the hangman: Theodore Durrant, John Miller, and Warden William Hale. The identity of these ghosts, and what each represents— the blameless, the botched, and the boss—is as telling as their possible existence.

When Warden Aguirre gave Lunt a second chance and reinstated him at the prison, the agreement came with a caveat: the former hangman would once again oversee executions. According to one source, Lunt welcomed a return to this duty, but once again, Lunt may have put on a face for the public.

According to another report, one apparently based on conversations with Lunt's friends and co-workers, he lived in fear of the next Hangman's Friday. "Some months ago he returned to the position and resumed his duties as hangman, although the prospect of arranging the rope on another man seemed to appall him. He constantly talked about this and brooded over it, and suddenly one morning the iron nerve snapped and he became a hopeless madman."[7]

Perhaps the most telling statement about Lunt's mindset came from Dr. R.W. Hill during a chance encounter inside the State Hospital for the Insane.

"I learn a new side to the character of hangman Lunt," Hill noted after visiting the troubled hangman about three weeks before he died. This "new side" included Lunt's habit of fortifying himself with alcohol before and after each hanging. The man known for his "wonderful nerve" began tippling on Hangman's Friday and continued his binge "for days afterward to keep down the blues."[8]

Bottle Blues

If Lunt downed a little liquid courage before noosing his subjects, it escaped notice of the press corps, the members of whom seemed to see and hear everything that occurred in the gallows room and almost certainly would not have missed a story about an inebriated hangman. On a stage as big as that of the San Quentin scaffold in the late 1800s, such clues as the scent of whiskey, bloodshot eyes, slurred speech, and teetering steps would have been obvious to anyone in the room.

Lunt may have taken a few nips but probably left the real imbibing to the short furloughs that followed each hanging. The image of a drunken hangman was not one that Warden Hale wanted the public to see, so it is conceivable that Lunt's drinking may have influenced the warden's decision to grant his hangman these brief respites from duty and may have been the catalyst in Lunt's dismissal from prison service in 1899.

Lunt's romance with the bottle predated his time as San Quentin's hangman, and when he tipped the bottle too frequently, his Mr. Hyde emerged and wreaked havoc on his career in law enforcement. A brief profile, published about a month before Lunt died, depicts him as a binge drinker. "He was a good officer," wrote a journalist for the *Evening Sentinel*, "barring occasions when he drank more than was good for him, which were not often. Through his weakness he lost his billet."[9] This quote is notable for several reasons: it came from one of Lunt's hometown papers, it indicates that his imbibing came in binges, and it notes that he lost his job or "billet" because of this "weakness."

Instead of a sot unable to saunter a few feet from a barstool, Amos Lunt apparently drank to excess only on occasion, and then to such excess that it cost him dearly. In a profile of the men who wore the star in Santa Cruz, former Police Chief J.E. Armstrong said of his predecessor, "Amos

Lunt then wore the star for part of one year, being duly discharged for naughty conduct."[10] By "naughty conduct," Armstrong was more than likely referring to Lunt's drinking sprees.

Dr. Hill's assessment of the troubled hangman indicates that Lunt continued his binge drinking in San Quentin and apparently used whiskey as a sort of nerve tonic. According to the profile in the *Evening Sentinel*, his habit eventually cost him his job at the prison when Warden Hale found him unfit for duty in 1899. For Amos Lunt, history had repeated itself. Once again, "His [Lunt's] old weakness overcame him and he lost his position."[11]

The unnamed *Evening Sentinel* writer concludes that Lunt's long-term romance with the bottle contributed to his mental implosion. "[Lunt's] work, his wont of employment and income while idle, added to the ravages his constitution had suffered from his periods of alcoholism, were too much for a constitution never robust."[12]

In an attempt to cleanse her husband's legacy, Laura Lunt condemned the story that Lunt used alcohol to cope with Hangman's Fridays as a pure fiction, but too many sources indicate otherwise.

Ghosts: The Blameless, the Botched, and the Boss

To paraphrase Arthur Conan Doyle's immortal Sherlock Holmes, when one eliminates the paranormal, what remains is the psychological; when eliminating the possibility of ghosts as a viable cause of Lunt's hallucinations, what remains is a rational basis behind his psychosis. Finding that rational basis, however, becomes a Sherlockian feat of detection.

Two sources in particular provide interesting insight into Lunt's breakdown: Dr. R.W. Hill's comments after seeing Lunt in the state hospital, and Laura Lunt's comments after his death.

> The hangman is now dying of softening of the brain and his mental sufferings are horrible to see. He is constantly crying out to the victims of his noose. He fancies that the spirit of Durrant and the eighteen other men he had hanged are hovering about him all the while, reproaching him for their taking off.
> Sometimes he thinks he sees the spirit of Warden Hale. In his shrieks of agony he calls out that he had sprung the trap only by express order of Warden Hale. He would put all the blame upon the warden. His agony is something terrible to see.[13]

The Blameless: The Ghost of Durrant

A big contributor to Lunt's agony, according to Dr. Hill, was the phantom of Theodore Durrant, who received mention in numerous items about Lunt's breakdown. Undoubtedly, area newspapers emphasized this aspect of Lunt's "haunting." Even in death, Durrant drew interest from the reading public and could help to sell newspapers.

If Lunt thought he received spectral visits from his most infamous subject, which appears likely, the haunting may have begun immediately after the hanging in 1898. The media circus during the execution of Durrant and the spotlight on his hangman, especially after his alleged "hot iron" remarks, meant that reporters would look for any interesting postscript to their stories.

Throughout the following weekend, reporters shadowed Durrant's parents, eavesdropped on the funeral, and interviewed principals in the case. A *Chronicle* reporter found his postscript at the wall of the state prison, where Amos Lunt resumed his guard duties on Monday, January 10, 1898. What the reporter found standing guard at the prison gate was not the narrator of "a hundred thrilling yellow stories"—a man happy to teach someone how to tie a noose—but instead a man still deeply shaken three days after Durrant's execution.

"The official executioner appeared for duty this morning [Monday, January 10, 1898] and resumed his station on the wall near the big arched entrance to the prison," the reporter noted. "He was restless, and his features had not resumed the placid look that is the hangman's normal expression."

Something about the Durrant execution remained with Lunt, which the *Chronicle* reporter described as "a creepy feeling." "Since the church belfry criminal dropped through the trap of the scaffold," the reporter explained, "the veteran hangman confesses to a creepy feeling in the vicinity of his spinal column."

The reporter alludes to the cause of Lunt's "creepy feeling" when he states, "the remembrance of those last words of the doomed murderer causes Lunt to seek a quiet corner in which to quiet his unstrung nerves."[14]

The ordeal of executing Durrant also deeply affected Captain W.C. Jamieson, who apparently had come to believe in the doomed man's innocence. According to one source, Jamieson refused to take part in any of the preparations, and during his final farewell to the condemned, he cried like a baby.[15]

Although Lunt was better at hiding his emotions than Jamieson, it appears likely that he too came to believe in Durrant's innocence, perhaps only after listening to Durrant's remarkable gallows speech, and the shame of hanging an innocent man came back to haunt him in the form of Durrant's ghost.

*   *   *

The Botched: The Ghost of Miller

Another hanging that bothered Lunt was that of John Miller, the hunchback nearly decapitated by the drop. While some question remains as to who measured the drop for the earliest hangings at San Quentin, Amos Lunt undoubtedly calculated the length of rope to snap Miller's misshapen neck, and he got it wrong.

"Another execution that troubled Lunt," wrote a Santa Cruz reporter just after the hangman's breakdown in October 1899, "was that of John Miller, the hunchback, who was given too long a drop and was nearly decapitated."[16]

Miller, who died almost instantly, did not a feel a thing. Lunt, on the other hand, may have felt a deep sense of shame, manifested in the specter of Miller, his head dangling from his neck by a sinew.

The Boss: The Ghost of Warden Hale

According to Dr. Hill, Amos Lunt also received spectral visits from his former boss. "Sometimes he thinks he sees the spirit of Warden Hale," Hill said.

Of all the ghosts that Amos Lunt claimed to see, perhaps the appearance of Warden Hale is the most indicative of his psychosis. During his rantings, as reported by Dr. Hill, Lunt pointed the finger at Hale for all that occurred in the San Quentin gallows room. "In his shrieks of agony," Dr. Hill recalled, "he calls out that he had sprung the trap only by express order of Warden Hale. He would put all the blame upon the warden."

In other words, Amos Lunt invoked the "Nuremberg Defense" to justify his actions as a hangman. Rather than feeling proud about his role in the official machinery of judicial punishment, Amos Lunt apparently felt a need to shift the onus to Hale.

Verification of Lunt's abnegation of responsibility comes from an unlikely source: the woman who tried to discredit Hill's observations. Contained in Laura Lunt's flurry of denials is a provocative statement: Amos Lunt did not even consider himself the hangman. He stretched the rope, tied the noose, calculated the drop, fitted the noose and cap, and signaled the rope cutting, but he did not release the trap, which in his later years provided enough of an excuse to shun the title of hangman. He added a series of justifications for good measure: he did not take part in the Death Watch or visit with the condemned in the death cells; rather, he sent cigars and other sundries to the men he would meet on the scaffold. Did these cigars represent empathy for the condemned, or regret?

If indeed Lunt expressed this disdain for the title of hangman to his wife, then he underwent a reversal that occurred at some point after the execution of Durrant. "I'm the hangman," he said when he introduced himself to journalist Alice Rix during their November 1897 tête-à-tête. During the interview, he graphically recreated the death procession, using a series of chairs in Captain Edgar's Office and a year later, he entertained the gallery at the Brandes trial with gallows humor when he offered his assessment of an appropriate drop for the prosecutor. These do not seem like the actions of a man burdened by a guilty conscience.

Yet, as early as the Rix interview, Lunt invoked the "just following orders" justification. He explained that he had "an awful strong feeling against the taking of human life," but when Rix pointed out the obvious contradiction by adding "except by hanging," Lunt "fidgeted." "I take my orders from the Warden," he responded. "When I obey his orders I do my duty."

"And later the Warden, speaking on the same subject," Rix explained, "told me he took his orders from the hanging Judge, and this one, I suppose, is equal to his responsibilities."

When Rix asked if Lunt believed in hanging as a just punishment, Lunt's response indicated his mindset about a year before his breakdown. "I may not be the one to judge, but I think it's the best way."[17]

When Frank Arbogast left the prison service, he echoed Lunt's "just following orders" justification. "I have simply done my duty," he said, "and left the question of whether it was right or wrong to the powers above me."[18] If any vengeful spirits visited the aging hangman in his sleep, he kept it to himself.

Amos Lunt may have even come to believe that he shouldered no responsibility for what occurred in the gallows room, but the party of 21 ghosts (the 20 condemned plus one) indicates that his internal justifications did not work. The ghosts, coupled with attempt to shift the blame to Hale through the "just following orders" excuse, suggests that Lunt may have felt a sense of guilt and possibly shame arising from his duties as hangman. This would explain the presence not only of the 20 men he hanged but also the man who ordered him to do it.

The Old Soldier

Over a century later, it is difficult to dissect the causes of Lunt's "melancholia" and equate them with a 21st-century diagnosis, although scouring the historical record for clues reveals some telling characteristics:

Continual and long-term tippling represents self-destructive behavior.

His lengthy hikes suggest a sense of isolation and detachment.

The visions of ghosts represent a sense of guilt.

One particular anecdote, about Lunt pointing his weapon at unseen enemies approaching the prison wall, suggests a degree of paranoia.

The spectral visits, which often occurred at night and disrupted his sleep, may represent what psychologists call "intrusive memories."

Based on these clues, it appears likely that the hangman of San Quentin suffered from post-traumatic stress disorder (PTSD). Each of the 20 ghosts that haunted Lunt represented a disturbing memory of what occurred on, and under, the scaffold. In the end, they got their revenge.

Appendix 1

Chronological List of Executions Performed by Amos Lunt

1. Friday, February 2, 1894: Lu Sing
2. Friday, April 20, 1894: P.J. Sullivan
3. Friday, June 7, 1895: Emilio Garcia
4. Friday, June 7, 1895: Anthony Azoff
5. Friday, June 7, 1895: P.J. Collins
6. Friday, July 26, 1895: William M. Fredericks
7. Friday, August 9, 1895: Fremont Smith
8. Friday, October 18, 1895: Hans Hansen
9. Friday, October 18, 1895: Thomas St. Clair
10. Friday, October 25, 1895: William Young
11. Friday, December 11, 1896: M.J. Miller
12. Wednesday, February 17, 1897: Chun Sing
13. Friday, April 23, 1897: F.J. Kloss
14. Friday, December 10, 1897: Harvey Allender
15. Friday, January 7, 1898: W.H.T. Durrant
16. Friday, March 11, 1898: Wee Tung
17. Wednesday, April 6, 1898: Benjamin L. Hill
18. Friday, May 27, 1898: J.J. Ebanks
19. Friday, October 14, 1898: John Miller
20. Friday, October 21, 1898: George W. Clark

Appendix 2
The Drop

Note: The following analysis pertains to record entries documenting the second through 21st executions conducted at San Quentin (the period of 1893–1898) only. The two sources discussed below also contain entries of hangings conducted outside the date range of this biography.

Two primary sources document the weight and drop of men hanged at San Quentin during the Lunt era: the Duffy (D) and the Sullivan (S) records.

The Duffy record refers to a register of condemned San Quentin inmates compiled by Warden Clinton T. Duffy and housed in the Marin History Museum. Each entry in the register contains basic information about the inmate, including drop for those executed. A duplicate of this record is held in the California State Archives under the title *Execution Books 1893–1967.*

The Sullivan record refers to *Album IV* of the Sullivan collection at the Anne T. Kent California Room in the Marin County Library. During a 40-year career at San Quentin, Daniel Sullivan—whose beat included "Murderer's Row" during most if not all of the Lunt era—compiled a collection including several volumes containing mug shots and information about prisoners. Sullivan's *Album IV* includes entries for inmates on "Murderer's Row" during the period of 1890–1912. For men hanged, in addition to height and weight, each entry page includes the length of drop and an outcome, although there is no description or definition of what constituted a "successful" or a "very successful" hanging or an indication if the absence of a designation indicated a failed execution.

For two of the men Lunt hanged—Emilio Garcia and John Miller—the Sullivan record lists no outcome. Because Lunt considered the Miller hanging, during which the rope nearly severed the condemned man's head, as an abject failure, the absence of an outcome for the Garcia hanging also appears to indicate a botched job.

The *Examiner*'s account of the triple hanging may provide a clue. "Meanwhile, on the other side of the door, Garcia swung beneath the gibbet.... The prison chaplain, Mr. Drahms, was on the platform. He stood with folded arms looking down on the form of the swaying murderer. Then the physicians clustered around Garcia and felt his pulse beats and listened for the last flutter of his heart. Garcia did not die easily. He was a sturdy little fellow, close knit and hard, but in thirteen minutes the doctors said he was dead."

This description may represent two completely different outcomes. On one hand, words such as "swung" and "swaying" hint at the possibility that the fall did not break Garcia's neck and that instead he died a slow death by asphyxiation. Indeed, the phrase "did not die easily" appears to support the notion of a bungled execution.

On the other hand, "swung" and "swaying" may represent the slight to-and-fro motion caused by a falling body coming to an abrupt halt in mid-air. And "did not die easily" may not denote a life-and-death struggle at the end of a rope but the natural ebbing of the pulse following the hanging. A 13-minute interval between the drop and the total cessation of pulse was consistent with and in some cases shorter than several of Lunt's other subjects. Patrick Sullivan's pulse beat for 12 minutes; Patrick Collins, 14; and according to one account, William Young's pulse did not cease until 17 minutes after the drop. The Sullivan record describes all three as "successful" hangings.

The *Oakland Tribune*'s coverage of the triple event published that same day—Friday, June 7 1895—appears to settle the debate. "His [Garcia's] neck was broken by the fall. He did not make a move after he fell." Had Garcia strangled to death, his body writhing, twisting, and spasmodically jerking on the end of the line, the reporters would most certainly have noted that fact. Such botched hangings always made good copy, ergo sold papers.

The Sullivan record's silence about an outcome in this particular case is a mystery.

The drops listed in both the Duffy and Sullivan records are identical except for two notable instances. The Duffy record's drop of 5'10" for William Fredericks—four inches longer than the 5'6" listed in the Sullivan record—is almost certainly an error. A drop of 5'6" for the 160-pound Fredericks is identical to drops given to men with comparable body weight such Garcia and Sing. Besides, a 5'10" drop would have been a long and possibly disastrous one for Fredericks. While reporters who witnessed hangings at San Quentin seldom discussed specific drops, they occasionally included a general number in their after-action articles. One such article provides support for the shorter of the two drops.

"He fell about five feet," a *Chronicle* reporter noted about the hanging of William Fredericks.

Likewise, the drop recorded for the hanging of Wee Tung on the Duffy record—5'4"—is almost certainly too short for a man weighing 133 pounds (barring a physical peculiarity). The hangman would have given him about the same drop—5'8" and 5'9" respectively—as that of Hansen and St. Clair, both of whom weighed 135 pounds. The 5'9" drop listed in the Sullivan record appears the correct one.

Anomalies aside, the information contained in both records is remarkably consistent, suggesting that either Clinton Duffy drew information from Sullivan's *Album IV* or that both emanate from a common source. The discrepancies discussed above, which suggest that the compilers and record-keepers possibly erred when transcribing numbers, tends to support the latter conclusion.

A third record, a register of hangings housed in the New York Public Library's archives, may provide a further clue. Like the Sullivan record, each entry in the two-volume set contains a notation about the hanging's outcome, and like the Duffy record, a brief synopsis of the subject's crime and disposition of his case. Unfortunately, the pages for the period from 1893 to 1902—those covered in this book—are missing. A detailed analysis of the extant entries and a comparison with both the Sullivan/Duffy records, which is beyond the scope of this book, may reveal the relationship, if any, among these three sources.

Whatever invisible strings connect these records, the original source for information about drop and outcome of the hangings during the Lunt era may have been a journal kept by the hangman himself. "The Haunting of Amos Lunt" provides a tantalizing clue. The author describes Lunt jotting a notation in a notebook following the hanging of Durrant: "'Very successful,' wrote the hangman in the little record book."

The "little record book" mentioned in the article may be a direct reference to *Album IV* of the Sullivan record or to the San Quentin register in the New York Public Library, either of which may have served as an official or quasi-official logbook.

The "little record book" may also refer to an original logbook kept by Lunt and later used as source material for all three. If Lunt kept such a record, its whereabouts remain unknown.

The following table compares the weight, height, and drop listed in the Duffy/Sullivan records along with the name of the officiating hangman (not included in either source) and the outcome (Sullivan record only).

Note: the executions of Eubanks and Sutton did not take place inside San Quentin, therefore they do not appear in San Quentin records. Because their hangings are discussed at length in this text, these entries are included for the purpose of comparison with drops calculated by Amos Lunt and Frank Arbogast.

Name	Weight (D/S)	Height (D/S)	Drop (D/S)	Hangman / Outcome (S)
James Eubanks	210	N.A.	5'0"	McDougall N.A.
Nathan B. Sutton	N.A.	N.A.	8'0"	Hale N.A.
Jose Gabriel (#15173)	140	5'3⅛" / 5'3½"	6'0"	McKenzie "Successful"
Lu Sing (#15372)	120	5'¼"	6'0"	Lunt "Successful"
P.J. Sullivan (#15866)	215	5'7½" / 5'7⅞"	5'0"	Lunt "Successful"
Anthony Azoff (#16016)	144/140	5'7⅝" / 5'6⅞"	5'8"	Lunt "about right"
Patrick J. Collins (#16258)	155	5'7"	5'6"	Lunt "Successful"
Emilio Garcia (#16287)	159	5'5⅜"	5'6"	Lunt [None]
W.M. Fredericks (#15960)	160	5'9" /5'9⅛"	5'10" / 5'6"	Lunt "Successful"
Fremont Smith (#15964)	220/180	5'9" / 5'8⅞"	5'6"	Lunt "Head nearly severed"
Hans Hansen	N.A./135	N.A. / 5'4½"	5'8"	Lunt "Successful"
Thomas St. Clair	135	5'4⅞"	5'9"	Lunt "Successful"
William Young (#16464)	145	5'3⅜"	5'9"	Lunt "Successful"
M.J. Miller (#16418)	148	5'6⅝"	5'6"	Lunt "Very Successful"
Chung Sing (#17107)	156	5'6¼"	5'6"	Lunt "Successful"
Frank Cooney Kloss (#16619)	140	5'5"	5'10"	Lunt "Very Successful"
Harvey Allender (#16969)	140	5'5½"	5'9"	Lunt "Very Successful"
William H.T. Durrant (#17260)	140	5'6⅛"	5'8"	Lunt "Very Successful"
Wee Tung (#17589)	133	5'2¼"	5'9" / 5'4"	Lunt "Very Successful"
Benjamin I. Hill (#17343)	190	5'7½"	5'2"	Lunt "Very Successful"
Joseph J. Ebanks (#17461)	160	5'8⅛" / 5'8½"	5'2"	Lunt "Successful"

Name	Weight (D/S)	Height (D/S)	Drop (D/S)	Hangman / Outcome (S)
John Miller (#17224)	163	5'2"	5'0"	Lunt [None]
George W. Clark (#17687)	127	5'8" /5'8¼"	5'3"	Lunt "Successful"
Manuel Chavez (#17401)	141	5'4⅛"	5'7"	Arbogast "Successful"
George C. Owens (#17654)	170	5'7"	5'4"	Arbogast "Very Successful"
Go See (#18366)	125	5'6¾"	5'8"	Arbogast "Successful"

Appendix 3
"The Official Table of Drops"

Inspired by several botched hangings in England, a committee led by Henry Bruce, the Baron of Aberdare, was formed in 1886 to study drops that would effectively fracture the cervical vertebrae. The committee produced a table based on 1,260 foot-pounds of force (1,260/weight of the subject=drop). In the succeeding years, this table underwent several evolutions. In 1892, the Home Office revised the drops based on the significantly reduced force of 840 foot-pounds and then in 1913, once again revised the table based on 1,000 foot-pounds of force. Because hangmen had routinely added length to the 1892 figures, the Home Office increased the force and subsequently length of drop for the 1913 revision. The following table contains an annotated combination of the three Home Office emanations. The original Home Office tables provide drops for each half stone (seven pounds) of bodyweight.

Weight in stones (pounds)	1886	1892	1913–
14 (196)	6'5"	4'3½"	5'1"
13 (182)	6'11"	4'7"	5'6"
12 (168)	7'6"	5'0"	5'11½"
11 (154)	8'2"	5'5"	6'6"
10 (140)	9'0"	6'0"	7'2"
9 (126)	9'6"	6'8"	7'11"
8 (112)	10'0"	7'6"	8'6"

The drops used in the first decade of hangings at San Quentin were based on a force consistent with those of the Home Office 1892 table. For example, Colonel McKenzie calculated a drop of 6'0" for Jose Gabriel, which equates to a force of 840 foot-pounds and matches the recommended drop for a person of ten-stone weight in the 1892 rendition of the Home Office's "Official Table of Drops." Three others among the first 20 hanged at San Quentin—Kloss, Allender, and Durrant—each weighed 140 and each received a slightly shorter drop of 5'10" (812 foot-pounds of force), 5'9" (805 foot-pounds), and 5'8" (793 foot-pounds) respectively. These shorter drops apparently worked. The Sullivan Record (see Appendix 2) characterized each of these hangings as "very successful."

Although the drops calculated for Kloss, Allender, and Durrant deviate from the 1892 Home Office table, it is tempting to conclude that the San Quentin hangmen knew about the table and may have used it as a guideline, making alterations as they saw fit. No official record of the source used by the early San Quentin hangmen exists, and the 1892 table would have been in force in England during Lunt's entire career on the scaffold. Whatever the case, the drops used by the hangmen in the San Quentin execution chamber during the late 19th century were shorter than those used by their English counterparts, even during the period covered by the 1892 table.

A close examination of the drops used at San Quentin during this period suggests that the hangmen, perhaps fearing the near decapitation that might result from a longer drop (and which occurred during William Hale's execution of Nathan B. Sutton), erred on the side of caution by using less rope. This shorter drop may have resulted from two primary factors: Hale's fear of repeating the Sutton debacle and the physical limitations of San Quentin's scaffold. The roof of the execution chamber capped the height of the scaffold and therefore limited the length of drop. Without cutting a hole in the floor, the San Quentin hangmen could not come close to the Home Office's recommended drops for the lightest subjects.

It bears noting that these numbers represent the science of hanging. Compensating for physical features or abnormalities, such as John Miller's misshapen neck, represents the art.

Chapter Notes

Preface

1. *San Francisco Call*, April 21, 1894.
2. *San Francisco Chronicle*, April 21, 1894.
3. According to The Great Register of Marin County of 1894, Lunt stood 5'11" and had blue eyes, brown hair, and a "light" complexion. Lunt, Amos. Entry No. 1530, The Great Register of Marin County—Year 1894. Also, Lunt, Amos. Entry No. 1584, The Great Register of Marin County—Year 1898. The Duffy and Sullivan records differ on P.J. Sullivan's height, with the former recording his height at 5'7½" while the latter places it at 5'7⅝". P.J. Sullivan, #15866, *Execution Books, 1893–1967*, F3717–1301–1302, San Quentin State Prison Records, R135, California State Archives, Office of the Secretary of State, Sacramento, California. Also, P.J. Sullivan, #15866, in Sullivan, Daniel. *San Quentin Prison—Album IV, Prisoner Mugshots.* Anne T. Kent California Room, Marin County Library, Marin County Civic Center, San Rafael, California.
4. *San Francisco Chronicle*, April 21, 1894.
5. *San Francisco Call*, April 21, 1894.
6. *Ibid.*
7. *Ibid.*

Introduction

1. *Sausalito News*, August 31, 1901.
2. F.F. Runyon, "In the Shadow of the Gallows: The Lockup," *Pasadena Evening Post*, December 22, 1927.
3. Pete Dotz, "Amos Lunt, the Hangsman of San Quentin Penitentiary, and His Fate," *Reno Gazette-Journal*, July 31, 1912.
4. When Lunt joined the prison service in 1891, Sullivan was employed as a guard. In the alphabetized "Payroll" of "Officers, Guards, and Employees" of San Quentin, dated July 1891 that forms part of Warden Hale's report to the prison board, Sullivan is listed as a guard earning $50 per month. San Quentin Prison Minute Book, 1891, page 166. *San Quentin Minute Books, 1874–1943.* State Board of Prison Directors Records. F3717: 987–1012. The California State Archives, Sacramento. He would later progress through the ranks, eventually becoming Turnkey. It is unclear when Sullivan began assisting with executions; the prison board's minutes list the ranks of employees but do not delineate their specific duties. Contemporary news reports of hangings conducted during the Lunt era, which are very detailed accounts, typically identify those who stood on the scaffold. The names "Captain Edgar," "Turnkey Jamieson," "Death Watch Guards [John D.] Jones and [Frank] Arbogast," "Warden Hale," "Father Lagan," and "Chaplain Drahms" appear often. Significantly, the name "Sullivan" is absent. This suggests that Sullivan's duties on the scaffold occurred only later, during Arbogast's turn as hangman. However, his duties during most if not all of Lunt's tenure as hangman included "Murderer's Row." An item in the *San Francisco Chronicle* of 1897 references him by name as the one "in his [condemned murderer Theodore Durrant] company yesterday."
5. *San Francisco Examiner*, September 29, 1895.
6. According to the piece in the October

24, 1899, edition of the *Santa Cruz Evening Sentinel*, Jamieson did not believe in Durrant's guilt and refused to fulfill his usual duties, so Lunt took over this vital aspect of the preparation, which he would continue until the end of his run as the hangman. "Prior to this execution," wrote the *Sentinel* reporter, "the duty of stretching rope and estimating the fall was assigned to Turnkey Jamieson. Jamieson believed Durrant innocent and refused to perform this office, so the ghastly work fell upon Lunt."

7. *San Francisco Chronicle*, December 10, 1897.

8. *Los Angeles Herald*, January 7, 1898; *Sacramento Record-Union*, January 7, 1898; *Los Angeles Times*, January 7, 1898; *Fresno Morning Republican*, January 7, 1898.

9. *Santa Cruz Evening Sentinel*, October 15, 1898.

10. Dr. W.F. McNutt, "Noose or Battery?" *San Francisco Examiner*, April 27, 1890.

11. *Oakland Tribune*, January 7, 1888.

12. *New York Herald*, July 8, 1865.

13. *San Francisco Examiner*, September 29, 1895.

14. *San Francisco Examiner*, September 29, 1895.

Chapter 1

1. Thomas Simpson Lunt, *A History of the Lunt Family in America* (Salem, MA: Salem Press, 1914) 146, Entry 941. According to Lunt, Amos Lunt married Mary E. Longfellow on November 24, 1845. A matrimony notice in the *Newburyport Herald* of November 28, 1845, gives the date of the wedding as Thursday, November 27, 1845. Amos Lunt's birthday of August 16, 1846, hints that either Mary became pregnant as soon as the couple exchanged vows or they had not waited for the formalities of a marriage ceremony to consummate their relationship.

2. In the 1850 U.S. Census, Lunt's occupation is listed as "mariner." 1850 U.S. Census, Essex County, Massachusetts, Newburyport, Sheet 66, line 6, Amos Lunt, NARA microfilm publication M432, Roll 313.

3. "FIVE DOLLARS REWARD. Lost on Friday the 5th, on Water-street, between Franklin and Winter streets, a Wallet, containing $32, in bills. Whoever may find the same and will leave it at the store of R. Griffith Jr., or at this office, shall receive the above reward." *Newburyport Herald*, December 12, 1845.

4. The Leon and Jeannette Rowland Collection at the UCSC Special Collections archive contains index cards recording basic biographical information for prominent Californians, including two entries (Box A-4, cards 629 and 630.01) detailing major events in the life of Amos Lunt, Sr. The two entries record a similar timeline but with a few conflicting dates. According to card 630, Lunt first traveled to California in May 1847; according to card 629, his first venture west occurred in 1849. Considering the birth of John T. in July 1848, the earlier date makes little sense unless someone other than Amos Lunt fathered the child. Before the opening of the transcontinental railroad, the one-way trip would have taken four months by land and nearly six by sea. Mary could not have been pregnant with John in May 1847. A late 1849 departure, however, would account for the birthdays of both John T. and Charles H. Lunt, born on July 9, 1850. His obituary in the September 20, 1886, edition of the *Santa Cruz Daily Surf* supports the latter date, stating that Lunt "came to California in '49." "Lunt, Amos, Sr." Cards 629–630, Box A-4, Rowland Card Collection Database, Leon and Jeannette Rowland Collection, UCSC Special Collections Archive.

5. Charles Lunt was born on July 9, 1850. "Charles H. Lunt," Entry 1671, page 214 in Thomas Simpson Lunt, *A History of the Lunt Family in America* (Salem, MA: Salem Press, 1914).

6. The two entries in the Rowland card collection both give 1851 as the date that Lunt, Sr., returned to Massachusetts. According to card 630, he traveled in late 1851 and remained in Massachusetts for six months. "Lunt, Amos, Sr." Cards 629–630, Box A-4, Rowland Card Collection Database, Leon and Jeannette Rowland Collection, UCSC Special Collections Archive.

7. This biographical information from Amos Lunt, Sr. Card 629, Box A-4, Rowland Card Collection Database, Leon and

Jeannette Rowland Collection, UCSC Special Collections Archive. The card entry for Amos Lunt, Sr., states that "she [Mary] didn't like the climate and returned to Massachusetts," but "climate" in this context may refer more to the atmosphere of San Francisco than the weather.

8. George W. Creasy, *The City of Newburyport in the Civil War: from 1861–1865* (Boston: Griffith-Stillings, 1903), 5.

9. Creasy's book presents brief biographies of the Newburyport veterans who served in the Civil War. His blurb about Amos Lunt on page 326 errantly gives his birth date as August 16, 1847 (not 1846).

10. According to Creasy, Lunt mustered out of service after the expiration of his enlistment, on August 4, 1864. According to *The Records of Members of the Grand Army of the Republic*, Lunt served until the end of the war and mustered out of service in Boston. William H. Ward, ed. *The Records of the Members of the Grand Army of the Republic, with a Complete Account of the Twentieth National Encampment* (San Francisco: H.S. Crocker, 1886), 483.

11. Entry 1670 for "John T. Lunt" in *A History of the Lunt Family in America* notes only that he died "young" and does not list a cause of death.

12. That the family lived together in Santa Cruz County is supported by the 1870 U.S. Census, which places them in the same household and describes 42-year-old Mary Lunt's occupation as "keeping house." The record also indicates that Amos Lunt, Sr., and his 20-year-old son Charles both worked in a sawmill in Soquel Township, while Amos Lunt, Jr., was apparently unemployed; his occupation is listed as "none." 1870 U.S. Census, Santa Cruz County, California, population schedule, Soquel Township, Soquel Post Office, P. 20, dwelling 146, family 146, Amos Lunt, NARA microfilm publication M593, Roll 89, Washington, D.C., National Archives and Records Administration.

13. On the 1880 U.S. Census, Lunt's occupation is listed as "farmer," although the California census of the same date lists his occupation as "lumberman." He is also listed as unmarried although his divorce from Mollie would not take place until October 1881. 1880 U.S. Census, Soquel Superior District, Santa Cruz County, California, population schedule, enumeration

district 90, P.495, P. 11, dwelling 99, family 105, Amos Lunt, NARA microfilm publication T9, Roll 313, Washington, D.C., National Archives and Records Administration.

14. The entry for "Amos Lunt, Jr." (entry 1669) in *A History of the Lunt Family in America* erroneously indicates that Lunt married Mary Milstead in 1875 and that she died in 1876, but an item in the *Santa Cruz Weekly Sentinel* of October 1, 1881, states "Amos Lunt, Jr., vs. Mollie Lunt—Divorce granted." "Amos Lunt, Jr." Entry 1669, page 214 in Thomas Simpson Lunt, *A History of the Lunt Family in America* (Salem, MA: Salem Press), 1914.

15. "Lunt, Amos, Jr." Card 630, Box A-4, Rowland Card Collection Database, Leon and Jeannette Rowland Collection, UCSC Special Collections Archive.

16. Lunt's advertisement in the *Santa Cruz Sentinel* of December 22, 1883, locates the saloon "opposite the plaza." Writing of Old Santa Cruz, Ernest Otto describes the location of Lunt's saloon as "The lower plaza," which he characterizes as "the center of business for many years." According to Otto, Lunt's saloon occupied a building that once housed a drug store. *Santa Cruz Sentinel*, April 16, 1939.

17. *Santa Cruz Sentinel*, December 22, 1883; *Santa Cruz Surf*, March 6, 1884.

18. Ernest Otto, "Old Santa Cruz," *Santa Cruz Sentinel*, December 17, 1944.

19. Otto describes saloons of "Old Santa Cruz" in columns appearing in the December 10 and December 17, 1944, editions of the *Santa Cruz Sentinel*. Otto was seven years old in 1880. 1880 U.S. Census, Santa Cruz City, Santa Cruz County, California, population schedule, enumeration district 88, P.449, P. 9, dwelling 76, family 80, Ernest Otto, NARA microfilm publication T9, Washington, D.C., National Archives and Records Administration.

20. The saloon, which Otto does not name, was operated by Bob Christy and Jimmie Handley. The two impresarios ran a small-scale entertainment complex, which included a small vaudeville theater and a second story where drunken patrons could crash. According to Otto, the saloon was ravaged by an angry mob. Ernest Otto, "Old Santa Cruz," *Santa Cruz Sentinel*, December 17, 1944.

21. *Santa Cruz Sentinel*, June 6, 1884.

O'Keefe apparently did not change the name of the saloon. In the same issue that announced the change of ownership, O'Keefe placed an advertisement for the Clipper: "Clipper Saloon: Best of Wines, Liquor & Cigars."

22. Otto states, "From one of the saloons the proprietor, Amos Lunt, gave up his business to become chief of police of Santa Cruz and went from here and became hangman at San Quentin," but Otto's timeline is confused. Lunt would not become chief of police until 1888. Ernest Otto, "Old Santa Cruz," *Santa Cruz Sentinel*, December 17, 1944.

23. *Santa Cruz Daily Surf*, July 11, 1887.

24. *Santa Cruz Sentinel*, June 12, 1884. 1880 U.S. Census, Santa Cruz City, Santa Cruz County, California, population schedule, enumeration district 88, P.449, P. 9, dwelling 76, family 80, Gertrude H. Otto, NARA microfilm publication T9, Washington, D.C., National Archives and Records Administration.

25. *Santa Cruz Sentinel*, June 12, 1884.

26. *Santa Cruz Sentinel*, May 22, 1885.

27. *Santa Cruz Sentinel*, March 11, 1885.

28. *Santa Cruz Sentinel*, March 18, 1885.

29. *Santa Cruz Sentinel*, March 13, 1885.

30. *Santa Cruz Sentinel*, March 18, 1885. William Pephfer was also known as William Pepper.

31. *Santa Cruz Sentinel*, March 22, 1885.

32. *San Francisco Examiner*, September 5, 1885.

33. According to a brief item in the June 1, 1886, edition of the *Santa Cruz Daily Surf*, Lunt assumed "his duties" that night.

34. In 1886, Amos Lunt, Sr., worked at Dougherty's Mill. *Santa Cruz Daily Surf*, September 20, 1886.

Chapter 2

1. According to an item in the June 1, 1886, *Santa Cruz Daily Surf*, "Amos Lunt, Jr., recently appointed a member of the Police Department, will assume his duties to-night."

2. The story occupied a full column in the May 4, 1887, edition of the *Santa Cruz Daily Surf*.

3. *Santa Cruz Sentinel*, February 15, 1887.

4. Armstrong's brief history of the Santa Cruz police chiefs appeared in *Santa Cruz Sentinel*, October 7, 1933.

5. *Santa Cruz Daily Surf*, November 5, 1887.

6. *Santa Cruz Daily Surf*, May 25, 1889.

7. *Santa Cruz Daily Surf*, May 27, 1889.

8. *Santa Cruz Sentinel*, October 7, 1933.

9. *Santa Cruz Sentinel*, August 24, 1901.

10. *Santa Cruz Daily Surf*, July 3, 1889.

11. *Santa Cruz Daily Surf*, July 13, 1889.

12. *Santa Cruz Daily Surf*, July 20, 1889.

13. *Santa Cruz Daily Surf*, March 22, 1890. Ernest Otto described the residence in "In Old Santa Cruz," one of a series of articles that appeared in *Santa Cruz Sentinel* in the 1940s. This segment ran in the May 6, 1945, edition.

14. *Santa Cruz Daily Surf*, January 9, 1891.

Chapter 3

1. Edward W. Bonney on May 9, 1862 (hanged by Colonel John W. McKenzie); Ramon Amador on September 9, 1871; and Lloyd Majors on May 24, 1884. *Oakland Daily Evening Tribune*, January 6, 1888.

2. The county jail was located in Oakland.

3. *Oakland Daily Evening Tribune*, January 6, 1888.

4. *Oakland Daily Evening Tribune*, January 6, 1888.

5. *Oakland Daily Evening Tribune*, January 6, 1888.

6. Coverage of the hanging consumed the entire front page of the January 6, 1888, edition of the *Oakland Daily Evening Tribune*, 2,000 copies of which appeared on the street within hours of the execution. One column listed all 250 invitees by name.

7. *Oakland Daily Evening Tribune*, January 6, 1888.

8. Note Sutton's use of the past tense—"executed"—instead of future tense—"will be executed." It is possible that the journalist later changed the text when he wrote his article following the event.

9. No documentary sources stating Sutton's exact height and weight exist. Contemporary sources disagree as to the length of drop. According to the *Oakland Daily Evening Tribune* writer, the drop was six feet, ten inches; according to his

colleague from the *San Francisco Chronicle*, the drop was eight feet.

10. *Oakland Daily Evening Tribune*, January 6, 1888.

11. *San Francisco Chronicle*, January 7, 1888.

12. *Oakland Daily Evening Tribune*, January 6, 1888.

13. *San Francisco Chronicle*, January 7, 1888.

14. *Ibid.*

15. Letter from N.B. Sutton to Sheriff Hale, dated January 4, 1888, quoted in the *Oakland Daily Evening Tribune*, January 6, 1888.

Chapter 4

1. *San Francisco Examiner*, December 16, 1891.

2. *San Francisco Examiner*, December 20, 1891.

3. *Ibid.*

4. *San Francisco Examiner*, January 20, 1891.

Chapter 5

1. When Warden John McComb's resignation became effective on April 1, 1891, Hale began his term as warden of San Quentin. San Quentin Prison Minute Book, 1891, 86–87. *San Quentin Minute Books, 1874–1943*. State Board of Prison Directors Records. F3717: 987–1012. The California State Archives, Sacramento, California.

2. Quoted in *San Francisco Examiner*, July 22, 1892.

3. In Ohio, where legislators had passed a similar law, hangings took place inside the walls of state penitentiaries, but county sheriffs still presided over executions. California legislators modeled their law on the Ohio precursor but removed county sheriffs by transferring the authority of overseeing executions to state prison wardens. *San Francisco Examiner*, May 12, 1891.

4. Quoted in *San Francisco Examiner*, July 22, 1892.

5. *Daily Alta*, April 12, 1891.

6. *San Francisco Examiner*, May 12, 1891.

7. During the period covered in this book, 1893–1898, 21 executions took place at San Quentin to just 11 at Folsom. San Quentin: 1893 (1); 1894 (2); 1895 (8); 1896 (1); 1897 (3); 1898 (6). Folsom: 1895 (1); 1896 (5); 1897 (2); 1898 (3). For a detailed discussions of hangings at Folsom, see April Moore, *Folsom's 93: The Lives and Crimes of Folsom Prison's Executed Men* (Fresno, CA: Craven Street Books, 2013).

Chapter 6

1. *San Francisco Chronicle*, February 28, 1893.

2. *San Francisco Examiner*, May 12, 1891.

3. *San Francisco Examiner*, May 30, 1891.

4. *Woodland [CA] Daily Democrat*, October 26, 1893.

5. John McNulty shot and killed James Collins on March 25, 1888; Sidney Bell murdered Samuel Jacobson on August 16, 1890; former police constable Joseph Wallace murdered Albert Rice on June 18, 1889; Charles Clark murdered Captain Duncan Logan on September 10, 1889; Ng Yuen murdered Li Lung on July 15, 1889. *San Francisco Examiner*, May 12. 1891. Clark cheated the hangman when he died in the county jail. Clark was described as "the consumptive murderer" by an *Examiner* journalist, and his tuberculosis ended his appeals, but the same reporter remarked that most of those on "Murderer's Row" needed daily medical attention "and no wonder," he said, "when one sees the gloomy holes in which they live and sniffs the vile air they breathe." *San Francisco Examiner*, July 12, 1891.

6. *San Francisco Examiner*, July 12, 1891.

7. The new law governing executions came into question as at least one attorney challenged its constitutionality. Carroll Cook, the attorney for condemned murderer John McNulty, argued that McNulty could not hang at a county jail because the new law repealed the old law, and he could not hang at a State prison because the new law represented "ex post facto legislation." *San Francisco Chronicle*, May 25, 1891. Commenting on the controversy from his cell in the county jail, McNulty quipped, "Time will tell whether Mr. Laumeister or Warden Hale will have the job of stretching my neck. It doesn't matter much to me which one gets the detail." Quoted in the *San Francisco Examiner*, July 12, 1891.

8. *Daily Alta*, April 12, 1891.

9. *Ibid.*

10. *Ibid.*

11. Lunt's appointment as a guard was one of ten approved by the State Prison Board during their meeting on May 9, 1891. San Quentin Prison Minute Book, 1891, 133. San Quentin Minute Books, 1874–1943. State Board of Prison Directors Records. F3717: 987–1012. The California State Archives, Sacramento, California.

Chapter 7

1. John C. Edgar, "Captain of the Yard's Report" In *Twelfth Annual Report of the State Board of Prison Directors of the State of California for the Forty-Second Fiscal Year, Ending June 30, 1891*. Sacramento: State Office, 1892, 26–27. In June 1891, the prison population contained 93 teenagers of the following ages: 14 (1), 16 (8), 17 (15), 18 (28), 19 (41).

2. *Ibid.*, 28.

3. San Quentin Prison Minute Book, 1891, 161. *San Quentin Minute Books, 1874–1943*. State Board of Prison Directors Records. F3717: 987–1012. The California State Archives, Sacramento, California.

4. Mansfield, I.L.R. "Report of the Physician." *Twelfth Annual Report of the State Board of Prison Directors of the State of California for the Forty-Second Fiscal Year, Ending June 30, 1891*. Sacramento: State Office, 1892, pp. 36–37.

5. The prison board minutes for May 1891 list 76 guards on duty. San Quentin Prison Minute Book, 1891, 129–130. *San Quentin Minute Books, 1874–1943*. State Board of Prison Directors Records. F3717: 987–1012. The California State Archives, Sacramento, California.

6. *San Francisco Chronicle*, March 29, 1892.

7. A small blurb in the January 21, 1899, *Marin County Tocsin* described him as "Amos Lunt, the well-known cliff climber."

Chapter 8

1. *San Francisco Examiner*, September 23, 1891; *Santa Cruz Surf*, September 22, 1891.

2. Eager to avoid any disruptions in the prison's routine, Hale scheduled Vital's execution for 5 a.m., before the rest of the population began the daily grind. *San Francisco Examiner*, July 22, 1892.

3. *Ibid.*

4. *San Francisco Examiner*, April 23, 1897.

5. *San Francisco Examiner*, July 22, 1892.

6. Anton Vital finally arrived at San Quentin two years later, on August 11, 1894. Following court action that had dragged on since 1892, Vital's new date with the hangman was set for Friday, October 12, 1894. Once again, he would escape his death sentence. Two days before Vital would have climbed the "stairway to Heaven," Governor Markham commuted Vital's sentence to life because of lingering questions about his sanity. Vital claimed, among other "powers," the ability to control weather phenomena such as blizzards and cyclones. *San Francisco Chronicle*, October 10, 1894. Sullivan's *Album IV* contains a page for Vital: Anton Vital, #14964, in Sullivan, Daniel. *San Quentin Prison—Album IV, Prisoner Mugshots*. Anne T. Kent California Room, Marin County Library, Marin County Civic Center, San Rafael, California.

Chapter 9

1. Jose Gabriel, #15173, *Execution Books, 1893–1967*, F3717–1301–1302, San Quentin State Prison Records, R135, California State Archives, Office of the Secretary of State, Sacramento, California. Also, Jose Gabriel, #15173, in Sullivan, Daniel. *San Quentin Prison—Album IV, Prisoner Mugshots*. Anne T. Kent California Room, Marin County Library, Marin County Civic Center, San Rafael, California. Also, Jose Gabriel, #15173, in Duffy, Clinton. *San Quentin Executioner's Log*. Object Identification: 1999.2872. The Marin History Museum, San Rafael, California. All three of these sources contain the same or similar information. Because the execution register housed in the California State Archives, which is a copy of the original housed in the Marin History Museum (the Duffy record), was the primary source consulted for this text,

succeeding endnotes concerning the weight of condemned convicts and their drops will cite this record.

2. *San Francisco Chronicle*, February 28, 1893.

3. The "Death Watch" over Jose Gabriel consisted of guards John Miller and T.K. Waters. *Oakland Tribune*, March 3, 1893.

4. *San Francisco Chronicle*, February 28, 1893; *Evening Bee*, March 3, 1893.

5. San Francisco vigilance committees hanged eight men from 1850--1856. For a detailed list, see "Executions in San Francisco, 1851-1890." *San Francisco Sheriff's Department History Research Project*.

6. *San Francisco Examiner*, March 3, 1893.

7. *Ibid.* For biographical details of McKenzie's achievements, see the *San Francisco Call*, March 28, 1898.

8. All of McKenzie's hangings occurred in San Francisco except for one: he hanged Edward Bonney in Alameda. During an interview with the *San Francisco Examiner*, McKenzie provided a brief resume of his experience with official hangings (he did not mention any hangings as part of his activities with vigilance committees). Based on this resume, it is possible to reconstruction a chronological list of McKenzie's hangings: June 10, 1859: William Morris ("Tipperary Bill"); September 21, 1860: James Whitford; March 1, 1861: Albert Lee; June 4, 1861: John Clarkson; May 9, 1862: Edward Bonney (in San Leandro, Alameda County); March 14, 1873: John Devine; July 25, 1873: Charles Russell; January 23, 1884: George Wheeler ("Wheeler the Strangler:). See *San Francisco Examiner*, March 3, 1893. For a thorough discussion of hangings in San Francisco, see "Executions in San Francisco: 1851-1890," *San Francisco Sheriff's Department History Research Project*.

9. *San Francisco Examiner*, March 3, 1893.

10. Jose Gabriel, #15173, *Execution Books, 1893-1967*, F3717-1301-1302, San Quentin State Prison Records, R135, California State Archives, Office of the Secretary of State, Sacramento, California. The Register and Descriptive List of Convicts under Sentence of Imprisonment in the State Prison of California records Gabriel's height as 5'2¾" Jose Gabriel, #15173, 116-117.

11. It appears that San Quentin prison authorities did not modify the scaffold or put a hole in the floor to increase the possible drop. Of the 20 men hanged by Lunt, only the first one—Lu Sing—received a drop of more than five feet, ten inches. Sing received a drop of six feet, most likely because Colonel McKenzie made the calculation and gave him the maximum allowable under San Quentin's scaffold (he also gave Jose Gabriel a six-foot drop). See *Execution Books, 1893-1967*, F3717-1301-1302, San Quentin State Prison Records, R135, California State Archives, Office of the Secretary of State, Sacramento, California. A news item in July 1893 named McKenzie as the hangman for Sing's execution, but he apparently bowed out at the last minute, and Hale subsequently replaced him with Lunt. *San Francisco Examiner*, July 10, 1893. According to a statement Hale made in 1895, after Lunt's seventh hanging, he named Lunt the San Quentin hangman the day before Sing's execution. *San Francisco Examiner*, September 29, 1895.

12. *Oakland Tribune*, March 3, 1893.

13. *San Francisco Examiner*, March 4, 1893.

14. *Oakland Tribune*, March 3, 1893.

15. *San Francisco Call*, March 4, 1893.

16. *Ibid.*

17. *Oakland Tribune*, March 3, 1893.

18. *Ibid.; Evening Bee*, March 3, 1893.

19. *San Francisco Examiner*, March 4, 1893.

20. *Ibid.*

21. *San Francisco Examiner*, September 29, 1895.

Chapter 10

1. *San Francisco Call*, February 3, 1894; *San Francisco Chronicle*, February 3, 1894. The *San Francisco Examiner's* February 3, 1894, article about the hanging records Sing's statement as "Good-by, all white men, good-by."

2. *San Francisco Examiner*, September 29, 1895. At the time this article was written, Lunt had hanged seven men.

3. Lu Sing, #15372, *Execution Books, 1893-1967*, F3717-1301-1302, San Quentin State Prison Records, R135, California State Archives, Office of the Secretary of State, Sacramento, California.

4. *San Francisco Examiner*, February 3, 1894.

5. *Ibid.*

6. Sing's execution was initially scheduled for Friday, July 14, 1893, but Coffey's legal efforts on his client's behalf led to a postponement.

7. *San Francisco Chronicle*, February 3, 1894.

8. *Ibid.*

9. The San *Francisco Chronicle* article of February 3, 1894, is the only account to contain these last words by Lu Sing.

10. Biographical detail from George C. Mansfield, *History of Butte County, California* (Los Angeles: Historic Record Company, 1918).

11. *San Francisco Examiner*, February 3, 1894.

12. *Ibid.*

13. *San Francisco Examiner*, September 29, 1895.

Chapter 11

1. This version is from the *Sacramento Record-Union*, November 18, 1892.

2. This version is from the *San Francisco Call*, April 21, 1894.

3. *San Francisco Chronicle*, April 20, 1894.

4. *Ibid.*

5. *San Francisco Chronicle*, April 21, 1894.

6. P.J. Sullivan, #15866, *Execution Books, 1893–1967*, F3717–1301–1302, San Quentin State Prison Records, R135, California State Archives, Office of the Secretary of State, Sacramento, California. Also, P.J. Sullivan, #15866, in Sullivan, Daniel. *San Quentin Prison—Album IV, Prisoner Mugshots*. Anne T. Kent California Room, Marin County Library, Marin County Civic Center, San Rafael, California.

7. He gave John Miller, who stood at 5'2" and weighed 163 pounds, a five-foot drop in 1898. It would prove to be too much rope for Miller. John Miller, #17224, *Execution Books, 1893–1967*, F3717–1301–1302, San Quentin State Prison Records, R135, California State Archives, Office of the Secretary of State, Sacramento, California.

8. *San Francisco Chronicle*, April 21, 1894.

9. Each of the papers that covered Sullivan's hanging reported a slightly different version of this episode. This one is from the *San Francisco Chronicle*, April 21, 1894.

10. *San Francisco Call-Bulletin*, April 21, 1894.

11. *Oakland Tribune*, April 20, 1894; *San Francisco Examiner*, April 21, 1894. Contemporary news accounts indicate that Lunt followed a procedure for the last steps in the hanging process: he slid the cap over the condemned man's head, leaving the face exposed, put the noose in place, and then pulled the cap down to conceal the man's face.

12. *San Francisco Call*, April 21, 1894; *San Francisco Examiner*, April 21, 1894.

13. *San Francisco Chronicle*, April 21, 1894.

14. *San Francisco Call*, April 21, 1894.

15. *Ibid.* The *Chronicle* reporter downplayed the cut, characterizing it as "an abrasion on the neck." *San Francisco Chronicle*, April 21, 1894.

16. *San Francisco Examiner*, April 21, 1894. According to this account, one of the witnesses attempted to take a photograph with "his Kodak." It is unknown if the witness managed to snap a picture, but it appears that photography was generally verboten at San Quentin hangings. Since newspapers of the era did not yet possess the technology to reproduce photographs, they sent sketch artists instead. These detailed renderings often accompanied featured articles and provide an invaluable chronicle of what occurred during hangings at San Quentin.

17. F.F. Runyon, "In the Shadow of the Gallows Prison Experiences: the Lock-Up." *Pasadena Evening Post*, December 22, 1927.

18. Lottie Lunt, born May 13, 1883; Arnold Lunt, born April 2, 1887. Thomas S. Lunt, *A History of the Lunt Family in America* (Salem, MA: Salem Press, 1914), 214.

19. Anthony Azoff, #16016, *Execution Books, 1893–1967*, F3717–1301–1302, San Quentin State Prison Records, R135, California State Archives, Office of the Secretary of State, Sacramento, California.

20. *Santa Cruz Sentinel*, October 16, 1894. The *Santa Cruz Surf* also ran a brief item about Lunt's visit in the October 15, 1894, edition.

Chapter 12

1. *San Francisco Examiner*, January 9, 1895. The article refers to Lunt as "Amos Lundt."

2. *Santa Cruz Sentinel*, January 13, 1895.

3. *San Francisco Examiner*, May 26, 1936.

4. San Quentin inmate Royall Douglass #19173 wrote "Garden of Death," a poem that rails against "laws that mock the laws of God,/And strangle men to death—". The poem first appeared in a 1911 compilation of Douglass' poetry titled *Drops of Blood*. See Royall Douglass, *Drops of Blood: Prison Verse by Royall Douglass, No. 19173* (Palo Alto, CA: Altruria Press, 1911).

5. Laurie also interviewed Rico Morasco, whose death sentence was later commuted to life imprisonment. Laurie's complete article was in the *San Francisco Examiner*, May 12, 1895.

6. Dormer's article appeared on page 10 of the May 12, 1895, edition of the *San Francisco Call*.

7. *San Francisco Call*, June 7, 1895.

8. *San Francisco Call*, June 9, 1895.

9. The *San Francisco Call* of March 26, 1895, published the portion of Azoff's statement in which he describes the robbery.

"We went to Boulder Creek at about noon and had dinner at the Foster House, Sprague paying for himself and for me, and after dinner we went up by the schoolhouse and sat down under a shade tree, when Sprague said he would go down and see the agent and make all the arrangements, so that there would be no trouble when we should go down after dark to carry out the plan he had suggested. We waited in the woods until about a quarter past 8 that night, when we left for the railway station-house. We walked along slowly and when we reached the station-house it had become quite dark. As we approached the railroad I could see that there were three large lamps burning in the station-house. Sprague gave me the piece of gunnysack and I approached the station from the rear. I noticed a boxcar standing on the track. I walked right up to the station-house and stepped into the door, while Sprague, stepping to one side of the door, remained outside.

"Almost immediately to the left of the door was the opening into the office of the station agent, and stepping up to the opening I looked in. The agent sat there, and when I laid the pistol down near the opening, and looked in he smiled and seemed to understand just what I was there for and seemed well pleased. I threw the gunny sack in through the opening and on the floor of the agent's office. He seemed to understand everything that was being done, and, carrying out the programme, I said, using if I remember correctly, the Irish brogue, 'Put all this month you have got into that sack.' Then Sprague who was standing by the door said to me, 'We will fire and then run over to my brother's.' I stood there for a moment to see how the agent was acting, as I did not understand why Sprague had stepped outside. The agent said nothing and only made me think from his action that everything was just as Sprague had stated, when just at that moment I heard a pistol-shot, which came from the place where Sprague stood, just outside the door. Thinking that he was carrying out his part of the programme I stood in the door and fired two shots in rapid succession and into the air.

"Almost before the noise of the last shot had died away I heard a whole volley ring out, and one bullet passed right near my head. I did not understand this for a moment, for it did not seem possible that Sprague could fire so many shots so suddenly, so I looked back into the agent's office and he was crouched down in one corner. I then stepped out and fired two more shots. All of this would hardly take ten seconds, and looking for Sprague I found that he had disappeared, and then, another shot being fired which broke the glass in the window and came near me, I knew instantly that something was wrong; that Sprague had put me in this trap for the purpose of benefiting himself, and that if I remained there another instant I should be killed. I stood in the light while all outside was dark.

"Realizing that moment the position I was in, and not knowing that any one had been hurt, I fled.

"Had I known at first, or had I imagined at first, that any one was firing at me of course I should not have stayed there in the light when I could have so easily run out in the darkness, as I did thereafter. I heard no one call to me and saw no one at or near the station excepting the agent and Sprague, and it was only while I was running that I knew there were many other people there from the fact that so many shots were fired in rapid succession.

"I fired but four shots. When I found so many people were firing at me I ran as rapidly as possible, and it being in the dark I tripped and fell and remained almost unconscious for some time. Finally I gathered myself together and everything being quiet I hastened along the road.

"I desire to say here that if any one shot Len Harris on that night it must have been Sprague for the purpose of carrying out his scheme of benefiting himself even at the loss of my life. He testified that a man arrested him and that when arrested he had a pistol in his hand, and I believe if the truth shall ever appear it will then be known that that pistol had been fired by Sprague, who knew where the officers were in concealment."

10. *San Francisco Call*, March 28, 1895.

11. *Oakland Tribune*, June 7, 1895. According to some accounts, Collins stabbed his wife 35 times.

12. The *San Francisco Examiner's* story about the Sarah Collins murder occupied three columns on page 12 of the October 9, 1893, edition. Hand-drawn sketches of her apartment and of the blood-drenched crime scene accompanied the story. News of Patrick Collins' execution received front-page coverage.

13. Kelly later recounted this conversation. *San Francisco Examiner*, October 9, 1893.

14. Anthony Azoff, #16016; Patrick J. Collins, #16258; Emilio Garcia, #16287. *Execution Books, 1893–1967*, F3717–1301–1302, San Quentin State Prison Records, R135, California State Archives, Office of the Secretary of State, Sacramento, California.

15. *San Francisco Chronicle*, June 8, 1895.

16. *San Francisco Examiner*, June 8, 1895.

17. *Ibid.*

18. *San Francisco Chronicle*, June 8, 1895. Writers from both the *Chronicle* and *Examiner* carefully noted Jack Harris' demeanor during the hanging of his father's murderer.

19. *San Francisco Examiner*, June 8,

1895. The *Chronicle* presents a different version of this incident. "After the body was cut down Harris nipped off a bit of the rope, which he carried away as a token of vengeance."

20. *San Francisco Examiner*, June 8, 1895.

21. *Oakland Tribune*, June 7, 1895; *San Francisco Chronicle*, June 8, 1895.

22. This portion is from the *San Francisco Examiner*, June 8, 1895. The other papers excluded this portion of Father Lagan's statement.

23. *San Francisco Examiner*, June 8, 1895.

24. Azoff, Anthony, #16016; Collins, Patrick, #16258; Garcia, Emillo [sic], #16287. Sullivan, Daniel. *San Quentin Prison—Album IV, Prisoner Mugshots.* Anne T. Kent California Room, Marin County Library, Marin County Civic Center, San Rafael, California.

25. *San Francisco Examiner*, June 8, 1895.

26. *Stockton Evening Record*, June 7, 1895.

27. *Oakland Tribune*, June 7, 1895.

Chapter 13

1. "The Haunting of Amos Lunt—Hangman," *San Francisco Call*, September 15, 1901.

2. *San Francisco Call*, July 26, 1895.

3. *San Francisco Chronicle*, July 27, 1895.

4. For the complete interview, see the *San Francisco Examiner*, July 26, 1895.

5. *Alameda Daily Argus*, July 26, 1895.

6. *San Francisco Examiner*, July 27, 1895.

7. *Ibid.* Michelson does not name "the guard," who is almost certainly Amos Lunt, the hangman. Lunt typically walked next to the condemned man in the procession to the gallows, and the *Call* writer identified the guard by name. "Fredericks himself was very pale, and Captain Lunt held him by one arm in case he should need support. His step, however, was firm and he glanced curiously upward at the rope as he ascended the gallows." *San Francisco Call*, July 27, 1895.

8. *San Francisco Chronicle*, July 27, 1895; *San Francisco Call*, July 27, 1895.

9. *San Francisco Chronicle*, July 27, 1895.

10. *Evening Bee*, July 26, 1895; *Evening Mail*, July 26, 1895. Lunt apparently took over from Hale the duty of signaling the concealed guards to sever the strings. This assertion is supported by coverage in the *Call*, which states that "Lunt... stepped back and raised his hand. The trap crashed..." July 27, 1895.

11. *San Francisco Chronicle*, July 27, 1895.

12. *Ibid.*

13. *San Francisco Examiner*, July 27, 1895.

Chapter 14

1. His name was spelled "Arbogast," but some news reports errantly spell it "Abrogast."

2. *San Francisco Examiner*, September 29, 1895.

3. *San Francisco Chronicle*, August 10, 1895.

4. *San Francisco Examiner*, August 10, 1895.

5. Fremont Smith, #15964; P.J. Sullivan, #15866; Patrick Collins, #16258; Emilio Garcia, #16287; *Execution Books, 1893–1967*, F3717-1301-1302, San Quentin State Prison Records, R135, California State Archives, Office of the Secretary of State, Sacramento, California.

6. *San Francisco Call*, August 9, 1895. The *San Francisco Examiner's* pre-hanging article of August 9, 1895, describes Smith as "strongly built."

7. *San Francisco Examiner*, August 9, 1895.

8. *San Francisco Call*, August 9, 1895.

9. *Ibid.*

10. *San Francisco Call*, August 10, 1895; *San Francisco Examiner*, August 10, 1895; *San Francisco Chronicle*, August 10, 1895.

11. *San Francisco Chronicle*, August 10, 1895.

12. *San Francisco Call*, August 10, 1895.

13. *Ibid.*

14. *San Francisco Examiner*, August 10, 1895.

15. *Ibid.*

16. *San Francisco Examiner*, September 29, 1895. The article may represent an atonement of sorts for the harsh comments

the newspaper published the day after Fremont Smith's hanging.

Chapter 15

1. "The usual number [of physicians] required to attend each man hanged is three, and the extra four were provided, it is said, in case of heart failure on the part of the executioner." *San Francisco Call*, October 19, 1895.

2. "Mucilage in Lieu of Virus," *Town Talk* 10, No. 515 (July 12, 1902): 15.

3. Hans Hansen; Thomas St. Clair. *Execution Books, 1893–1967*, F3717-1301-1302, San Quentin State Prison Records, R135, California State Archives, Office of the Secretary of State, Sacramento, California.

4. *San Francisco Examiner*, October 13, 1895.

5. *San Francisco Chronicle*, October 18, 1895.

6. *San Francisco Examiner*, October 18, 1895. The article in the *Examiner* does not mention Lunt's role in altering the scaffold, but an article in the *Chronicle* of the same date states, "In the chamber adjoining the condemned cell a new double scaffold, the first of its kind ever seen within the walls of San Quentin prison, has been built. From the stout crossbeam dangle two ropes. They are stretched taut with heavy weights. The traps have been tested by the prison hangman, Amos Lunt, who has supervised the erection of the scaffold at the request of the United States Marshal, and have been pronounced satisfactory."

7. *San Francisco Call*, October 16, 1895.

8. Hans Hansen and Thomas St. Clair in Daniel Sullivan, *San Quentin Prison—Album IV, Prisoner Mugshots*. Anne T. Kent California Room, Marin County Library, Marin County Civic Center, San Rafael, California. Anthony Azoff, #16016. Execution Books, 1893–1967, F3717-1301-1302, San Quentin State Prison Records, R135, California State Archives, Office of the Secretary of State, Sacramento, California. William H.T. Durrant, #17260, hanged in 1898, would also receive a drop of 5'8". He weighed 140 pounds.

9. Some news accounts have Lunt and a Death Watch guard simultaneously noosing the two men, while others criticize the

procedure for a slight delay caused by Lunt working the knot on one man and then the other. Given the importance that Lunt placed on placement of the noose in the September 29 interview, and in considering the criticism that he faced for failing to tighten the knot around Fremont Smith's neck, it appears more likely that Lunt noosed both St. Clair and Hansen.

10. *The San Francisco Examiner*, October 19, 1895.

11. *San Francisco Examiner,* October 18, 1895.

12. *Ibid.*

13. *San Francisco Call*, October 16, 1895.

14. *San Francisco Examiner*, October 19, 1895.

15. *San Francisco Examiner*, October 18, 1895.

16. *Ibid.*

17. St. Clair's statement appeared in its entirety in the October 19, 1895, edition of the *San Francisco Chronicle* and the October 19, 1895, edition of the *San Francisco Call.*

18. *San Francisco Call*, October 19, 1895.

19. *Ibid.*

20. *San Francisco Chronicle*, October 19, 1895.

21. *Ibid.*

22. *Ibid.* According to the *Call*'s article of the same date, Hansen was noosed first and "for a full minute he remained a prey to untold emotions while St. Clair was being made ready." This account suggests that Lunt either noosed both men or had to oversee Miller's noosing of St. Clair.

23. *San Francisco Call*, October 19, 1895. The *Call* took a decidedly negative stance on the executions. Their writer lapsed into editorializing when he wrote, "The execution can be termed a success only because of the fact that the men are dead. The proceedings were exceedingly repugnant to the American mind." This stance may in part explain the harsh criticism of both the hanging and the officials involved.

24. According to a piece in the *San Francisco Chronicle* of October 19, 1895, "Hansen died quietly after nine minutes. After the life had left him the body of St. Clair was still wriggling. It was not until fourteen minutes had elapsed that everything was quiet." This statement suggests

that St. Clair's body displayed physiological reactions for at least ten minutes, although it is difficult to take it at face value since no reporters had witnessed the hanging and this description was likely added to titillate readers.

25. *San Francisco Chronicle*, October 19, 1895.

26. *Ibid.*

Chapter 16

1. William Young, #16464, *Execution Books, 1893–1967*, F3717–1301–1302, San Quentin State Prison Records, R135, California State Archives, Office of the Secretary of State, Sacramento, California. Lunt would hang six men in 1898.

2. *San Francisco Call*, October 26, 1895.

3. Details of the inquest of Pierre Latestere are from the *Monterey Cypress*, March 31, 1894.

4. William Young, #16464, *Execution Books, 1893–1967*, F3717–1301–1302, San Quentin State Prison Records, R135, California State Archives, Office of the Secretary of State, Sacramento, California.

5. *San Francisco Examiner*, October 26, 1895.

6. *San Francisco Chronicle*, October 26, 1895.

7. *San Francisco Call*, October 26, 1895.

8. *Ibid.* The article does not mention Lunt by name, instead attributing the quote to "the hangman."

9. News accounts of hangings at San Quentin invariably report, down to the minute, the interval between the drop and the cessation of the victim's heartbeat. These accounts typically agree, but in the case of William Young, the accounts vary widely. According to a piece in the *Examiner* from October 26, Young's heartbeat lasted for seven-and-a-half minutes but the body was left hanging for a total of 17 minutes. The *Chronicle*'s account of the same date states that Young's heartbeat lasted for 16½ minutes, while the *Call*'s account gives a time of 17 minutes. Because the body was typically cut down very shortly after detection of the final heartbeat, the latter two accounts are likely the more accurate, although at 17 minutes, Young's pulse lasted well beyond the nine others who proceeded him to the gallows.

10. The anecdote is preserved for posterity in the December 14, 1895, edition of the *Santa Cruz Sentinel*.

Chapter 17

1. Miller's original execution was scheduled for September 27, 1895. *San Francisco Examiner*, December 6, 1895.

2. This position gained some traction among those familiar with the case. "His attorneys," wrote a *Call* reporter, "enlisted much sympathy for him from people who believed that young Greene should have been hanged." *San Francisco Call*, December 12, 1896.

3. *San Francisco Examiner*, December 12, 1896.

4. The *Call's* coverage of December 12, 1896, conveyed this snippet of Father Lagan's words. The *Chronicle's* story of the same date did not quote the priest, instead stating, "Father Lagan stepped forward and told the spectators that Miller had requested him to say that he died an innocent man." The *Marysville Daily Democrat* and the *Evening News* ran stories quoting Lagan as saying, "He will expiate with his life the crime of which he was accused, but was less guilty than some." The *Marysville Daily Democrat*, December 12, 1896; *Evening News*, December 11, 1896.

5. *San Francisco Chronicle*, December 12, 1896; *San Francisco Examiner*, December 12, 1896.

6. *San Francisco Call*, December 12, 1896.

7. *Alameda Daily Argus*, January 15, 1897.

8. News of the Roe hanging, with sketches of the gallows, occupied almost an entire page in the January 16, 1897, edition of the *San Francisco Chronicle*.

9. *Record Union*, January 16, 1897.

10. *San Francisco Chronicle*, January 15, 1897.

Chapter 18

1. Chun Sing, #17107, *Execution Books, 1893–1967*, F3717–1301–1302, San Quentin State Prison Records, R135, California State Archives, Office of the Secretary of State, Sacramento, California. Also, Chun Sing, #17107, The Register and Descriptive List of Convicts under Sentence of Imprisonment in the State Prison of California records, 278–279.

2. *San Francisco Chronicle*, February 18, 1897.

3. *Ibid.*

4. All three major San Francisco newspapers reported these as Chun Sing's final words.

15. *San Francisco Call*, February 18, 1897.

6. *San Francisco Chronicle*, February 18, 1897. The *Chronicle* erred in describing the Sing execution as Lunt's 11th.

7. William H.T. Durrant, #17260, *Execution Books, 1893–1967*, F3717–1301–1302, San Quentin State Prison Records, R135, California State Archives, Office of the Secretary of State, Sacramento, California. For a detailed account of the Durrant case, see Robert Graysmith, *The Bell Tower: The Case of Jack the Ripper Finally Solved...in San Francisco* (Washington, D.C.: Regnery Publishing, 1999). Graysmith builds a case for Durrant's innocence and provides an alternate suspect in Pastor John Gibson. For trial testimony, see Edgar D. Peixotto, *Report of the Trial of William Henry Theodore Durrant, Indicted for the Murder of Blanche Lamont, before The Superior Court of the City and County of San Francisco, Including a Full History of the Case* (Detroit: The Collector Publishing Company, 1899).

Chapter 19

1. Frank Cooney Kloss, #16619, *Execution Books, 1893–1967*, F3717–1301–1302, San Quentin State Prison Records, R135, California State Archives, Office of the Secretary of State, Sacramento, California. The Register and Descriptive List of Convicts under Sentence of Imprisonment in the State Prison of California records Kloss' profession as "actor." Frank Cooney Kloss, #16619, p. 237–238, entry 5. Inmate Indexes 1851–1940, San Quentin State Prison Records, F3717: 1135–41. California State Archives, Office of the Secretary of State, Sacramento, California.

2. Sources differ about the details of Kloss' crime. According to the San Quentin Execution Books, Kloss did not try to

rouse Deady, instead stabbing him twice in the throat. Newspaper accounts of his hanging, however, describe him slashing Deady's throat and severing the jugular vein. According to the *Oakland Tribune* of April 21, 1897, Deady died a few hours later from blood loss, although someone with a severed jugular vein would exsanguinate in seconds, not hours.

3. *San Francisco Examiner*, April 23, 1897.

4. Sattler described the origin of the term "walking days" when he described the pepper plot to a reporter. "On certain days in the week prisoners are released from their cells for exercise. We call it 'walking day.' Prisoners on the lower corridor are taken out one day and those on the upper corridor on another, so there can be only one-half the prisoners on the floor at one time." *San Francisco Examiner*, April 23, 1897.

5. *San Francisco Examiner*, April 23, 1897.

6. *Ibid.*

7. *Ibid.*

8. *Chico Enterprise*, March 14, 1944.

9. Runyon recounted the incident in two stories written 30 years later. See F.F. Runyon, "In the Shadow of the Gallows, Prison Experiences by F.F. Runyon: The Yellow Story," *Pasadena Evening Post*, December 23, 1927; F.F. Runyon, "In the Shadow of the Gallows, Prison Experiences by F.F. Runyon: The Turned-Down Story," *Pasadena Evening Post*, December 24, 1927.

10. Lottie Lunt was born on May 13, 1883.

11. *San Francisco Examiner*, April 23, 1897.

12. *San Francisco Examiner*, April 24, 1897.

13. *Ibid.*

14. Death Watch guard J.D. Jones recalled Kloss' assertion in a statement that he made after the hanging which was published in the April 24, 1897, edition of the *Examiner*.

15. *San Francisco Examiner*, April 24, 1897.

16. *Oakland Tribune*, April 23, 1897; *San Francisco Call*, April 24, 1897.

17. This is most likely a reference to a statement printed in April 23, 1897, edition of the *San Francisco Examiner* and

repeated in the *Oakland Tribune* of the same date: "A few days ago when the crippled and aged mother of the condemned man went to San Quentin to bid him good-by his curses and foul words shouted at her shocked the death watch as few incidents have power to do."

18. *San Francisco Examiner*, April 24, 1897.

19. *Oakland Tribune*, April 23, 1897.

20. *San Francisco Call*, April 24, 1897. The *Examiner* quoted Kloss as saying, "Make a good job of it." *San Francisco Examiner*, April 24, 1897.

21. *Oakland Tribune*, April 23 1897.

22. *San Francisco Examiner*, April 24, 1897.

23. *Ibid.*

24. *San Francisco Examiner*, April 24, 1897.

25. F.F. Runyon, "In the Shadow of the Gallows, Prison Experiences by F.F. Runyon: The Turned-Down Story," *Pasadena Evening Post*, December 24, 1927.

Chapter 20

1. F.F. Runyon, "In the Shadow of the Gallows, Prison Experiences by F.F. Runyon: The Turned-Down Story," *Pasadena Evening Post*, December 24, 1927.

2. *San Francisco Call*, May 14, 1897; *Oakland Tribune*, May 14, 1897.

3. *Oakland Tribune*, May 14, 1897.

4. *San Francisco Call*, May 14, 1897.

5. F.F. Runyon, "In the Shadow of the Gallows, Prison Experiences by F.F. Runyon: The Turned-Down Story," *Pasadena Evening Post*, December 24, 1927.

6. *Alameda Daily Encinal*, May 15, 1897.

Chapter 21

1. *San Francisco Examiner*, November 11, 1897.

2. William H.T. Durrant, #17260, *Execution Books, 1893–1967*, F3717–1301–1302, San Quentin State Prison Records, R135, California State Archives, Office of the Secretary of State, Sacramento, California.

3. *San Francisco Examiner*, November 11, 1897.

Chapter 22

1. Alice Rix, "Lund tells how a man should be hanged," *San Francisco Examiner*, November 21, 1897. Because the Rix interview offers a rare insight into the mind of a man who seldom spoke about his work, most of Lunt's responses are reproduced here verbatim, albeit with added or altered attribution (e.g. "Lunt explained"). In her subsequent article, Rix added interjections, commentary, and descriptions of Lunt's behavior during the interview. These are included, with attribution, only when relevant.

2. *San Francisco Examiner*, September 29, 1895.

3. Rix's interview ran with the title, "Lund tells how a man should be hanged," and errantly spells the hangman's name "Lund." *San Francisco Examiner*, November 21, 1897.

Chapter 23

1. *San Francisco Examiner*, December 11, 1897.

2. *Evening News*, December 10, 1897; *Sacramento Evening Bee*, December 10, 1897; *San Francisco Chronicle*, December 10, 1897.

3. *Evening News*, December 10, 1897.

4. *San Francisco Chronicle*, December 11, 1897.

5. Harvey Allender, #16969, *Execution Books, 1893–1967*, F3717–1301–1302, San Quentin State Prison Records, R135, California State Archives, Office of the Secretary of State, Sacramento, California. Harvey Allender, #16969, p. 266–267, entry 7. Inmate Indexes 1851–1940, San Quentin State Prison Records, F3717: 1135–41. California State Archives, Office of the Secretary of State, Sacramento, California.

6. *Evening News*, December 10, 1897. The reporter erred when he said that Allender received a foot more of rope "than that used for heavy men." Lunt had given his shortest drop, at 5'0," to P.J. Sullivan.

7. *San Francisco Chronicle*, December 10, 1897.

8. *Ibid.*

9. *San Francisco Examiner*, December 11, 1897.

10. *Evening News*, December 10, 1897.

11. *San Francisco Examiner*, December 11, 1897; *Sacramento Evening Bee*, December 10, 1897.

12. *Sacramento Evening Bee*, December 10, 1897.

13. The eight are named in the *Sacramento Evening Bee*'s December 10, 1897, story about the Allender hanging: Searcy, #17259 (San Bernardino); Durrant, #17260, Knott, #17497 and Miller, #17224 (San Francisco); Chavez, #17401, and Ebanks, # 17461(San Diego); Hill, #17343 (Oakland); and Fellows, #17469 (Riverside). Of these eight, only Durrant, Miller, Ebanks, and Hill would eventually hang at San Quentin. See also *San Francisco Chronicle*, December 10, 1897.

Chapter 24

1. *Scranton Tribune*, January 7, 1898.

2. *San Francisco Chronicle*, January 7, 1898. According to the *San Francisco Examiner*, "die like a Durrant" was a reference to relatives who had died valiantly in combat. *San Francisco Examiner*, January 7, 1898.

3. *San Francisco Examiner*, January 7, 1898.

4. *San Francisco Examiner*, January 8, 1898. The edition contained a facsimile of Durrant's note to Alice Rix.

5. *San Francisco Chronicle*, January 7, 1898.

6. *Ibid.*

7. *San Francisco Chronicle*, January 8, 1898.

8. William H.T. Durrant, #17260, *Execution Books, 1893–1967*, F3717–1301–1302, San Quentin State Prison Records, R135, California State Archives, Office of the Secretary of State, Sacramento, California. The *Call* erred in reporting, "The fall provided for Durrant is seven feet." *San Francisco Call*, January 7, 1898.

9. *San Francisco Examiner*, January 7 1898.

10. *San Francisco Chronicle*, January 8, 1898.

11. *Ibid.*

12. *Ibid.*

13. *Ibid.*

14. *Ibid.*

15. *San Francisco Call*, January 8, 1898.

16. *San Francisco Examiner,* January 8, 1898.

17. *San Francisco Call,* January 8, 1898; *San Francisco Chronicle,* January 8, 1898; *San Francisco Examiner,* January 8, 1898.

18. *San Francisco Chronicle,* January 8, 1898.

19. *San Francisco Call,* January 8, 1898; *San Francisco Chronicle,* January 8, 1898; *San Francisco Examiner,* January 8, 1898. Reporters jotted down the words as Durrant spoke them, which led to variations in the reporting of the final speech. The *Examiner's* transcript differs slightly from the *Chronicle's.*

20. *San Francisco Chronicle,* January 8, 1898.

21. *San Francisco Examiner,* January 8, 1898.

22. *San Francisco Chronicle,* January 8, 1898.

23. *San Francisco Examiner,* January 8, 1898.

24. A sidebar titled "A Ghastly Banquet" detailed the grief-stricken Durrants eating lunch beside their son's coffin and contained the graphic description of Theodore Durrant's face when the black hood was removed. Unlike the other two San Francisco papers, the *Call* did not run sketches of Durrant's final moments on the scaffold. In a sidebar on the front page of the January 8, 1898, edition, the editors explained that they considered such art "sensationalism" and as such "injurious" and only necessary to satisfy "a morbid craving." However, "A Ghastly Banquet," apparently considered neither sensational nor injurious, ran at the top of page one.

25. *San Francisco Chronicle,* January 8, 1898.

26. *San Francisco Examiner,* January 8, 1898.

27. *San Francisco Chronicle,* January 8, 1898.

28. Both physicians gave lengthy statements to the *Call,* January 8, 1898.

29. *San Francisco Chronicle,* January 8, 1898.

30. Michelson's piece appeared in the January 8, 1898, edition of the *Call.*

31. *San Francisco Chronicle,* January 8, 1898.

32. *San Francisco Chronicle,* January 10, 1898.

Chapter 25

1. *San Francisco Examiner,* February 8, 1898. The Belew case captivated the pages during the first week of February 1898. The entire front page of the February 6, 1898, edition of the *Examiner* was devoted to the case and contained a detailed discussion of Belew's admissions.

2. Located at the intersection of Dupont and Jackson Streets.

3. Lu Sing, #15372, Thomas St. Clair, and Wee Tung, #17589, *Execution Books, 1893–1967,* F3717–1301–1302, San Quentin State Prison Records, R135, California State Archives, Office of the Secretary of State, Sacramento, California. Also, Wee Tung, #17589, The Register and Descriptive List of Convicts under Sentence of Imprisonment in the State Prison of California, p.23, entry 4.

4. *San Francisco Call,* March 12, 1898; *San Francisco Examiner,* March 12, 1898.

5. *Santa Cruz Sentinel,* March 12, 1898.

6. *San Francisco Examiner,* March 12, 1898.

7. *San Francisco Chronicle,* March 12, 1898.

Chapter 26

1. *San Francisco Examiner,* April 7, 1898; *San Francisco Chronicle,* April 7, 1898. *San Francisco Call* of April 7, 1898, recorded a variant of Hill's speech.

2. *San Francisco Call,* April 6, 1898.

3. Benjamin L. Hill, #17343, Fremont Smith, #15964, and P.J. Sullivan, #15866, *Execution Books, 1893–1967,* F3717–1301–1302, San Quentin State Prison Records, R135, California State Archives, Office of the Secretary of State, Sacramento, California. Also, Benjamin I. Hill, #17343, The Register and Descriptive List of Convicts under Sentence of Imprisonment in the State Prison of California, p.2, entry 10.

4. *Oakland Tribune,* January 13, 1896.

5. *San Francisco Call,* April 6, 1898.

6. *San Francisco Examiner,* April 6, 1898.

7. *Ibid.*

8. *San Francisco Chronicle,* April 7, 1898.

9. *San Francisco Examiner,* April 7, 1898.

10. *San Francisco Chronicle*, April 7, 1898.

11. *San Francisco Examiner*, April 7, 1898.

Chapter 27

1. *San Francisco Examiner*, May 27, 1898.

2. *San Francisco Examiner*, May 28, 1898.

3. Joseph Japheth Ebanks, #17461, Benjamin I. Hill, #17343, Chun Sing, #17589, and W.M. Fredericks, #15960, *Execution Books, 1893-1967*, F3717-1301-1302, San Quentin State Prison Records, R135, California State Archives, Office of the Secretary of State, Sacramento, California. Also, Joseph Japheth Ebanks, #17461, The Register and Descriptive List of Convicts under Sentence of Imprisonment in the State Prison of California, p.12, entry 8.

4. *San Francisco Chronicle*, May 27, 1898.

5. *San Francisco Examiner*, May 27, 1898.

6. Joseph Japheth Ebanks, #17461, *Execution Books, 1893-1967*, F3717-1301-1302, San Quentin State Prison Records, R135, California State Archives, Office of the Secretary of State, Sacramento, California.

7. *San Francisco Examiner*, May 27, 1898.

8. *San Francisco Examiner*, May 28, 1898.

Chapter 28

1. *Santa Cruz Evening Sentinel*, October 15, 1898.

2. *San Francisco Examiner*, October 15, 1898.

3. John Miller, #17224, *Execution Books, 1893-1967*, F3717-1301-1302, San Quentin State Prison Records, R135, California State Archives, Office of the Secretary of State, Sacramento, California.

4. John Miller, #17224, *Execution Books, 1893-1967*, F3717-1301-1302, San Quentin State Prison Records, R135, California State Archives, Office of the Secretary of State, Sacramento, California. John Miller, #17224, p. 288, entry 10. Inmate

Indexes 1851-1940, San Quentin State Prison Records, F3717: 1135-41. California State Archives, Office of the Secretary of State, Sacramento, California.

5. The *San Francisco Examiner* of October 15 put his weight at 185, while the *Evening Sentinel* of the same date put it at 200.

6. *San Francisco Examiner*, October 15, 1898.

7. *San Francisco Chronicle*, October 15, 1898.

8. *San Francisco Examiner*, October 15, 1898.

9. *San Francisco Examiner*, October 14, 1898.

10. *San Francisco Examiner*, October 15, 1898.

11. SanIbid.

12. *Ibid.*

13. *San Francisco Chronicle*, October 15, 1898.

14. *Santa Cruz Evening Sentinel*, October 15, 1898.

15. *San Francisco Examiner*, October 15, 1898.

Chapter 29

1. 1870 U.S. Census, Clay County, Illinois, p. 26, lines 6-18, Lavina Kneff (line 8), William Clark (line 13), and George Clark (line 15), NARA microfilm publication M593, Roll 196. Entries for the Anderson Kneff family (lines 6-10) and the Joel Clark family (lines 11-18) are listed next to each other.

2. According to Lavina, George visited the Kneff household once a month before she married his brother, but his visits increased to once a week during the first year of Lavina's marriage. Often he would spend the night. The *San Francisco Examiner*'s coverage of the trial from January 28, 1898, included a detailed account of Lavina's testimony, which included her account of the affair with George.

3. According to a *San Francisco Chronicle* article about George Clark's hanging, his intimacy with Lavina predated her marriage to William Clark and continued to within a few weeks of his murder. *San Francisco Call*, October 22, 1898. For a full transcript of Lavina Clark's testimony, see the *San Francisco Chronicle*, January 28, 1898.

4. *San Francisco Examiner*, January 28, 1898.

5. *Ibid.*

6. George W. Clark, #17687, *Execution Books, 1893–1967*, F3717-1301-1302, San Quentin State Prison Records, R135, California State Archives, Office of the Secretary of State, Sacramento, California. Also, George Clark, #17687, The Register and Descriptive List of Convicts under Sentence of Imprisonment in the State Prison of California records, p. 31, entry #6.

7. *San Francisco Chronicle*, October 22, 1898.

8. *San Francisco Examiner*, October 20, 1898.

9. *San Francisco Examiner*, October 22, 1898.

10. *San Francisco Call*, October 22, 1898. "The execution was witnessed by about seventy-five persons—an unusually large number," reported the *Call*.

11. The reporters present at Clark's hanging wrote diverging accounts of his mien on the scaffold, which presents an interesting example of how eyewitnesses tend to see different things. The *Examiner's* account of October 22, 1898, presents Clark as calm and collected. The *Chronicle's* account of the same date describes him as near collapse. "This said, Clark weakened rapidly, and when the guards strapped his ankles his limbs were trembling violently." The reporters also heard different things from their place five feet below. According to the *Examiner's* representative, Lunt thought Clark wanted to say something, but he was just saying a few final prayers. According to the *Call's* representative, "Just as the black cap was about to be placed over his head Clark feebly asked to be permitted to speak a few words. Hangman Lunt removed the noose, but Clark's throat contracted and he was unable to utter a sound."

12. *San Francisco Chronicle*, October 22, 1898.

Chapter 30

1. An item in the *Marin County Tocsin* of January 21, 1899, states, "Amos Lunt, the well known cliff climber, was fortunate to win $1,000 on a 25-cent lottery ticket."

2. *Santa Cruz Evening Sentinel*, January 27, 1899.

3. *San Francisco Examiner*, January 26, 1899; *Los Angeles Record*, January 27, 1899; *San Francisco Call*, January 27, 1899.

4. *San Francisco Examiner*, January 26, 1899.

5. These excerpts of Lunt's testimony are from the *Oakland Tribune*, March 22, 1899. Of all the newspapers that covered Lunt's testimony during the Brandes trial, the *Tribune* does the best at preserving the Q & A of the original trial.

6. Brown was mistaken. Allender dropped 5' 9." Harvey Allender, #16969, *Execution Books, 1893–1967*, F3717-1301-1302, San Quentin State Prison Records, R135, California State Archives, Office of the Secretary of State, Sacramento, California. These excerpts of the trial testimony are from the *San Francisco Call*, March 22, 1899. The *Call*, like most newspapers reporting trial testimony, condensed the typical Q & A into blocks of text.

7. *San Francisco Examiner*, March 22, 1899.

8. Charles Duff, *A Handbook on Hanging* (London: Putnam, 1961), 78. Duff's treatise on hanging, first published in 1928, went through several printings and was even translated into German by Bertolt Brecht. According to the printing details in the 1961 "finally revised edition," the Nazis found the book offensive and burned it in 1933. John Ellis began his career in 1907 and executed the notorious Dr. Crippen. He resigned his post in 1924. His first suicide attempt occurred later that same year. In 1932, he succeeded by slicing his throat with a razor.

9. *Oakland Tribune*, March 22, 1899; *San Francisco Call*, March 22, 1899; *San Francisco Examiner*, March 22, 1899.

10. *Record-Union*, April 2, 1899.

11. *San Francisco Call*, May 4, 1899.

12. Details of the raid are from the*San Francisco Call*, May 28, 1899.

13. *San Francisco Call*, November 13, 1913.

14. Manuel Chavez, #17401, *Execution Books, 1893–1967*, F3717-1301-1302, San Quentin State Prison Records, R135, California State Archives, Office of the Secretary of State, Sacramento, California.

15. *Santa Cruz Evening Sentinel*, April 17, 1899.

16. *San Francisco Chronicle*, April 16, 1899.

17. *Santa Cruz Evening Sentinel*, April 17, 1899.

18. George C. Owens (#17654), *Execution Books, 1893–1967*, F3717–1301–1302, San Quentin State Prison Records, R135, California State Archives, Office of the Secretary of State, Sacramento, California.

19. *San Francisco Examiner*, October 7, 1899.

20. *Santa Cruz Evening Sentinel*, October 10, 1899.

Chapter 31

1. *San Francisco Call*, October 23, 1899.

2. An item under the headline "Hangman Lunt Improving" in the *San Francisco Chronicle* of October 25, 1899, presented an optimistic outlook for Lunt's treatment. "Dr. J. Henry Barbat [sic] announced last evening that Hangman Lunt of San Quentin Prison was rapidly regaining his health of mind and body. The physician said that his patient was suffering from nervous exhaustion, with occasional spells of melancholia, but with careful treatment and a much-needed rest, he would soon be in a condition to go back to his duties."

3. *San Francisco Call*, October 23, 1899; *San Francisco Chronicle*, October 23, 1899.

4. *San Francisco Call*, October 31, 1899.

5. *Santa Cruz Sentinel*, October 25, 1899.

6. *Santa Cruz Sentinel*, August 24, 1901.

7. According to an article in the *San Francisco Chronicle* from October 31, 1899, Lunt had lost 32 pounds in the previous two months, hinting that his mental troubles had begun to impact his physical health long before his reinstatement to the prison service in early October.

8. *San Francisco Call*, October 31, 1899.

9. Go See's execution took place on Friday, January 5, 1900. Daniel Sullivan, *San Quentin Prison—Album IV, Prisoner Mugshots*. Anne T. Kent California Room, Marin County Library, Marin County Civic Center, San Rafael, California.

10. Dr. Hill, who mistakenly states that Lunt hanged 19 men ("the spirit of Durrant and the eighteen other men,") recalled his visit to a reporter in the

Riverside Independent Enterprise, August 24, 1901.

11. *Sausalito News*, August 31, 1901.

12. *San Francisco Call*, September 15, 1901.

Chapter 32

1. *Sausalito News*, August 31, 1901.

2. Amos Lunt was laid to rest in the Santa Cruz Memorial Park in plot G-62.

3. *Santa Cruz Sentinel*, September 25, 1901.

4. *Santa Cruz Evening Sentinel*, September 25, 1901.

Chapter 33

1. *Grass Valley* (CA) *Morning-Union*, January 5, 1902.

2. Pete Dotz, "Amos Lunt, the Hangman of San Quentin Penitentiary, and His Fate," *Reno Gazette-Journal*, July 31, 1912. The Dotz article occupied three columns of the Editorial Page.

3. F.F. Runyon, "In the Shadow of the Gallows: The Lockup," *Pasadena Evening Post*, December 22, 1927.

4. *San Francisco Examiner*, July 12, 1900.

5. *Riverside Independent Enterprise*, August 24, 1901.

6. *San Francisco Call*, November 28, 1913.

7. The *San Francisco Call* ran a brief, two-paragraph biography on December 22, 1900.

8. The ads appeared in the *Marin Journal* throughout 1902–1903 and gave her address as "17 Marin Street, San Rafael."

9. 1940 U.S. Census, Amador County, California, Judicial Township 2, The Preston School of Industry, Sheet 9B, lines 79–80, Lottie Lunt (line 79), Laura J. Lunt (line 80), NARA microfilm publication T627, RG29.

10. For a short biography, see the *Sacramento Evening Bee*, January 30, 1908.

11. August Drahms, *The Criminal: His Personnel and Environment, a Scientific Study* (New York: MacMillan, 1900).

12. *Los Angeles Times*, January 11, 1927.

13. Father Lagan's obituary ran in the December 24, 1904, editions of the

San Francisco Call and the *San Francisco Examiner*.

14. *Oroville Daily Register*, April 28, 1922.

15. In a full-page exposé published in the July 7, 1902, edition of the *San Francisco Examiner*, Edwin H. Clough describes Dr. Lawlor's methods of maintaining law and order inside the home.

16. *San Francisco Call*, July 21, 1902.

17. *San Francisco Examiner*, February 28, 1930.

18. *San Francisco Examiner*, March 3, 1930.

19. *Detroit Times*, May 26, 1936.

20. *San Francisco Examiner*, May 26, 1936.

21. *Tonopah Daily Bonanza*, April 26, 1908.

22. "I never expect to attend another," he said after Fredericks' hanging. *San Francisco Examiner*, July 27, 1895.

Chapter 34

1. "The Haunting of Amos Lunt—Hangman," *San Francisco Call*, September 15, 1901.

2. *Sausalito News*, August 31, 1901.

3. *Ibid.*

4. *San Francisco Chronicle*, January 11, 1898.

5. *Oakland Tribune*, March 22, 1899.

6. *San Francisco Chronicle*, December 10, 1897.

7. *Sausalito News*, August 31, 1901.

8. *Riverside Independent Enterprise*, August 24, 1901.

9. *Santa Cruz Evening Sentinel*, August 24, 1901.

10. *Santa Cruz Sentinel*, October 7, 1933.

11. *Santa Cruz Evening Sentinel*, August 24, 1901.

12. *Ibid.*

13. *Riverside Independent Enterprise*, August 24, 1901.

14. *San Francisco Chronicle*, January 10, 1898.

15. "Prior to this execution the duty of stretching the rope and estimating the fall was assigned to Turnkey Jamieson," wrote an *Evening Sentinel* reporter on October 24, 1899. "Jamieson believed Durrant innocent and refused to perform this office, so the ghastly work fell upon Lunt."

16. *Santa Cruz Evening Sentinel*, October 24, 1899.

17. *San Francisco Examiner*, November 21, 1897.

18. *San Francisco Call*, November 28, 1913.

Bibliography

Newspapers

Alameda (CA) *Daily Encinal*
Alameda Daily Argus
Chico Enterprise
Daily Alta
Detroit Times
Evening Bee (Sacramento)
Evening News (Sacramento)
Fresno Morning Republican
Grass Valley (CA) *Morning-Union*
Los Angeles Herald
Los Angeles Times
Marin County Tocsin
Marin Journal
Marysville Daily Democrat
Monterey Cyprus
Newburyport Herald
Oakland Daily Evening Tribune
Oakland Tribune
Oroville Daily Register
Pasadena Evening Post
Reno Gazette-Journal
Riverside Independent Enterprise
Sacramento Record-Union
San Francisco Call
San Francisco Call-Bulletin
San Francisco Chronicle
San Francisco Examiner
San Francisco Town Talk
Santa Cruz Evening Sentinel
Santa Cruz Sentinel
Santa Cruz Surf
Sausalito News
Scranton Tribune
Stockton Evening Record
Tonopah Daily Bonanza
Woodland Daily Democrat

Books/Websites

Creasy, George W. *The City of Newbury-port in the Civil War: from 1861–1865.* Boston: Griffith-Stillings, 1903.

Douglass, Royall. *Drops of Blood: Prison Verse by Royall Douglass, No. 19173.* Palo Alto, CA: Altruria Press, 1911.

Drahms, August. *The Criminal: His Personnel and Environment, a Scientific Study.* New York: Macmillan, 1900.

Duff, Charles. *A Handbook on Hanging.* London: Putnam and Company, 1961.

"Executions in San Francisco, 1851–1890." *The San Francisco Sheriff's Department History Research Project.* www.sfsdhistory.com.

Graysmith, Robert. *The Bell Tower: The Case of Jack the Ripper Finally Solved...in San Francisco.* Washington, D.C.: Regnery, 1999.

Lunt, Thomas Simpson. *A History of the Lunt Family in America.* Salem, MA: Salem Press, 1914.

Mansfield, George C. *History of Butte County, California.* Los Angeles: Historic Record Company, 1918.

Moore, April. *Folsom's 93: The Lives and Crimes of Folsom Prison's Executed Men.* Fresno, CA: Craven Street Books, 2013.

Peixotto, Edgar D. *Report of the Trial of William Henry Theodore Durrant, Indicted for the Murder of Blanche Lamont, before The Superior Court of the City and County of San Francisco, Including a Full History of the Case.* Detroit: The Collector Publishing Company, 1899.

Ward, William H., ed. *The Records of*

the *Members of the Grand Army of the Republic, with a Complete Account of the Twentieth National Encampment.* San Francisco: H.S. Crocker, 1886.

Documents

Duffy, Clinton. *San Quentin Executioner's Log.* Object Identification: 1999.2872. The Marin History Museum, San Rafael, California.

Execution Books, 1893–1967, F3717-1301–1302, San Quentin State Prison Records, R135, California State Archives, Office of the Secretary of State, Sacramento, California.

The Great Register of Marin County— Year 1894.

The Great Register of Marin County— Year 1898.

Inmate Indexes 1851–1940, San Quentin State Prison Records, F3717: 1135–41. California State Archives, Office of the Secretary of State, Sacramento, California.

1880 US Census, NARA microfilm publication T9, Roll 313, Washington, D.C., National Archives and Records Administration.

1850 US Census, NARA microfilm publication M432, Roll 313.

1870 US Census, NARA microfilm publication M593, Roll 89, Washington, D.C., National Archives and Records Administration.

Rowland Card Collection Database, Leon and Jeannette Rowland Collection, UCSC Special Collections Archive.

San Quentin Prison Minute Book, 1891. San Quentin Minute Books, 1874–1943. State Board of Prison Directors Records. F3717: 987–1012. The California State Archives, Sacramento, California.

Sullivan, Daniel. *San Quentin Prison— Album IV, Prisoner Mugshots.* Anne T. Kent California Room, Marin County Library, Marin County Civic Center, San Rafael, California. (Available online at marinlibrary.org.)

Twelfth Annual Report of the State Board of Prison Directors of the State of California for the Forty-Second Fiscal Year, Ending June 30, 1891. Sacramento: State Office, 1892.

Index

Numbers in **bold italics** indicate pages with illustrations